Cultural Tourism in a Changing World

TOURISM AND CULTURAL CHANGE
Series Editors: Professor Mike Robinson, *Centre for Tourism and Cultural Change, Leeds Metropolitan University, UK* and Dr Alison Phipps, *University of Glasgow, Scotland, UK*

Understanding tourism's relationships with culture(s) and vice versa, is of ever-increasing significance in a globalising world. This series will critically examine the dynamic inter-relationships between tourism and culture(s). Theoretical explorations, research-informed analyses, and detailed historical reviews from a variety of disciplinary perspectives are invited to consider such relationships.

Other Books in the Series
Irish Tourism: Image, Culture and Identity
    Michael Cronin and Barbara O'Connor (eds)
Tourism, Globalization and Cultural Change: An Island Community Perspective
    Donald V.L. Macleod
The Global Nomad: Backpacker Travel in Theory and Practice
    Greg Richards and Julie Wilson (eds)
Tourism and Intercultural Exchange: Why Tourism Matters
    Gavin Jack and Alison Phipps
Discourse, Communication and Tourism
    Adam Jaworski and Annette Pritchard (eds)
Histories of Tourism: Representation, Identity and Conflict
    John K. Walton (ed)

Other Books of Interest
Managing Educational Tourism
    Brent W. Ritchie
Marine Ecotourism: Issues and Experiences
    Brian Garrod and Julie C. Wilson (eds)
Natural Area Tourism: Ecology, Impacts and Management
    D. Newsome, S.A. Moore and R. Dowling
Progressing Tourism Research
    Bill Faulkner, edited by Liz Fredline, Leo Jago and Chris Cooper
Recreational Tourism: Demand and Impacts
    Chris Ryan
Shopping Tourism: Retailing and Leisure
    Dallen Timothy
Sport Tourism Development
    Thomas Hinch and James Higham
Sport Tourism: Interrelationships, Impact and Issues
    Brent Ritchie and Daryl Adair (eds)
Tourism Collaboration and Partnerships
    Bill Bramwell and Bernard Lane (eds)
Tourism and Development: Concepts and Issues
    Richard Sharpley and David Telfer (eds)

For more details of these or any other of our publications, please contact:
Channel View Publications, Frankfurt Lodge, Clevedon Hall,
Victoria Road, Clevedon, BS21 7HH, England
http://www.channelviewpublications.com

TOURISM AND CULTURAL CHANGE 7
Series Editors: Mike Robinson and Alison Phipps

Cultural Tourism in a Changing World

Politics, Participation and (Re)presentation

Edited by

Melanie Smith and Mike Robinson

CHANNEL VIEW PUBLICATIONS
Clevedon • Buffalo • Toronto

Library of Congress Cataloging in Publication Data
Cultural Tourism in a Changing World: Politics, Participation and (Re)presentation
Edited by Melanie K. Smith and Mike Robinson.
Tourism and Cultural Change: 7
Includes bibliographical references and index.
1. Heritage tourism. 2. Heritage tourism–Social aspects. I. Smith, Melanie K.
II. Robinson, Mike. III. Series.
G156.5.H47C857 2006
338.4' 791–dc22   2006017791

British Library Cataloguing in Publication Data
A catalogue entry for this book is available from the British Library.

ISBN 1-84541-044-0 / EAN 978-1-84541-044-5 (hbk)
ISBN 1-84541-043-2 / EAN 978-1-84541-043-8 (pbk)
ISBN 1-84541-045-9 / EAN 978-1-84541-045-2 (Ebook)

Channel View Publications
An imprint of Multilingual Matters Ltd

UK: Frankfurt Lodge, Clevedon Hall, Victoria Road, Clevedon BS21 7HH.
USA: 2250 Military Road, Tonawanda, NY 14150, USA.
Canada: 5201 Dufferin Street, North York, Ontario, Canada M3H 5T8.

Typeset by Datapage Ltd.
Printed and bound in Great Britain by MPG Books.

Contents

Acknowledgements

We would dearly like to thank all of the contributors to this book and in particular our four coordinating editors: Jim Butcher, Stroma Cole, Nikki MacLeod and László Puczkó.

Thanks are also due to the Association for Tourism and Leisure Education (ATLAS) and go also to Sami Grover and the production team at Channel View Publications for their assistance and patience.

Melanie Smith and Mike Robinson

Contributors

John Akama, Department of Tourism, Moi University, Kenya
jsakama@yahoo.co.in

Josie Appleton, Spiked-Online, UK
Josie.Appleton@spiked-online.com

Tanuja Barker, School of Tourism and Leisure Management,
University of Queensland, Australia
tanuja.barker@uq.edu.au

Jenny Briedenhann, Faculty of Leisure and Tourism,
Buckinghamshire Chilterns University College, UK
jenny.briedenhann@neweconomics.org

Kevin Burns, Dundalk Institute of Technology, Ireland
Kevin.Burns@dkit.ie

Jim Butcher, Faculty of Business and Sciences,
Canterbury Christ Church University
b.j.butcher@canterbury.ac.uk

Stroma Cole, Faculty of Leisure and Tourism,
Buckinghamshire Chilterns University College, UK
stroma.cole@bcuc.ac.uk

René van der Duim, Department of Environmental Sciences,
Wageningen University, The Netherlands
rene.vanderduim@wur.nl

Anya Diekmann, Department Gestion et Analyse du Tourisme,
IGEAT, Université Libre de Bruxelles, Belgium
adiekman@ulb.ac.be

Rodrigo de Azeredo Grünewald, Sociology and Anthropology
Department, Federal University of Campina Grande, Brazil
gru@ch.ufcg.edu.br

Catherine Kelly, Heritage, Arts and Tourism Division,
Business School, University of Greenwich, UK
C.Kelly@greenwich.ac.uk

Jane Lovell, Canterbury City Council, UK
j.lovell@cant.gov.uk

Fiona Candon, Western Development Commission, Ireland
candon@wdc.ie

Nicola MacLeod, University of Greenwich, London
N.E.Macleod@gre.ac.uk

Frances McGettigan, Athlone Institute of Technology, Ireland
fmcgettigan@ait.ie

Barbara Marciszewska, Academy of Physical Education and Sport,
Gdansk, Institute of Tourism and Recreation, Poland
marcisz@awf.gda.pl

Géraldine Maulet, Department, Gestion et Analyse du Tourisme,
IGEAT, Université Libre de Bruxelles, Belgium
gemaulet@ulb.ac.be

Satu Miettinen, University of Art and Design, Helsinki, Finland
samietti@uiah.fi

Karin Peters, Department of Environmental Studies,
Wageningen University, The Netherlands
karin.peters@wur.nl

László Puczkó, Xellum Consulting Ltd, Budapest, Hungary
lpuczko@xellum.hu

I. Nyoman Darma Putra, Indonesian Literature, Faculty of Letters,
Udayana University, Bali, Indonesia
grass@indo.net.id

Stéphanie Quériat, Department Gestion et Analyse du Tourisme,
IGEAT, Université Libre de Bruxelles, Belgium
squeriat@ulb.ac.be

Pranhill Ramchander, Technikon SA, Department of Marketing and Tourism, South Africa
pramchan@tsa.ac.za

Tamara Rátz, János Kodolányi University College, Székesfehérvár, Hungary
tratz@uranos.kodolanyi.hu

Mike Robinson, Centre for Tourism and Cultural Change, Sheffield Hallam University, UK
mike.robinson@shu.ac.uk

Frans Schouten, NHTV Breda University of Professional Education, The Netherlands
schouten.f@nhtv.nl

Melanie Smith, University of Greenwich, London
M.K.Smith@gre.ac.uk

Marion Stuart-Hoyle, Department of Sport, Tourism and Lesiure, Canterbury Christ Church University College, UK
m.stuart@canterbury.ac.uk

Arvid Viken, Finnmark University College, Norway
arvid.viken@hifm.no

Agung Suryawan Wiranatha, Research Centre for Culture and Tourism, Udayana University, Bali, Indonesia
baligreen@indo.net.id

Chapter 1

Politics, Power and Play: The Shifting Contexts of Cultural Tourism

MIKE ROBINSON and MELANIE SMITH

Introduction

Contexts are important, not only because they embed specific phenomena in more general historical circumstances, but because they themselves change both in a temporal sense and also in their social and political validity as interpretative frameworks for actions and events. The emphasis in this chapter is to provide some degree of context for the concept of cultural tourism and the remaining chapters of the book, which explore the ways in which culture(s) is/are mobilised *for* tourists and read *by* tourists within particular settings. In utilising the term cultural tourism we are explicitly acknowledging both the cultural nature of, and the role of, tourism as a process and set of practices that revolve around the behavioural pragmatics of societies, and the learning and transmission of meanings through symbols and embodied through objects. In this vein it is useful to acknowledge the normalising perspective of Levi-Strauss (1988), which recognises the implicitness of culture not as something set against life, or overlain over it, but as substituting itself to life as a constructing power and transformational process which is processual, and practical; life builds culture, builds life. Tourism, as an expression and experience of culture, fits within this form of historical contextualisation and also assists in generating nuanced forms of culture as well as new cultural forms. In this sense it is not difficult to see that use of the term 'cultural tourism' is problematic. As Urry (1995) suggests, tourism is simply 'cultural', with its structures, practices and events very much an extension of the normative cultural framing from which it emerges. Cultural tourism *is* tourism, and clearly, as this book demonstrates, it is far more than production and consumption of 'high' art and heritage. It reaches into some deep conceptual

1

territories relating to how we construct and understand ourselves, the world and the multilayered relationships between them.

Tourism as an international system of exchange displays particular tensions around the interface between space and experience that reaches into the conceptual heart of globalisation. The global structural·realities of tourism are very much framed by the idea of the nation state and have their roots in the modern political geographies and nation-building agendas of the late 19th, and the first decades of the 20th century. Despite growing interest in the notion of regionalism whereby the region acts as the focal point for 'culture building and identification' (Frykman, 2002), it is the idea of the nation that still holds primacy in the metanarratives of international tourism. Each nation, no matter what their position in any notional global political league table, promotes tourism as an actual and potential source of external revenue, a marker of political status that draws upon cultural capital, and as a means to legitimise itself as a territorial entity. Thus, national governments have offices for tourism that quite willingly promote the idea of a national 'brand'. Wandering around the World Travel Market in London, or the International Travel Convention in Berlin, one can be forgiven for thinking that ideas of mobility, transnational flows and deterritorialisation had no currency whatsoever. Exhibition stands forcefully exist as microcosms of nations, albeit with regional and subregional constituent parts. Tour operators act as buyers of essentially 'national' products. Developers negotiate with national government offices under national legislative frameworks. National airlines retain highly visible and symbolic meaning for both host community and tourists, and despite the presence of multinational hotel chains, many hotel groups remain firmly structured around particular national characteristics and ideologies.

Of course, a 'tourism of nations' perspective is riven with the fault lines of conflict and contestation. Nevertheless, it is a reality that maps onto Westernised cognitive frameworks of cultural resemblance, which have themselves been shaped by essentialising histories of the nation-state. Counter, and in parallel, to this metastructural view, are the social realties of 'doing' tourism and 'being' a tourist, which exist not within and between bounded territories but with far more immediate, intimate, and to the tourist, more meaningful spaces. Here the focus is upon experience and the *in situ* production of spaces that facilitates such experiences for tourists; a point largely accommodated by the babel of globalisation theorists who have challenged ideas of national boundaries. The thesis which proffers notions of boundary dissolution (language and religious boundaries included), the compression of time and space, and the emergence of 'landscapes' fashioned along cultural and ethnic lines (Appadurai, 1990), positions the tourist as part of a larger 'flow' of people, ideas and objects. Things and containers such as 'Spain' or 'France', and even their regions, relinquish their importance in the light of processes and actions, and what become more important for the tourist are not the metanarratives and ideological frameworks of nationhood, nor the notions of cultural resemblance and difference, but rather the outcomes of individual and social encounter, interaction and engagement.

This tension inherent in international tourism is not reducible to some binary opposition between modes of production versus modes of consumption. It is not some battle between historical fact and socio/anthropological interpretation. Nor is it about the relativism of where anyone happens to be standing. Rather, it is very much a movement along a continuum between two sets of equally valid, albeit discursive practices functioning at and between macro and micro levels. International tourism exists as a suitably vague umbrella term that is locked into the continuities of the modern nation-state *and* operates through the experiences and practices of the individual tourist. Cultural tourism is, *de facto*, caught up in the movements and flows of the world and this is evident when we come to look at the various cases set out in this book. For, despite having specific geographic foci and particular genealogies, the various cultural developments and conflicts discussed are sculpted through their exposure to, and encounters with, peoples from 'other' places and pasts.

Culture as Resource and the Resourcefulness of Culture

The most distinguishing feature of mature capitalist systems over recent decades has been the re-creation of economies around the symbolic value of culture(s). The political roles of culture as representing and enforcing national ideologies and particular hierarchies of power, together with its social roles as entertainment and as a form of communal intellectual glue, while still present, have been overtaken by its centrality in economic life. Scott (1997: 323) neatly summarises this fundamental shift arguing that:

> ...capitalism itself is moving into a phase in which the cultural forms and meanings of its outputs become critical if not dominating elements of productive strategy, and in which the realm of human culture as a whole is increasingly subject to commodification, i.e. supplied through profit-making institutions in decentralized mar-

kets. In other words, an ever-widening range of economic activity is concerned with producing and marketing goods and services that are infused in one way or another with broadly aesthetic or semiotic attributes.

Culture, in its widest sense, provides a set of material and symbolic resources that are abundant in supply (arguably infinite), and highly mobile (Rojek & Urry, 1997). The resource of culture is certainly at the basis of international tourism and indeed has facilitated its growth and allowed various societies and sections of societies to participate in the development process. However, in treating culture as a resource we should not neglect aspects of agency, as the value and priority of culture(s) relates not only to its intrinsic worth, but to the ways that it is used (Keating, 2001). This in turn begs questions about ownership of, and access to, culture (Robinson, 2001), and also raises issues with regard to the ways in which culture is 'read' by particular typologies of tourists. So-called 'cultural products', as Therkelsen (2003: 134) points out: 'generate associations and meanings that are influenced by the cultural backgrounds of the potential tourist.' In this sense, tourists do not encounter culture as some value-neutral form or process. Rather, they decode culture(s), in social spaces and times in relation to particular formal and informal knowledge regimes accrued through exposure to formulated tourism packages and through the normative processes of socialisation (Robinson, 2005).

In a European context, conventional conceptions of what we understand to be 'culture' have largely been dictated by our postenlightenment sensibilities regarding the romantic, the beautiful, the educational, and also, by extension, the moral. It is not surprising that what is now heralded as 'cultural tourism' broadly follows the patterns of the 'grand tour' of the 18th and 19th centuries indulged in by the social elite. Motivating factors of education, social betterment and basic human curiosity remain but have been complemented by a range of other factors which have assisted in the on-going development of cultural tourist centres. Importantly, the rise of the low-cost airlines across Europe has played a key role in stimulating tourism within more recently acknowledged cultural centres such as Budapest, Krakow and Ljubljana. Though well established cities of culture such as Paris, Rome, Venice and Athens maintain their primacy from the early days of tourism, cheap flights have created new opportunities for people to experience heritage and the arts, particularly in some smaller places such as Girona, Bratislava and Riga. This apparent democratisation of cultural tourism has also been helped along by highly competitive and increasingly sophisticated marketing campaigns, mainly within urban contexts. The European Cities of Culture campaign, with its strong emphasis on destination branding, has been particularly successful in this way and has acted to endorse the idea that culture is a highly 'moral' product and also, through its ability to attract tourists, is economically beneficial.

In this vein, the concept of cultural tourism seems to be taking hold everywhere. Former heavily industrial centres have moved from being economies of production to economies of symbolic cultural consumption, and industrial heritage sites would seem to substitute all too easily for sites of manufacturing. The number of festivals and cultural events has increased exponentially over recent years and there has also been substantive growth in the number of museums and cultural attractions as destinations have sought to compete for the growing markets of culture-hungry tourists. But the on-going ferment and frenzy to create new displays of cultural capital and to attract the 'cultural tourist' – that is the well educated, largely White, high-spending, middle-class tourist – raises a number of longstanding issues relating to how we use culture to make sense of, and gain meaning from, a rapidly changing world.

An important point of perspective to bear in mind is that while cultural tourism is certainly a growing segment of international tourism, the vast majority of tourists could be said to be culture-proof (Craik, 1997) in that they are not seeking the exotic, culture or heritage, but relaxation, warm weather and various forms of hedonistic activity. Beach holidays remain as popular as ever with tour operators continually seeking to develop virgin stretches of coastline, while theme parks (50 years after the opening of Disneyland), as a destination and a model of tourism development, are flourishing. This is not to say that the individuals that go to make up so-called 'mass' tourism are somehow devoid of any interest in culture(s). But it does remind us that tourism reflects a certain degree of polarisation between the persistence of culture as somehow elevated and special in society, and the culture of the ordinary and the everyday.

Culture, as the social critic Raymond Williams pointed out, is one of the most problematic words to define, but despite elaborations and attempts by anthropologists over the years to widen our understanding of the term culture away from elitist notions, it would seem that, in the context of tourism we are, in the main, reproducing the idea of 'high' culture from the 18th and 19th centuries. Nor is this restricted to European tourism. We have exported our aesthetic preferences and conceptions of culture to other places. In the Middle East, for instance, rich as it is with centuries of history and cultural diversity, we have inscribed our predilections for romantic ruins that we can recognise onto national tourist strategies. A country like Jordan, for example, is locked into the promotion of its Greco-Roman sites and the Natabean city of Petra, as 'must-see' places. However, such sites are hardly representative of the culture(s) of the Jordanian/Arab peoples, shaped as they have been by Ottoman culture and complex historical relations with the West. At one level this is playing to the market. At another level it is obscuring the very essence of local and national identity.

We should not be surprised at our own preferences for culture as expressed in the iconic and the spectacular. As tourists we have but little time in any one location and instinctively we gravitate to what is heralded as being the exceptional, rather than the norm, and what we recognise through our own aesthetic frames. It is also not surprising that a destination eager to capitalise on the economic rewards of tourism should prioritise its cultural high points. The question, however, is one of extent. For in privileging some aspects of culture to tourists, we exclude others and close off tourism as a development option for some destinations and communities.

The Politics of Playfulness, Creativity and Change

Wallerstein (2000) writes of multiple temporalities, universalisms and particularisms in the context of cultural development in the 21st century. Although total relativism is not a necessarily desirable condition (universalisms relating to fundamental human rights might need to be prioritised, for example), this affords enormous scope for tolerance, political change and innovation. Though this can lead to a superficial democratisation of culture (Wallerstein, 2000), and problematises how we define who are 'we' and who are the 'others', it nevertheless forces our attention to the rapidity and restlessness of change and shifting power relations.

Relativism and pluralism go a long way in characterising culture(s) as a set of resources and it is thus not surprising that cultural tourism constantly seems to generate interconnected and apparently intractable moments of contestation in the way we represent and receive culture as both tourists and hosts. How, for example, how can we privilege womens' or Black history without doing the same for men or Whites? How can we balance the iconic signification of culture with the intimate? How do we celebrate cultural difference and diversity in ways that retain meaning for tourists and visited communities? Both relativism and essentialism still create major challenges in the context of truth and reconciliation, especially when interpreting or representing one's past in the present. Alexander *et al*. (2004) note how cultural traumas (e.g. the Holocaust) leave indelible marks on their groups' consciousness, memories and identity, which can be both solidifying or disruptive, but rarely unanimous. People come to terms with their past in different ways, but the development of a (cultural) tourism industry also necessitates the acceptance of responsibility in terms of interpretation and representation of events. The 20th century is widely regarded as one of the most violent and tragic in modern history, thus there is much to come to terms with and to (re)present.

Culture is a serious process and a serious state, and many of the chapters of this book bring out the ways in which the ephemeral tourist experience touches upon the deepest and most persistent of struggles. At the same time, postmodern societies are equally meant to be 'playful' in their approach to tourism (Rojek, 1993). As a leisure industry, tourism is based on a sense of escape from the existential burden of history and contemporary reconciliation. Human coping strategies also include the freedom and hedonistic expression afforded by tourism. The 21st century, and its concomitant globalisation born of new media, technology and regenerative creative industries, lends itself easily to a proliferation of exciting touristic developments. For example, Junemo (2004) describes how a growing destination like Dubai is the epitome of playfulness, a place where globalisation is not a threat, but has been embraced wholeheartedly both in urban and tourism planning. Sheller and Urry (2004) refer to the playfulness of places, which are always on the move, consisting of different mobilisations of memories, emotions, performances, bodies, etc. There are multiple contested meanings of place as described earlier with regard to interpretations of history, but these can also be used in creative ways to transform and regenerate, or even to create new destinations. More than one of the case studies in this book refer to the ways in which culture as heritage, and culture as contemporary creativity are being used simultaneously (not always without conflict) in the redevelopment or repositioning of destinations. Some of the more playful and creative aspects of cultural tourism development arguably need to take their place alongside the more sombre reminders of our dissonant pasts.

Mobility and playfulness are clearly still predominantly influenced by power and capital, but as Turner and Rojek (2001) note, there has been a democratisation of mobility, in which travel has become almost a citizenship right. It is worth noting too, that communities are as fluid and mobile as their cultures. Many cultural theorists write of 'deterritorialisation' and groups occupying 'the borderlands' (i.e. those who do not fit into established master discourses of nation, race, ethnicity, etc). A sense of place is now as much a psychological concept as a physical or geographical one, especially for diasporic cultures. Place, like identity, is also constantly being negotiated. As stated by Meethan (2001), cultures and societies are not passive recipients of tourism, they are also sites of contestation and resistance. Postcolonial discourse often emphasises the 'loss' of cultures (usually referring to indigenous cultures), but questions should be asked about for whom it is a loss? There is a Western tendency to fossilise cultures as heritage and to prioritise the built environment. There is something of a postimperial obsession with physical symbols or legacies that represent the past (e.g. buildings, statues, memorials). Even where these are now displaced and dissonant (for example, in former communist countries), they may be preserved and placed in tourist 'statue parks' (e.g. in Hungary). By contrast, Fisher (2004) notes how indigenous peoples in neocolonial societies tend to describe their heritage more in terms of intangible, *præcolonial* traditions or 'essence' of place.

It is in such contexts that we have to position cultural tourism as creatively evolving and evolving creatively. In doing so, what we refer to as cultural tourism is becoming far more inclusive, breaking away from some of the more established notions of culture as loci of symbolic power and elitist expressions of apparent 'good taste', and moving toward more inclusive, democratic and experiential interpretations. There are perhaps two key reasons for this movement, or, more aptly, drifting. The first relates to the nature of the tourist experience itself. Destinations, their peoples and cultures are *experienced* by the tourist and not just gazed upon. Observing tourists reveals that they actually spend considerably less time than we think in formalised cultural settings such as galleries, museums and historic buildings. Rather more time is spent in restaurants, cafes, bars, shops, the airport and the hotel. Indeed, tourists spend large amounts of time 'walking around' and 'people watching', and in the process observing and encountering aspects of the host's culture in the form of everyday practices and behaviours. Far from being culture proof, it is particularly these aspects of ordinary life that tourists absorb and on their return home constitute their narratives of memory of experience. From the point of view of the host community and indeed the host tourist authorities, this aspect of culture is easily overlooked as not being of any significance and hence devoid of political currency. It is informal, *ad hoc*, impossible to manage and control and yet it is of critical importance in shaping the tourist experience. But it is easy to forget that what is considered to be ordinary in one cultural setting is exotic to another. As a normative part of the touristic process people encounter the cultures of others, through shopping, eating and drinking etc., but this in itself can become an out-of-the-ordinary experience. In Britain, for example, the still-popular activities of going to a pub or of eating fish and chips are transformed into special activities for many overseas tourists. Ordinary as they may be, these are authentic activities in themselves and can be said to be close to the heart of British culture, however they seldom appear on the cover of promotional brochures.

A second reason for the trend towards less elitist cultural forms relates to the realities of generational replacement and increasing distance away from so-called 'high-brow' culture. Each generation produces its own cultures, the potential of which has still not been fully recognised by the tourism sector. On the one hand this does create problems as various established cultural forms and traditions are becoming threatened with extinction. On the other hand, new cultural forms are created. Again, it is sometimes all too easy to dismiss these as being outside of 'culture'. In the context of European history and culture, the notion of fast food would seem to have little in the way of cultural value and any distinctive pull for tourists. However, in the USA, a nation with a relatively short documented history, the birthplace of Kentucky Fried Chicken in Corbin, Kentucky, boasts a museum and an authentically reconstructed cafe, and many tourists. Their cultural experiences revolve around what they can relate to and what they feel connected with, albeit in a different environment. This does not make them unappreciative of the other cultural products, but it does illustrate the point that cultures *do* change in relation to the market.

Recognising and promoting the culture of the ordinary and the everyday is not to deny the importance of the 'high' arts, heritage and classical performances. Rather, it is to recognise the realities of cultural change and different forms of creativity, and the importance of the overall experience in tourism. But what does all of this mean for the future development of cultural tourism and the communities and economies it purports to serve?

For the increasing number of tourists roaming the surface of the planet it creates an ever-expanding number of experiences and possibilities. All tourism is 'cultural' in this sense. As tourists, and as people, in a globalising world we are increasingly in contact with 'other' cultures, able to experience the uniqueness of each and the commonalities of all. Cultural tourism in this way can be a powerful mechanism to understanding other places, peoples and pasts, not through selective, high-profile cultural sites and activities that may not necessarily be representative of the societies they operate in, but through a more democratic and ubiquitous approach to cultures. In these terms even mass tourism has important and forgotten cultural elements. Our first encounter with another culture is most likely to be with the menu, the waiter and the food in a restaurant near a resort.

It is 'popular', everyday culture that increasingly infuses domestic and international tourism patterns. Television soap operas now hold more influence on travel patterns than classical opera. Tourists are more likely to visit a destination with literary connections because they have seen a film than because they have read the book. Football, and sport generally, has the power to define new tourist opportunities. Different shopping and dining experiences are arguably more central to the overall cultural experience than museum visits. Now, all of this may not be a popular perspective with the guardians of 'high' culture, but for the tourism authorities of those destinations off the main tourist routes (and in many cases these overlap with the very places which need economic and cultural development), the everydayness of culture, in both material and symbolic ways, provides an important set of resources.

At one level the cultural landscape has transformed considerably since the early days of tourism and travel. The canvas of culture has broadened, become more accessible and more creative. On another level, the basics of culture have remained in place and its important dimensions relate to the changes it constantly undergoes and the fact that it is lived, experienced, shared and exchanged.

Themes and Cases

The rationale for this publication was that whilst there are several interesting books that cover the more theoretical aspects of cultural tourism and its relationship to heritage and the arts (see for instance: Hughes, 2000; McKercher & Cros, 2002; Smith, 2003), there are few books that provide detailed, supporting case studies. Those that do are built upon here in updated contexts, for example, the work of Richards (1996; 2001) and Robinson and Boniface (1999). In terms of geographical and spatial coverage, this book is not comprehensive, but it does take examples from all three worlds as described by Denning (2004); the capitalist, the communist and the postcolonial. Hopefully this will provide the reader with some awareness of the political, social and cultural frameworks that influence each of these worlds or regions.

Though the book is broadly divided into four thematic sections, covering cultural policy and politics, notions of community participation and empowerment, issues of authenticity and commodification, and interpretation in cultural tourism, they all point up the contested processes of transforming and mobilising culture for touristic purposes in relation to changing contexts. Each section is fronted with an exploration of some of the conceptual issues relating to these themes followed by illustrative case studies. The themes addressed here are clearly not exhaustive but frequently emerge as being key to any discussions relating to cultural tourism. Sigala and Leslie (2005) provide good coverage of the more managerial and commercial aspects of cultural tourism (for example, attractions management, marketing, sustainability, new technology).

In the introduction to the first section, *Politics and Cultural Policy*, Jim Butcher provides an overview of the links between cultural politics, cultural policy and cultural attractions. For Butcher, the contemporary policy and political settings for culture and cultural tourism *per se* are problematised by increasing pluralism, democracy and social inclusion. In a postmodern context, the rise of populism and political correctness increasingly raise questions relating to 'universal' versus 'particular' cultures. As mentioned above, heightened relativism, whilst able to generate new creative forms, may also lead to an overly narrow interpretation or representation of human cultures. It might also engender a decline in standards or an instrumentalist approach to cultural development.

The spaces that cultural tourism occupies are frequently shared with and/or inherited from other functions and other symbolic uses, and as such are subject to contestation. Catherine Kelly discusses heritage tourism development in the contested political spaces of Ireland. She considers the attraction of the Ulster–American Folk Park in Omagh, County Tyrone, which focuses on emigration trails to the USA, and compares and contrasts the viewpoints of visitor groups from both Southern and Northern Ireland. This exemplifies the varying perceptions of visitors when confronted with a dissonant heritage site in a politically sensitive location, and suggests strategies for interpreting and representing multiple cultures and identities.

Arvid Viken describes how the Rosendal Barony in Norway has been redeveloped as a museum and heritage attraction for tourism, focusing in particular on the implications for local communities. He highlights some of the tensions between conservation and local developments, and the elitism of the venue and its visitors, which are seen by some to perpetuate old social divisions. He argues that in this case social history is generally underplayed or not critical enough and emphasises some of the ubiquitous conflicts inherent in national heritage developments, together with their local, social implications.

Barbara Marciszewska demonstrates how cultural tourism policy in post-1989 Poland is increasingly moving away from so-called 'high' culture and heritage towards more populist cultural activities. She notes that this is partly a result of low local incomes limiting cultural consumption, as well as a demand for new touristic experiences, especially in cities. The case also notes that a concerted effort is needed by governments to support and fund cultural development, and to make the necessary links to tourism policy.

All three cases in this section demonstrate different aspects of cultural tourism politics, but a shift can be seen in all three contexts away from a single definition of 'culture' or 'heritage' towards a more plural or populist approach. Increasingly, the viewpoints of different communities, audiences and visitors appear to be taken into consideration when developing cultural tourism policies and attractions and while government support is not always forthcoming, such issues are at least being raised on political agendas.

In the second section, *Community Participation and Empowerment*, Stroma Cole discusses 'ethnic tourism', and questions definitions and meanings of community, commodification and empowerment. Whilst it is often assumed that 'commodification' has a negative connotation, it can also engender positive changes. In addition, mechanisms for community participation are increasing, yet there is still a need to understand the true nature of empowerment and its impact on local communities. The case studies in this section focus on the complex inter-relationships between locality, community, traditions and identity, and though good practice is noticeable it is seen that the development of cultural tourism cannot be separated from the historical and contemporary political realities that impact upon communities and that can either help or hinder participation and empowerment.

A key issue within the context of postcolonial societies relates to the difficulties of reconciling global and local forces. This is explored by Rene van der Duim, Karin Peters and John Akama as they compare Maasai tourism projects in Kenya and Tanzania. In outlining the political and power structures that have traditionally framed much of the development of cultural tourism in Africa, they point to gaps between apparent local participation and true empowerment and the need for closer analysis of stakeholder relationships.

Overcoming long-standing imbalances of power between social groups is part of the groundwork for establishing cultural tourism. Also within this section Jennifer Briedenhann and Pranill Ramchander discuss the development of 'township tourism' in post-apartheid South Africa. They focus on the relatively under-researched aspect of local resident perceptions of the impacts of township tourism in Soweto, which reveals that although many of the positive impacts are recognised and appreciated, there is still clearly a need for better mechanisms for local community inclusion, participation and empowerment.

In situations where there is a more level playing field between stakeholders, cultural tourism is arguably easier to establish. Frances McGettigan, Kevin Burns and Fiona Candon discuss a case study of Kiltimagh in rural Ireland, where European Commission initiatives have encouraged 'bottom-up' approaches to community development. Here a partnership approach provided an effective framework for community involvement and has demonstrated the increasing importance of the more intangible aspects of community and tourism development, such as quality of life and pride of place. Also in the case of an advanced political context, Satu Miettinen looks at the status of Lappish communities in Finland with regards to arts and crafts production, traditional heritage and tourism development. She highlights positive examples of small villages in which local producers have managed to improve their arts and crafts businesses as a result of training and networking, and how local women have been instrumental in developing cultural and heritage tourism. Overall, development has been largely successful due to high levels of community participation and empowerment.

Leading the third section on *Authenticity and Commodification*, Nicola MacLeod discusses the complex and contradictory nature of authenticity and commodification, which are recurrent themes in tourism literature. She revisits previous theories and sheds new light on these phenomena in a postmodern context, questioning the very premise on which concerns about these issues have traditionally been based. The case studies in this section illustrate the different ways in which both tourism products and tourist experiences are affected by these notions in contemporary contexts. Each questions changing perceptions of authenticity and commodification, both in theory and practice, suggesting that tourists often think that they want authenticity, but in fact are not all that comfortable when it involves too much 'reality'. Indeed, as Grünewald notes in this volume, many tourists are simply happy to take home beautiful souvenirs, however 'acculturalised' they may be.

For indigenous people, traditional (albeit changing) processes may constitute 'authenticity' far more than the products that are created.

Frans Schouten examines different forms of authenticity in both Western and non-Western contexts, focusing in particular on the souvenir industry in Bali and the Netherlands. He notes the very different perceptions of products and processes in terms of tradition and identity, and the power structures that determine the 'authentication' of tourist souvenirs.

Rodrigo de Azeredo Grünewald explores the ways in which tourism growth in regions of Brazil (namely amongst the Pataxó people) has altered arts and crafts production. He suggests that native objects are rarely imbued with the same 'functional authenticity', but they can still retain internal significance at the same time as acquiring new meanings. Conscious ethnic identity construction is an important element of social vitality, and tourism can often enhance rather than compromise this process.

Tanuja Barker, Darma Putra and Agung Wiranatha discuss Balinese dance and some of the difficulties of retaining indigenous meanings whilst providing touristic performances. It is clear that a divergence of opinions has emerged amongst local dance groups as to how far performances should be adapted to suit tourists' needs; however they note that much of the recent controversy relates to economic rather than social issues (e.g. the exploitation of dancers for low wages). They rightly conclude by emphasising the importance of respecting indigenous perspectives on authenticity and its manifestation in performing culture.

The final section focuses on *Interpretation* within cultural tourism and László Puczkó provides an overview of the changing nature of interpretation within the tourism attraction sector. Using a framework of theory from applied psychology, he explains some of the tools and techniques that have been developed in recent years in order to refine the process of interpretation to meet the needs of both individual and collective users. He argues that interpretation requires a complex blend of both a scientific and a fundamentally human approach if it is to be successful. The case studies in this section go on to describe some of the difficulties of implementation, due to political agendas, social sensitivities and economic necessity. Together they highlight the ways in which cultural tourism attractions are being forced to reconsider issues of interpretation and (re)presentation in the light of new political and social agendas, the changing needs of visitors, and increasing competition. A certain degree of openness and flexibility is required on the part of managers as they adapt and respond to these developments.

Tamara Rátz examines the controversies inherent in managing dissonant heritage sites, focusing on a case study of the House of Terror in Budapest, Hungary. She emphasises problems of political bias and selective interpretation, issues of local resonance versus tourist detachment, and the limitations of representing complex historical events. Overall, her contribution highlights some of the common problems facing many heritage attractions that are based on the darker and more tragic elements in our collective pasts.

Josie Appleton suggests that some of the recent political agendas in the UK have led to a dilution and distortion of the role and function of museums, many of which have turned from traditional collections management towards social inclusion. Whilst this is arguably a noble intention, she contests the notion that museums should become all things to all people, and akin to other visitor attractions, which do not purport to have an educational function.

Anya Diekmann, Géraldine Maulet and Stéphanie Quériat discuss the extent to which caves in Belgium are being standardised as visitor attractions. Whilst they accept that it is often more difficult to differentiate between natural (as opposed to cultural) attractions, they question the need for more creative and innovative approaches to presentation. This includes the interpretation of the sites, provision of additional facilities, attractions or events, and marketing.

Marion Stuart-Hoyle and Jane Lovell discuss some of the issues that are common to many heritage cities, which are moving towards the development of more contemporary and experiential attractions. They examine some of the strategies being used to engage visitors, enhance their experience and lengthen their stay, at the same time as preserving the heritage.

Conclusion

This book does not claim to offer any definitive solutions to the issues that it raises. However, it does seek to locate the phenomenon that is cultural tourism as part of a wider set of contexts that are historically embedded but are changing constantly. This is the case for both the development of tourism 'products' as expressions of culture, and in the way that culture is consumed by the tourist. Moreover, it invites the reader to read cultural tourism as a political process, or at least a set of economic transactions that have political impacts. Many of the case studies considered here reveal an ongoing process of negotiation between different social groupings relating to access to various configurations of places, peoples and pasts as cultural resources, and rights to utilise and express these in particular ways. As part of this process we can witness creative and innovative developments within cultural tourism, together with challenges and changes to the very political and social frameworks that shape it.

References

Alexander, J.C., Eyerman, R., Giesen, B., Smelser, N.J. and Sztompka, P. (2004) *Cultural Trauma and Collective Identity.* Berkley: University of California Press.
Appadurai, A. (1990) Disjuncture and difference in the global cultural economy. *Public Culture* 2 (2), 1–24.
Craik, J. (1997) The culture of tourism. In C. Rojek and J. Urry (eds) *Touring Cultures – Transformations of Travel and Theory* (pp. 113–137). London: Routledge.
Denning, M. (2004) *Culture in the Age of Three Worlds.* London: Verso.
Fisher, D. (2004) A colonial town for neo-colonial tourism. In C.M. Hall and H. Tucker (eds) *Tourism and Postcolonialism: Contested Discourses, Identities and Representations* (pp. 126–139). London: Routledge.
Frykman, J. (2002) Place for something else. Analysing a cultural imaginary. *Ethnologia Europaea – Journal of European Ethnology* 32 (2), 47–68.
Hughes, H. (2000) *Arts, Entertainment and Tourism.* Oxford: Butterworth-Heinemann.
Junemo, M. (2004) "Let's build a Palm Island!" Playfulness in complex times. In M. Sheller and J. Urry (eds) *Tourism Mobilities: Places to Play, Places in Play* (pp. 181–191). London: Routledge.
Keating, M. (2001) Rethinking the region. Culture, institutions and economic development in Catalonia and Galicia. *European Urban and Regional Studies* 8 (3), 217–234.
Levi-Strauss, C. (1988) *The Savage Mind.* London: Weidenfeld & Nicolson.
McKercher, B. and du Cros, H. (2002) *Cultural Tourism: The Partnership Between Tourism and Cultural Heritage Management.* New York: The Haworth Press.
Meethan, K. (2001) *Tourism in Global Society: Place, Culture, Consumption.* London: Palgrave.
Richards, G. (ed.) (1996) *Cultural Tourism in Europe.* Wallingford: CABI.
Richards, G. (ed.) (2001) *Cultural Attractions and European Tourism.* Wallingford: CABI.
Robinson, M. (2001) Tourism encounters: Intra-cultural conflicts in the world's largest industry. In A. Nezar (ed.) *Consuming Heritage, Manufacturing Tradition – Global Forms and Urban Norms* (pp. 34–67). London: Routledge.
Robinson, M. (2005) The trans-textured tourist: Literature as knowledge in the making of tourists. *Tourism Recreation Research* 30 (1), 73–81.
Robinson, M. and Boniface, P. (eds) (1999) *Tourism and Cultural Conflicts.* Wallingford: CABI.
Rojek, C. (1993) *Ways of Escape: Modern Transformations in Leisure and Travel.* London: Palgrave Macmillan.

Rojek, C. and Urry, J. (eds) (1997) Transformations of travel and theory. In: C. Rojek and J. Urry (eds) *Touring Cultures – Transformations of Travel and Theory* (pp. 1– 19). London: Routledge.

Scott, A.J. (1997) The cultural economy of cities. *International Journal of Urban and Regional Research* 21 (2), 323– 339.

Sheller, M. and Urry, J. (eds) (2004) *Tourism Mobilities: Places to Play, Places in Play.* London: Routledge.

Sigala, M. and Leslie, D. (eds) (2005) *International Cultural Tourism: Management Implications and Cases.* Oxford: Butterworth-Heinemann.

Smith, M.K. (2003) *Issues in Cultural Tourism Studies.* London: Routledge.

Therkelsen, A. (2003) Imaging places. Image formation of tourists and its consequences for destination promotion. *Scandinavian Journal of Hospitality and Tourism* 3 (2), 134– 150.

Turner, B.S. and Rojek, C. (2001) *Society and Culture: Principles of Scarcity and Solidarity.* London: Sage.

Urry, J. (1995) *Consuming Places.* London: Routledge.

Wallerstein, I. (2000) 'Cultures in conflict? Who are we? Who are the others?', *Y.K. Pao Distinguished Chair Lecture,* Center for Cultural Studies, Hong Kong University of Science and Technology, 20 September.

Part 1
Politics and Cultural Policy

Chapter 2

Cultural Politics, Cultural Policy and Cultural Tourism

JIM BUTCHER

Introduction

Many writers have written about important political dimensions of tourism on a range of topics. However, as Hall recognises, the political nature of this massive global industry, at both macro and micro political levels, is underacknowledged (Hall, 1994: 4).

More specifically, there are important political issues connected to *cultural* tourism. For example, the role of museums and the commercialisation of heritage are often part of debates about national identity in ways that mass tourism is not (Herbert, 1995; Lowenthal, 1998). Also, museums, galleries and heritage sites, along with other objects of the cultural tourist's fascination, are regulated through state cultural policy, policy that is very much the product of a wider contested cultural politics. As McGuigan argues, cultural policy should be considered, formulated and criticised in the light of wider cultural politics, rather than viewed as a technical question of implementing given objectives (McGuigan, 1996, 2004).

This chapter takes as its framework a simple proposition – that *cultural policy* provides the bridge between *cultural politics* on one hand and *cultural attractions* on the other. The chapter considers the following question: 'What are the broad cultural political influences, influential in the trajectory of cultural policy making around the world, that inform cultural policy specifically related to cultural tourism?'

Any attempt to answer this broad question is inevitably general and provisional, but no less important for that. Here it is argued that the notion of a singular culture, often linked to nation, and positioned in the liberal humanist tradition, has in recent decades been challenged by *cultures* in the plural, linked to multiple identities, often critical of the supposed elitism of liberal humanism. This is a broad trend that has influenced social and political thought, and shaped debates about culture

21

and cultural policy. It is a trend reflected in policies related to cultural tourism, such as the importance of cultural diversity in the development and marketing of 'cultural cities' (Landry, 2000), the evolution of museums to reflect a wider variety of historical experience (Walsh, 1992), and the trend in UNESCO to promote a diversification away from economically developed countries and towards traditional cultures in its choice of World Heritage Sites (UNESCO, 1994).

We begin by considering what cultural policy is, and its importance with respect to the development of cultural tourism.

Cultural Policy and its Relevance to Cultural Tourism

Cultural policy has been defined as 'the institutional supports that channel both aesthetic creativity and collective ways of life' (Miller & Yudice, 2002: 1). These institutional supports may be regarded as the ways in which governments support, or fail to support, artistic output, and output that is considered part of a place's 'cultural capital', referring to a place being perceived as exhibiting positive cultural connotations, and hence being attractive to prospective cultural tourists (see Throsby, 2000).[1] Historic buildings, cultural events, galleries, museums and also the planning and design of public spaces contribute to cultural capital, and are all part of the remit of the public sector – hence the importance of policy.

Cultural capital also includes the nurturing and marketing of an intangible 'sense of place' – in the cultural city, it may be more 'the grit and the glitter, the diversity, the excitement and stimulation of human activity, than interesting settings and events which attracts the cultural tourists' (Richards, 2001: 40). Hence place marketing has also grown in importance in cultural policy (Murray, 2001).

Whilst the provision of cultural tourism attractions may be just one aspect of a national or regional cultural policy, it has become important, especially with the growth of leisure travel, a development that effectively makes the objects of cultural policy – museums, galleries, festivals etc. – also the objects of the tourist's desires, and hence a vehicle for economic development and regeneration. For example, Picard (1996: 180) discusses a striking case of the intimacy between cultural policy and tourism, discussing the way in which the Balinese state's promotion of cultural tourism has 'entrust[ed] the fate of Balinese culture to the cause

---

[1] A different, but related, meaning applied to the term is that of Bourdieu, who views cultural capital as a knowledge of high culture that positions the cultured individual apart from, and above, others (Bourdieu, 1990).

of the tourism industry'. The role of cultural tourism in national identity is also briefly discussed by Steinberg (2001: 41), who cites the case of India, where tourism promotion has been related to the greater goal of 'rehabilitating the Indian personality through the revival of traditional cultures', a process incentivised in parts of rural India by cultural tourism revenues. Even the UK's Millennium Dome (and numerous other Millennium attractions around the world) could also be cited in this context, as it was widely regarded as an attempt to provide a *unifying* celebration of, and reflection on, British culture, and one that would regenerate a part of East London through tourism (see McGuigan, 2004).

Case: The history debate in Germany

An interesting example of the implications for cultural policy, and cultural attractions, of a nation's cultural politics, is that of Germany. Germany's intensely problematic recent history gave rise to a strong sense of a need for reflection in West German cultural policy, and in the new post-reunification Germany after 1991 (Parkes, 1997: pt. 3). A prominent example of the ensuing debates on this theme was the *Historikerstreit* (History debate) that took place in the late 1980s, notably between conservative historian Ernst Nolte and liberal social theorist Jurgen Habermas. The former argued that German identity should be premised upon the broad sweep of German history, emphasising the country's progressive role as well as the experience of WWII (Furedi, 1992). For Habermas, WWII and the Holocaust were specific, recent aspects of history that imposed a duty upon Germany to learn from its recent past and develop a political culture in the light of this (Furedi, 1992) – the German term *vergangenheitsbewältigung* (coming to terms with the past) sums up this outlook (Schoenbaum & Pond, 1996). Hence the debate polarised around two versions of German identity, drawing differentially on Germany's past, and more specifically, the importance of the past in shaping contemporary German political culture.

The terms of this debate also framed the discussions about Germany's museums and memorials in the 1980s and subsequently – how much space should be devoted to WWII in national museums? Where should new memorials to Germany's victims be sited, and whose suffering should they reflect? In the early 1980s the plans to build the Museum of German History in West Berlin, and the House of History of the Federal Republic in Bonn, caused controversy, with some seeing the museums as opportunities for Germany to critically confront its past, and others emphasising the forging of a more self-confident national identity

(Furedi, 1992). Such questions are clearly fraught given the role of the Holocaust as a moral touchstone for contemporary society. Hence the contestation of cultural policy is bound up with competing conceptions of German identity, and cultural tourism attractions are implicated in this.

Liberal Humanism and Cultural Policy

The ideology underpinning cultural policy in the modern era is generally considered to have been that of liberal humanism (Jordan & Weedon, 1995: ch. 2). Liberal philosophy is characterised by an emphasis on the rights of the individual (often *vis a vis* the state), to realise him or herself to the full, whilst humanism considers reason as the common driver of progress for all humanity. Implicit in liberal humanism is a universal conception of culture as being the best and finest that human society has achieved in the arts, science and knowledge – a common standard against which all societies can be considered and to which all people can aspire. Yet the post-WWII period has witnessed a questioning of this outlook, and this questioning informs many of the debates in contemporary cultural policy, including those pertaining to cultural tourism.

The liberal humanist view of culture was famously defined by 19th-century educationalist Mathew Arnold in his 1867 polemic *Culture and Anarchy* thus: culture is 'the pursuit of our total perfection by means of getting to know, on all matters which most concern us, the best which has been thought and said in the world' (Arnold, 1971: 6). Further, Arnold argued that society should 'make the best that has been thought and known in the world current everywhere', and that 'the aim of the cultured individual' is to carry 'from one end of the society to the other, the best knowledge, the best ideas of their time' (Arnold, 1971: 44).

This vision was in the Enlightenment tradition, which upheld a *universal* conception of human culture, rather than one that takes as its starting point *different* cultures. Museums, art appreciation, music – in so far as they were supported by the state – developed around Arnold's themes in developing Western societies, and the legacy remains strong today. In the UK, for example, cultural policy has in the past been very much in this tradition. From the Acts of Parliament establishing public libraries (1850) and public museums (1849), funding for arts and culture have been infused with Arnold's notion of culture and being a cultured individual (Jordan & Weedon, 1995). A similar tradition is evident in the USA, France and other industrial societies (Yudice & Miller, 2002).

Challenges to Liberal Humanism

In opposition to Arnold's notion of culture, opponents have invoked *cultures* in the plural. In has been widely argued in recent decades that the liberal humanist worldview served to legitimise the power of Western societies and the elites within them (Jordan & Weedon, 1995). Its critics argue that it takes the experience of the West, and projects this as a universal standard for all societies and the cultures within them, in the name of 'civilisation' or 'progress' (Jordan & Weedon, 1995), and as such, that it is 'eurocentric' (p. 32–33). It presents, some argue, culture as a hierarchical ladder, whereby the way to progress was, and is, to take a step towards the values and beliefs emanating from the most economically advanced capitalist countries.

For example, two writers from the cultural studies field comment ironically on what they view as a eurocentric liberal humanist conception of culture:

> 'Beauty, ...morality, ... virtue, ...intellect, ...perfection ... (universal) standards' – here in a nutshell are virtually all of the values of the West's well-established dominant cultural institutions. Think of the BBC, Oxford University, Harvard, London's Museum of Mankind, New York's Museum of Modern Art, The Tate Gallery, The Louvre ... Thanks to the benevolent institutions of western colonialism and cultural imperialism, the potential for this enlightenment and perfection is not simply limited to individuals within Western societies. It is available to all the world's people. (Jordan & Weedon, 1995: 26)

Jordan and Weedon are critical of the Enlightenment-influenced view of 'universal' culture and take a different view. They characterise their view as pluralist (accepting and reflecting different cultures), inclusive (enabling previously excluded cultures to be part of society's cultural mainstream) and ultimately democratic (enabling all sections of society to contribute to its future) (Jordan & Weedon, 1995).

Raymond Williams has identified a number of ways of looking at 'culture', which can be invoked to help understand the tension between the liberal humanist outlook and the pluralist approach with regard to cultural policy (Williams, 1976: 80). Culture can be:

(1) a *general* process of intellectual, spiritual and aesthetic development (which we might associate with liberal humanism);

(2) a *particular* way of life, whether of a people, a period or group (which suggests a pluralist approach); and
(3) the works and practices of intellectual and especially artistic activity.

It is the third definition that is normally associated with cultural tourism. However, whilst traditionally this artistic and intellectual activity, in the form of the work in galleries, the contents of museums, great architecture etc. was linked to the first definition, as exemplary of a *general* process, there is today also an emphasis on cultural sites as reflecting *particular* ways of life, particular strands of culture. This latter outlook is in line with Williams' second definition. Cultural policy, and cultural tourism sites, have been influenced by this trend. For example, consider the following statement from an influential UK arts monitoring group, putting forward a view that contests the 'singular' liberal humanist view with a pluralist one:

> The UK is made up not of a singular culture, but of a multiplicity of cultural groups and interests ... part of the individual's sense of identity arises from the groups to which they belong. 'British culture' is neither a singular concept nor a set of neat packages labelled 'youth culture', 'woman's culture', and so on: it is a kaleidoscope constantly shifting and richly diverse. (National Arts and Media Strategy Monitoring Group, 1992; cited in Jordan & Weedon, 1995: 27)

Cultural policy has, of course, always been contested – this is not new. In the past this was the case through projects of the political Right and Left, through nationalism and regionalism and by different social groups. These were generally political (as opposed to cultural) projects that often shared the Enlightenment-influenced outlook of liberal humanism. Today, however, the liberal humanist tradition itself, which influenced both official cultural policy, and the arguments of those contesting it, has been challenged by more pluralistic notions of culture that take as their starting point *cultures* as opposed to *culture*. The results of this have been challenges to the mainstream made by social and ethnic groups, or policy makers claiming to act on their behalf, on the basis of claiming a distinctive cultural space, and this has been institutionalised through the growth of multicultural arts and other policies in economically advanced societies and supranational bodies such as the EU and UN.

The context for the growth of this politics of culture is the decline of the grand political projects and ideologies of the elites and, indeed, their opponents, especially in the post-Cold War era (Furedi, 1992). Universal political projects such as socialism or capitalism do not exert the same influence over contemporary consciousness. Rather, identity has increasingly become analysed and understood as multiple, fluid *identities* (Giddens, 1991). Hence politics has become increasingly influenced by a *cultural* politics, which often involves challenging official culture and traditional notions of national identity (Malik, 1996). Jordan and Weedon (1995) show that since the late 1960s dominant cultural institutions have been repeatedly challenged for their 'elitist' stance, and have adopted a new agenda prominently featuring 'diversity'. These criticisms of liberal humanism are increasingly influential within cultural policy, and therefore shape policy pertaining to cultural tourism too. Smith's (2003) book on cultural tourism contains numerous examples of policies and initiatives that seek to redress the balance from grand towards excluded narratives, or from a liberal humanist outlook towards pluralism.

Case: Culture wars in the USA

The USA is an important case to consider in the above respect, given its roles as the most economically advanced and powerful nation in the world and the leading Cold War protagonist, and its global cultural role (today considered by many critics of cultural globalisation to be detrimental to cultural diversity around the world). The end of the Cold War pulled the rug from under American identity, which had rested on America's role as leader of the 'free world' against communism (Furedi, 1992). With no Cold War through which to articulate a sense of what it is to be American, conservatives turned to multiculturalism and political correctness as scapegoats for America's relative decline (Malik, 1996).

For example, Adam Meyerson, editor of the conservative *Policy Review* argued that 'the greatest ideological threat to western civilisation comes from within the West's own cultural institutions' (cited in Malik, 1996: 181). One prominent such institution in the USA is the National Endowment for the Arts, which became the focus of the infamous 'Culture Wars' in the 1980s and subsequently. Under the Reagan administration especially, conservatives railed against what they saw as the dilution of tradition and American values in art, a process they saw as sponsored by the Endowment, whilst liberals defended its pluralist approach (McGuigan, 1996: 7–11).

The Culture Wars are implicated in debates on cultural tourism attractions. For example, when the Smithsonian Institute developed an exhibition in 1995 on the 50th anniversary of the atomic bombing of Hiroshima and Nagasaki, many objected that it was anti-American, as it emphasised Japanese casualties, thus implicitly questioning the notion that the bombing was a just military action – a bomb for peace. Yet in 2003, Japanese veterans and liberals objected to another exhibition featuring the Enola Gay, the aircraft that dropped the atom bomb on Hiroshima, on the opposite grounds, that it was uncritical of the bombing and did not show the devastating human results of the technology on display (Rennie & Joyce, 2003).

The criticisms of the liberal humanist outlook are briefly considered below in terms of the advocacy of alternative narratives, populism and postmodernism. A brief defence of liberal humanism follows this.

Alternative Narratives

Sociologist Stuart Hall argues that 'the emergence of new subjects, new genders, new ethnicities, new regions, new communities' has given hitherto invisible groups 'the means to speak for themselves for the first time' (Hall, 1991: 34). Hall is typical of many in seeing the emergence of the voices of those hitherto excluded within mainstream culture as a democratic trend, against hegemonic national identities. Those contesting liberal humanism in cultural policy typically adopt Hall's outlook and apply it to state-sponsored cultural output. For example, Miller and Yudice (2002) view official cultural policy as often incorporating the subordination of one group of people by the elites, and hence regard challenges to this as potentially empowering for minorities or even majorities excluded from official manifestations of culture. Such a view is influential in the arts and cultural establishments in the UK, USA and elsewhere too.

Sociologist Axel Honneth offers an analysis that is useful here, drawing on ideas developed by German political sociologist Jurgen Habermas. Honneth argues that social struggles have increasingly come to take the form of *struggles for recognition* of one's culture on the part of minority or excluded groups (Honneth, 1996). If successful, such widened recognition of plural cultures has the potential to develop a more democratic, representative public discourse, which can influence policy and culture more generally. In this vein, arguments for reflecting greater diversity in museums and cultural attractions often invoke the need to recognise and give voice to different cultures. Campaigners, minority groups and liberal policy makers have pushed for just such wider recognition in cultural attractions such as museums, galleries, visitor attractions, festivals, carnivals and other expressions of culture.

For example, recent years have witnessed the 'phenomenal' growth of visitor attractions and museums focussed on the issue of slavery (Dann & Seaton, 2001a: 13). Butler argues that such sites can provide an opportunity for Americans to reflect on their inglorious past and adopt a more critical sense of what America stands for: 'It is necessary for people, both as individuals and as members of a society to see, touch and feel their past errors, so that when they are confronted by a similar evil in the present or the future, they can challenge it before it becomes institutionalised and the surrounding culture becomes desensitised to its dangers' (Butler, 2001: 174). It has been argued that such sites can potentially boost the cultural representation and self-esteem of Black Americans, although this is regarded as highly problematic due to issues such as how the past is portrayed and the commercial interests some-times involved (Dann & Seaton, 2001a). Hence heritage attractions are posited as having an important role in including the excluded and challenging dominant ideas that constitute national identity.

The growth of tourist attractions around the theme of native American Indians in the USA, interest in Aboriginal tourism in Australia, and the increased number of museums focussing on the experience of minorities in the UK are other examples of the growth in supply of *alternative* historical narratives, often critical (or with the potential to be critical) of previously dominant aspects of national identity.

Supranational cultural policy making can be a significant arena for developing world nations in the above respect. Miller and Yudice (2002: 191) argue that 'culture has clearly been a key site of critique by those excluded from the bounty of modernity'. For example, developing world countries have utilised UNESCO fora to stake cultural claims, such as their demand that UNESCO's Decade of Culture, 1988–97, should adopt a multiethnic definition of culture rooted in diversity, rather than one rooted in universal values (Miller & Yudice, 2002).

Yet the growth of demands for recognition – be they originating from groups deemed excluded or from critical policy makers claiming to act on their behalf – can become difficult. One author refers to this fraught process in the following terms:

> Whose culture shall be the official one and whose shall be subordinated? What cultures shall be regarded as worthy of display and which shall be hidden? Whose history shall be remembered and whose forgotten? What image of social life shall be projected and which shall be marginalised? What voices shall be heard and which

silenced? Who is representing whom, and on what basis? This is the
realm of cultural politics. (Jordan & Weedon, 1995: 4)

The quote alludes to contentious issues that animate those concerned
with cultural policy and shape the cultural attractions sector.

Populism

It is worthy of note that the advocacy of a broadening of cultural
policy to include hitherto excluded narratives is often explicitly
presented as anti-elitist. For example, one author refers to 'culture rising
up from below, not passed down from above' as 'an important
characteristic of the new cultural planning impetus, the new movement
from community enrichment' (Von Eckardt, cited in Smith, 2003: 153).
Further, '[t]his assures popularity, pluralism and whatever the antonym
for elitism is' (p. 153). As well as the growth of such populist sentiments,
boundaries between high and mass culture have become blurred (Urry,
1990). What is considered excellent, or valid, involves a wider diversity
of cultural forms, often rooted in the experience of 'the people'.

For example, populism is implicit in France's *ecomusée* model,
developed in the 1970s, and influential since, which seeks to present a
people's, industrial history in the form of a museum. This is not high
culture, but a *people's* culture, reflecting the distinctive experience of
people in a particular locality or industry (Walsh, 1992). Walsh argues
that such museums can engage visitors in a way other museums may
not, through relating to the lived experiences of their ancestors in their
daily lives (Walsh, 1992). This sentiment has influenced the growth of
museums and attractions whose focus is on ordinary people and
everyday lives (Miller & Yudice, 2002: 152).

Postmodernism

Another way of viewing the shift from liberal humanism to greater
cultural diversity is to consider the influence of the postmodern condition on both the tourist and the policy-making organisations. While the
characterisation of contemporary society or culture as 'postmodern' is a
point of dispute amongst sociologists and others, many consider that
some aspects of postmodernism are in evidence in cultural policy and in
culture generally – a declining sense of a cultural hierarchy, a blurring of
boundaries between different cultural forms, and the growing sense that
culture is fluid and relative (McGuigan, 1996: 30). As such, postmodern-

ism could be seen as a counter to the hierarchy of modern social order, and for this reason, a progressive cultural development.

In this vein Harvey (1989: 48) argues that '[t]he idea that all groups have a right to speak for themselves, in their own voice, and have that voice accepted as authentic and legitimate [...] is essential to the pluralistic stance of post-modernism'. Further, he argues that by decentring the liberal humanist discourse of modernism in this way, hitherto marginal groups can occupy centre stage, and engage in a more democratic social dialogue (Harvey, 1989). Such sentiments fuel attempts by policy makers to reflect a wider diversity of social experience through cultural attractions.

A Defence of Liberal Humanism

Yet whilst the anti-elitism implicit in postmodernism could be regarded as democratic, opening up 'culture' to a greater number and diversity of voices, it could also be seen as limiting. Some have argued that a celebration of diversity in the cultural sphere can translate into a decline of standards through the view that all cultural forms are relative, and can only be judged in their own, culturally specific, terms. If we reject humanism in favour of such relativism then how can culture transcend difference and aspire to reflect universal themes? The tension between a conception of universal human culture, and the more relativistic direction favoured by many critical cultural policy makers, is an important axis around which cultural policy is disputed.

This issue has been well expressed by cultural critic Kenan Malik. He argues that the cultural 'ladder' characteristic of Victorian England (and characteristic of liberal humanism generally) has been taken down and turned on its side, with all cultural expressions at the same level and therefore equal (Malik, 1996). Yet far from tackling inequality, this process reproduces it in a new, cultural form, by defining people by their differences and denying the idea of human progress (Malik, 1996). Applying Malik's argument to cultural attractions one could argue that whilst a diversity of voices can now be heard in the arts and culture, it becomes harder for them to articulate anything beyond their own *particular* cultural terms of reference – there is little chance for anyone, regardless of cultural or economic background, to ascend a ladder placed on its side.

Following this logic, others have argued that the anti-elitist populism of sections of today's cultural establishment compartmentalises historical and cultural artefacts and artistic expression into distinct categories, and restricts the potential for culture from any origin to aspire to be truly, universally great (Appleton, 2001). For example, in the British Museum in London, the Rosetta Stone is surely a historical artefact with universal significance, with great import for all humanity, regardless of the perceived demands of the people, or the perceived needs of different communities and cultures. Further, the museum itself is valued for its role as a repository of artefacts reflecting *human* culture and history, not *particular* cultures or histories.

A rather different argument put forward by some critical of liberal humanism's critics is that 'the people' in populist cultural policy comprise a stage army mobilised rhetorically to justify a vain attempt by disconnected elites to connect with their constituencies. In this vein, cultural critic Clare Fox argues, with reference to the British context, that cultural populism in the arts is often a self-conscious and patronising attempt to create social connectedness that singularly fails to challenge or inspire (Fox, 2004).

And is liberal humanism necessarily at odds with the trend towards pluralism and populism? A middle ground has been considered by Miller and Yudice (2002) and recently by the former Head of the British Museum Robert Anderson (2001), one that can combine the sense of aesthetic standards and universal significance, whilst also accepting the efficacy of populist (socially inclusive?) trends in cultural policy. Anderson (2001) asserts that it is important to maintain culture that is not historically contingent in places such as the British Museum, whilst accepting a more populist approach elsewhere. Hence perhaps the issue is less the variety of different types of cultural attraction, and more the conflation of the mission of the museum with that of the theme park (Swarbrooke, 2000) or with the objectives traditionally assigned to social policy (Appleton, 2001).

Case: The UK and social inclusion

The UK is striking for the extent to which cultural policy has become influenced by populism and the aim of addressing the claims of hitherto excluded sections of the community. Notably, this outlook is central to the social inclusion agenda, through which cultural policy is increasingly required to 'socially include' those previously excluded in a variety of ways (Matarrasso, 1997). In the name of 'joined up government', a social inclusion unit was established on the inception of the New Labour government in 1997, seeking to promote inclusion across all government departments. Principally through the Department for Culture, Media and

Sport, cultural policy has become profoundly influenced by the emphasis on social inclusion. Cultural attractions as diverse as the Millennium Dome, the British Museum and Magna (one of a new breed of hybrid 'edutainment'-oriented, publicly funded visitor attractions) have all adapted to the social inclusion agenda, a significant aspect of which is that cultural attractions should reflect and reach out to the diversity of culture – different religions, ethnicities and levels of formal educational attainment. The erstwhile boundaries between cultural policy and social policy have been significantly eroded, and cultural attractions are deemed to have a direct role in tackling social problems. Their funding is often linked to addressing these wider, social goals.

Conclusion

Wider ideological trends have shaped the cultural tourism sector as they inform many of the debates about heritage sites, galleries, museums and so forth that comprise cultural tourism attractions. Cultural policy, developed through liberal humanism, has tended to adapt to criticisms that it has excluded alternative narratives and is elitist. A cultural attractions sector that to a greater extent reflects cultural diversity and cultural populism has emerged in the light of this.

Criticisms of these trends can take the form of a conservative desire to preserve the exclusivity of high culture. Yet equally they can represent a humanist desire to uphold the universal value of great art, scientific advance and an understanding of human history, regardless of the origin of the artefact or the audience.

The following chapters in this section consider further a number of themes on cultural tourism politics and policy. Catherine Kelly's chapter looks at heritage politics, focusing on a case study of the Ulster American Folk Park in Northern Ireland. Barbara Marciszewska's chapter considers the approach in new EU member state Poland to cultural tourism, and the socioeconomic significance of this growing sector. Finally, Arvid Viken's chapter provides an interesting case study, looking at the micro-political dynamics of the development of Norway's only barony as a tourist attraction.

References

Anderson, R. (2001) The access issue is nothing new. In J. Appleton (ed.) *Museums For the People: Conversations in Print* (pp. 44–46). London: Institute of Ideas.

Appleton, J. (2001) Museums for 'the people'? In J. Appleton (ed.) *Museums For the People: Conversations in Print* (pp. 10–26). London: Institute of Ideas.

Arnold, M. (1971) *Culture and Anarchy.* Cambridge: Cambridge University Press (originally published 1875).

Bourdieu, P. (1990) *Distinction: A Social Critique of the Judgement of Taste* (R. Nice, trans.) London: Routledge.

Butler, D.L. (2001) Whitewashing plantations: The commodification of a slave free antebellum South. In G.M.S. Dann and A.V. Seaton (eds) *Slavery, Contested Heritage and Thanatourism* (pp. 163– 176). New York: Haworth Press.

Dann, G.M.S. and Seaton, A.V. (2001a) (eds) *Slavery, Contested Heritage and Thanatourism.* New York: Haworth Press.

Dann, G.M.S. and Seaton, A.V. (2001b) Slavery, contested heritage and Thanatourism. In G.M.S. Dann and A.V. Seaton (eds) *Slavery, Contested Heritage and Thanatourism* (pp. 1– 31). New York: Haworth Press.

Fox, C. (2004) The politics of art. *The Liberal* (2), 16– 17.

Furedi, F. (1992) *Mythical Past Elusive Future: History and Society in an Anxious Age.* London: Pluto.

Giddens, A. (1991) *Modernity and Self Identity: Self and Society in the Late Modern Age.* Cambridge: Polity.

Hall, C.M. (1994) *Tourism and Politics: Policy, Power and Place.* New York: Wiley.

Hall, S. (1991) The local and the global. In A.D. King (ed.) *Culture, Globalization and the World System: Contemporary Conditions for the Representation of Identity.* Basingstoke: MacMillan.

Harvey, D. (1989) *The Condition of Postmodernity.* Cambridge: Blackwell.

Herbert, D.T. (ed.) (1995) *Heritage, Tourism and Society.* London: Pinter.

Herbert D.T. (1995) Heritage places, leisure and tourism. In D.T. Herbert (ed.) *Heritage, Tourism and Society* (pp. 1– 20). London: Pinter.

Honneth, A. (1996) *The Struggle for Recognition: The Moral Grammar of Social Conflicts.* Cambridge: Polity.

Jordan, G. and Weedon, C. (1995) *Cultural Politics: Class, Gender, Race and the Postmodern World.* Oxford: Blackwell.

Landry, C. (2000) *The Creative City: A Toolkit for Urban Innovators.* London: Earthscan.

Lowenthal, D. (1998) *The Heritage Crusade and the Spoils of History.* Cambridge: Cambridge University Press.

Malik, K. (1996) *The Meaning of Race: Race, History and Culture in Western Society.* London: Macmillan.

Matarasso, F. (1997) *Use or Ornament? The Social Impact of Participation in the Arts.* Stroud: Comedia.

McGuigan, J. (1996) *Culture and the Public Sphere.* London: Routledge.

McGuigan, J. (2004) *Rethinking Cultural Policy.* Milton Keynes: Open University Press.

Miller, T. and Yudice, G. (2002) *Cultural Policy.* London: Sage.

Murray, C. (2001) *Making Sense of Place: New Approaches to Place Marketing.* London: Comedia.

Parkes, S. (1997) *Understanding Contemporary Germany.* London: Routledge.

Picard, D. (1996) *Bali: Cultural Tourism and Touristic Culture.* Singapore: Archipelago Press.

Rennie, D. and Joyce, C. (2003) Enola Gay flies into new A-bomb controversy. *Daily Telegraph* archives. On WWW at http://www.telegraph.co.uk/news/main/filed on 21/08/03. Accessed 20.7.04.

Richards, G. (ed.) (2000) *Cultural Attractions and European Tourism*. Oxford: CABI.

Schoenbaum, D. and Pond, E. (1996) *The German Question and Other German Questions*. London: Palgrave.

Smith, M. (2002) *Issues in Cultural Tourism Studies*. London: Routledge.

Steinberg, C. (2001) Culture and sustainable tourism. In *Recognising Culture: A Series of Briefing Papers on Culture and Development*, Comedia, Department of Canadian Heritage and UNESCO, supported by the World Bank.

Swarbrooke, J. (2000) Museums: Theme parks of the third millennium? In M. Robinson *et al*. (eds) *Tourism and Heritage Relationships: Global, National and Local Perspectives* (pp. 417–432). Sunderland: Business Education Publishers Ltd.

Throsby, D. (2000) *Economics and Culture*. Cambridge: Cambridge University Press.

UNESCO (1994) Report from expert meeting on global strategy, Convention Concerning the Protection of the World Cultural and Natural Heritage, 18th session, 12–17 November. On WWW at http://unesco.org/archive/global94.htm. Accessed 20.10.04.

Urry, J. (1990) *The Tourist Gaze*. London: Sage.

Walsh, K. (1992) *The Representation of the Past: Museums and Heritage in the Post-Modern World*. London: Routledge.

Williams, R. (1976) *Keywords*. London: Fontana.

Chapter 3
Heritage Tourism Politics in Ireland

CATHERINE KELLY

Introduction

The ways in which heritage objects are selected, put together, and written or spoken about have political effects. These effects are not those of the objects *per se*; it is the use made of these objects and interpretive frameworks that can open up or close down historical, social and cultural possibilities; ... by legitimating difference, museum pedagogy can become a critical pedagogy (Hooper-Greenhill, 2000). The importance of insightful and inclusive cultural policy that acknowledges such legitimisation of difference is crucial in spaces of contested identity and multiple heritage(s). Ireland is only one such space in an increasing number of global zones of conflict where concepts of 'heritage and national cultural identity' have become fragmented, blurred and often violently challenged. As tourism increasingly seeks out cultural products, the politics of heritage representation for-self, versus for-others, becomes more and more loaded.

This chapter will address issues relating to the representation of emigration history and heritage using a specific heritage site case study situated within Northern Ireland. Heritage is a much debated concept with definitions ranging from 'anything simply inherited from the past, ... an incorporation of the natural and the built environment' (Duffy, 1994: 77) to 'a commodified product using a selection of resources from the past for the products of modern demands ... a specific use of history, not a synonym for it' (Ashworth & Larkham, 1994: 47). These authors also argue that the heritage commodity is a product that can be used by consumers/visitors and therefore contains particular messages. 'These messages stem from the conscious choices of resources, products and packaging, which are performed on the basis of sets of subjective values, consciously or not, of those exercising these choices' (Ashworth & Larkham, 1994: 20). In recent decades many writers have discussed 'dominant ideology hypotheses' in relation to culture and other issues, whereby governments and/or ruling elites project legitimising messages to compound their positions. Bourdieu's concepts of 'cultural capital' can be extended to include heritage, and as such, forms part of a process of national politicocultural power relations.

On the island of Ireland, where concepts of 'national', 'heritage' and 'cultural identity' are contested and problematic, the role of cultural organisations, policy formulators and heritage tourism sites takes on added significance. 'In Northern Ireland, culture is one of many terrains on which political struggles are waged. Culture is seen as one battlefield on which the broader political struggle can be fought, the interests of one's own national community advanced, and those of the other retarded' (Thompson, 2003: 1). It should not, however, be assumed that dominant state organisations and others do not *acknowledge* the difficulty of variable definitions, uses and interpretations of both 'culture' and 'heritage'. A multiplicity of quite different ideologies can (and do) exist, and can be conveyed through the same heritage, rather than any specific coherent political programme intended to support any distinctive prevailing view of society. Whether national conflicts are reconcilable through proactive, inclusive cultural heritage policy is arguable and remains to be seen in many places, but questions of identity and difference appear to be ubiquitous in the landscape of contemporary political theory (O'Neill, 2003). Problems of diverse heritage representation are not exclusive to divided states such as Ireland; Graham *et al*. (2000), note that this imagining of an internal national homogeneity – which draws inevitably upon a particular representation of heritage and a mythology of the past for its coherency and legitimisation – has conditioned Western conceptualisations of political space for more than two centuries.

Moving from the conceptual to the applied, the politics of representation become crucial at the practical level of heritage (and other 'tourist') sites and exhibition design and layout. The process of heritage interpretation should, insists Harrison (2000), be simply about moving knowledge from specialists to the general public in a clear and effective way. What is said and what is not, in complex settings becomes loaded, and more importantly, *how* messages are portrayed takes on added significance. The task for curators, educators and exhibition developers is to provide experiences that invite visitors to make meaning through deploying and extending their existing interpretive strategies and repertoires, using their prior knowledge and their preferred learning styles, and testing their hypotheses against those of others, including experts (Hooper-Greenhill, 1995).

The politics of educated elitism is often played out in the cultural and tourism sectors where dominant ideologies are often reinforced by personnel with high cultural capital and influence. O'Neill (2003) further argues that conflicts of national identity typically call into question the legitimacy of the state, the justice of its key institutions and the inclusiveness of the ethos in which those institutions are embedded. This idea is developed by Graham *et al*. (2000: 96) who note that 'heritage is polyvocal, although the selection and transmission of messages raises the question of privileged viewpoints'. The state must, comments Thompson (2003), be seen as complicit in the shaping of cultural forms, and not simply taking ready-formed cultural identities and making them manifest in the public realm. Bearing this in mind, we must assess the importance of museums, heritage and tourism spaces in roles of the *creation* and authentic reflection of cultural identities. In certain global locations, museums and other cultural sites have been given a proactive role in reconciliation processes, which is a marked redefinition of their traditional purposes. Viewpoints vary amongst practitioners and academics about the degree of onus that should be displaced from the central State for such a key function.

Chappell (1989) suggests that visitors are ready to be challenged about major issues from the past and present and that good museums and heritage sites must not be passive or regressive but rather, should have things to say that ultimately advance the discussion about social relations and economic structures. Furthermore, Ellis (1995) comments that museums have been urged to adopt a political stance in their exhibitions that explore social problems and Karp (1992) concurs that they cannot be impartial observers in clashes over contested identities. If the understanding of culture suggests a critical role for museums in picturing and presenting inclusive, equitable societies (Sandell, 2002), then the structures and organisations related to cultural conveyance must be closely examined. Whether this is an appropriate expectation for cultural sites, many with largely tourism-driven motives, remains problematic.

Cultural Heritage Policy Context

It is beyond the remit of this chapter to attempt an in-depth review and critical assessment of the history of cultural heritage structures in Ireland, but a contemporary overview is needed as cultural context for the case study review that follows. The government department in charge of cultural matters in Northern Ireland is the Department of Culture, Arts and Leisure (DCAL). DCAL was formed as a result of political devolution and for the first time in Northern Ireland a government has created a focus for culture, arts and leisure. Of relevance to this research is the administration of 'museums and heritage' by DCAL (including the built heritage, landscape and archaeology, local history and heritage based attractions). DCAL (2001) acknowledges the value of culture in its own right but also comments that it can 'help to promote social inclusion and improve community relations by bringing people together, and helping communities to learn about and understand themselves and one another'. Amongst other functions, DCAL's strategy includes working with local District Councils to develop integrated local plans for culture, arts and leisure. A range of other governmental and nongovernmental organisations are partnering DCAL in these development plans.

Pertinent to this work is the MAGNI organisation, Museums and Galleries of Northern Ireland, which is within the Culture & Creative Industries division of DCAL (Figure 3.1). Established in 1998, MAGNI comprises the main museums, galleries and heritage sites in the province (including this chapter's Ulster American Folk Park case study). MAGNI's main functions are 'through its collections, to promote the awareness, appreciation and understanding by the public of: art, history and science, the culture and way of life of people; and the migration and settlement of people' (DCAL, 2004).

Key operational programmes and documents for DCAL include the aforementioned Local Cultural Strategies, as well as the recent 'Local Museum and Heritage Review' (2002). The latter was an attempt to

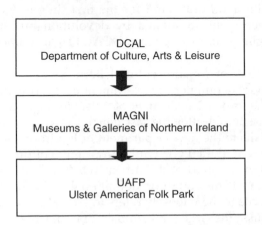

Figure 3.1 Cultural organisational structures, Northern Ireland

stocktake and devise strategies for future museum and heritage development within the new cultural department in Northern Ireland.
Amongst its key findings was the proposal to set up a new 'Heritage
Sub Group' within a wider Cultural Forum. Again, definitional and
conceptual challenges surrounding the meaning of 'heritage' will have
great significance as this proposal is developed in real terms. Even
the initial departmental response to the proposal (DCAL/DoE, 2002)
acknowledges that 'overlapping responsibilities for heritage mean that
the involvement of others will be necessary to ensure that the definition
reflects the needs of the museum, heritage, tourism and cultural sectors.'
Furthermore, as museum and heritage sites take on added roles of
cultural education in society, the politics of inclusion and representation
must be addressed and somehow expressed. Recent education consul-
tancy documents, such as 'A Culture of Tolerance: Integrating Education'
(1998) and 'Towards a Culture of Tolerance: Education for Diversity'
(1999), have proposed ways in which to appreciate cultural diversity and
to promote 'cultures of tolerance'. DCAL's own document, 'What Culture
Can Do For You' (2003), states clearly that museums achieve educational
benefits by 'educating people about their history, which helps inform
them about their personal identities'. Working together with other
governmental departments will, it seems, be a necessary focus for a
successful integrative cultural-heritage-museums sector.

'Parity of esteem' emerged as a solid phrase during the Northern
Ireland peace process. This term can be applied to not just the new,
transparent political structures, but also to good practice strategies for
attractions in the renegotiated cultural landscape. As a newly formed
department with a cultural remit for the first time in Northern Ireland
(and in a government stimulated by devolution but struggling with
political wranglings and stoppages), DCAL has an immense task on its
hands.

In the Republic of Ireland, cultural heritage matters are dispersed
somewhat through a number of governmental departments and agencies
(Figure 3.2). The former Department of Arts, Heritage, Gaeltacht and the
Islands was disbanded after the last general election and the remit for
heritage now falls to the new Department of Environment, Heritage and
Local Government (DEHLG), whilst arts and culture fall within the
Department of Arts, Sport and Tourism (DAST). The differentiation of
these functions calls into question definitional and conceptual problems
once more. 'Heritage' here loosely refers to the natural and built heritage
of Ireland, while 'the arts', film, music and the main museums and
galleries ('cultural institutions' unit) are managed by a separate minister.

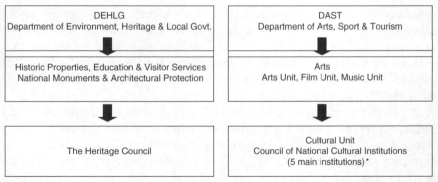

DEHLG Department of Environment, Heritage & Local Govt.	DAST Department of Arts, Sport & Tourism
Historic Properties, Education & Visitor Services National Monuments & Architectural Protection	Arts Arts Unit, Film Unit, Music Unit
The Heritage Council	Cultural Unit Council of National Cultural Institutions (5 main institutions)*

see above

Figure 3.2 Republic of Ireland governmental organisations for culture and heritage

DELG states that 'Ireland is endowed with a rich heritage... and that heritage is inextricably linked with our sense of identity and affirms our historic, cultural and natural inheritance' (DEHLG, 2003).

The Heritage Council, a semi-state organisation (under DEHLG) exists to 'propose policies and priorities for the identification, protection, preservation and enhancement of the national heritage' (Heritage Council, 1995; Starrett, 2000). Confusingly, the Heritage Fund is administered by DAST and provides financial support to the republic's five National Cultural Institutions (the National Archives, National Gallery of Ireland, National Library of Ireland, National Museum of Ireland and the Irish Museum of Modern Art). The merging of tourism and arts/culture in the new department has engendered interesting debate about the politics of commodification.

Tourism Frameworks in Ireland

Tourism in Ireland is unusual insofar as many external visitors perceive the destination as a single unit – 'the island of Ireland', whilst in reality it is governed by two separate nation states and their respective ministries. Arguably, political violence in Northern Ireland has sporadically marred the entire island's reputation in terms of a safe visitor destination, despite the containment of trouble to the North-eastern corner of the country. Northern Ireland, in particular, has attempted to redress any negative imbalance since the Good Friday Peace Agreement (1999) through various economic and cooperative programmes. The EU has heavily funded investment schemes for the region and encourages cross-border cooperation not only for sociocultural peace-forging schemes, but also for island-wide initiatives for tourism and general economic development. Programmes include the *Northern Ireland Programme for Building Sustainable Prosperity*, the *EU Programme for Peace and Reconciliation in Northern Ireland and the Border Region of Ireland*, *INTERREG* (I–III) and *EQUAL*.

A North–South Ministerial Council was established under the Good Friday Agreement which comprises ministers from the Northern Ireland Assembly (the devolved self-ruling 'parliament' which has some statutory powers) and the Irish Government. The aim of the Council is to develop consultation, cooperation and implementation on matters of mutual interest to the two states. Tourism is one of six key areas identified for cooperation between existing government departments and other bodies (other areas include transport and the environment – both of which play a vital role in sustainable tourism development on the island as a whole).

The Northern Ireland Tourist Board (NITB) and Bórd Fáilte (BF) are the semi-state bodies that carry out the practical functions of their respective government departments (Table 3.1). Such functions include consumer information/liaison (tourist information centres, accommodation approval etc.) as well as product development, industry marketing and strategic research and development. Both jurisdictions rely heavily upon diasporic tourism visitation, particularly from mainland Britain and North America. *Visiting friends and relatives* (VFR) makes up almost a third of the Republic's tourism profile and almost a half of Northern Ireland's. In the case of US visitors, impacts from the New York 9/11 terrorist attack have been heavily felt. Arguably, tourism in global destinations that have been the centre of past political strife suffers exponentially during – and for a considerable time after – such crises.

Table 3.1 State tourism organisations in Ireland

Northern Ireland	*Republic of Ireland*
DETI	DAST
Department of Enterprise Trade & Investment	Department of Arts, Sport and Tourism
↓	
Northern Ireland Tourist Board	Bórd Fáilte (Fáilte Ireland)

In both states, tourism visits and contribution to the exchequer rose in 2003 and all market destinations showed a slight rise (Table 3.2). Interestingly, NITB separates visitors from the Republic of Ireland in its statistics, but BF classes Northern Ireland visitors with its general 'Britain' figures.

In terms of the 'heritage-tourism product', Ireland tends to promote its historic culture, landscape, traditions and people. Similarities exist North and South of the border in this respect. In Northern Ireland, the Giant's Causeway is a World Heritage Site and is the number one visitor attraction and in the Republic, Newgrange (Neolithic Burial Tomb) is the most visited World Heritage Site. Many museums and heritage centres focus on Ireland's largely rural culture and traditions (outside Dublin and Belfast), and the natural landscape is heavily promoted. Increasingly, non-fixed forms of heritage expression through music, dance and festivals are attracting high visitor numbers. O'Connor (2003) refers to the role Irish dance has played (particularly *Riverdance*) in the globalisation of Irish culture, whilst McGovern (2003) comments on the world popularisation of the 'Irish pub experience', emphasising the appeal of premodern nostalgia. Whilst political strife has calmed somewhat in recent years (the touristic promotion of 'feel-good Irishness' centred around drink and music has helped to blur *some* of the negative imagery), 'identity' remains a complex concept for Irish people themselves to contend with. Relationships between heritage, tourism and authenticity are *de rigeur* in contemporary cultural tourism analyses, but in the case of Ireland, the processes of commodification, selection and representation take on added political significance. In particular, heritage sites that choose to narrate contentious and/or partial sociocultural histories often enter an arena of complexity. Where visitor sites attract domestic, diasporic and overseas tourists, each with their own schemata of Irish heritage, the implicit politics of cultural/tourism space should be a key consideration. This chapter looks next at a specific example of how one particular tourism site in Northern Ireland elicited debate among a mixed group of visitors about the politics of representation in heritage tourism.

Assessing Multiple Heritage(s): The Ulster–American Folk Park

The Ulster–American Folk Park (UAFP), located in Omagh, Co. Tyrone, was used in a recent cross-border study to elicit debate and discussion on how multiple Irish histories and identities might best be

Table 3.2 Ireland's tourism revenue and visitor origin profile

2003 (latest figures available)	Republic of Ireland		Northern Ireland	
Tourism value to the economy	€4.1 billion		£2.74 million	
Total visits	6.2 million		1.95 million	
Visitors by main market area		% Change 2002		% Change 2002
	Britain		Britain	
	3.5 m	+ 3%	1.3 m	+ 16%
	Europe (Germany and France comprise half)		Eire	
	1.4 m	+ 8%	340,000	+ 3%
	North America		Europe	
	0.9 m	+ 6%	115,000	+ 5%
			North America	
			97,000	No change

Source: Data compiled from Northern Ireland Tourist Board and Failte Ireland figures

represented in public/tourist heritage spaces. The Folk Park was established in 1976 as Northern Ireland's contribution to the American bicentenary. It was themed around the portrayal of the emigrant trail to America, and in particular, on the story of the Mellon family – a Presbyterian success story of accomplishment in the New World. Large-scale emigration from Ireland to North America began in the 1720s and throughout the remainder of the 18th century involved many settlers who sought land and a new way of life. Many of the early (Ulster) pioneers were Presbyterian and became known in their adopted country as Scotch–Irish. Interrupted only by the American War of Independence (1775–83) and the Napoleonic Wars (1793–1815), the great tide of emigration continued into the 19th century as America began to attract immigrants from all parts of Ireland.

The Great Famine in Ireland (also known as 'the potato famine' or simply 'the famine') lasted from 1845 to 1849 and brought lasting demographic change to the island of Ireland. Pre-Famine emigration to the USA in the 17th and 18th centuries is thought to have been in the region of 1.5 million people. The five-year period of the famine itself is thought to have contributed at least another 1.5 million to the American population, not including those who died in transit (UAFP website, Museums and Galleries Northern Ireland website). The UAFP claims, according to the informational literature, to 'tell the story of these emigrants and their everyday lives through the reconstruction of original and replica buildings' (UAFP website). The juxtaposition of historical data on 'pre'/'during-famine' emigration figures followed by the above statement suggests a museum concerned with the telling of a comprehensive range of migration histories; however, this is questionable at the UAFP. 'If a museum or a site is to have an educational value... they must also honestly represent the more shameful events of our past... if interpretation is to be a social good, then it must alert us to the future through the past (Uzzell, 1989; quoted in Tunbridge & Ashworth, 1996).

The UAFP centres its story of emigration largely around the enterprise success of Judge Thomas Mellon, who was originally from Co. Tyrone, and who went on to found a vast industrial empire in Pennsylvania. 'His experiences *are typical of many emigrants*' the UAFP explanatory literature tells us, 'and it is fitting that his boyhood home should provide the centrepiece of the Ulster–American Folk Park.' Over the past 25 years the park has grown and now claims to be 'the largest museum of emigration in Europe and stands as a permanent symbol of the many links which have been forged down the centuries between Ireland and America' (UAFP website). Along with the outdoor–indoor folk park, the site also contains a complementary indoor museum exhibition entitled 'Emigrants' and houses the Centre for Migration Studies (CMS), which serves as a research resource for migration records and archives. In 1998, the UAFP joined with the Ulster Folk and Transport Museum, Armagh Museum and the Ulster Museum to form the National Museums and Galleries of Northern Ireland (MAGNI). In 2003, the UAFP ranked ninth in Northern Ireland's top 20 tourist attractions and recorded 126,170 visitors (NITB, 2004).

Research case study

As an academic working within the emerging field of heritage studies in the Republic of Ireland, the author felt the need for constant negotiation, assessment and justification of the term 'national heritage', which is not as problematic, perhaps, in other countries. The UAFP was chosen as a case study site for a practical research exercise that brought together two visitor groups – one from the Republic or 'South' of Ireland and one from the North, to discuss and critique differential heritage representations and issues of cultural identity. The visitor groups in this instance were final-year geography and heritage studies students from Southern and Northern Irish universities. 'Educational tourists' make up an important part of all heritage and museum site visitor numbers in Ireland, and indeed globally. The role of Irish universities in cross-border cooperation and education is an important one and here 'visitor-studies' take on added meaning in the context of the peace process and creating new or emerging cultural representations. Buckley and Kenney (1994: 129), in their work on Northern Ireland, also concur that 'schools and museums should enable individuals of different ethnicities to explore their own and each others' cultural heritage'.

Specifically, the aims of the field study were to (a) facilitate communication and interaction between students from both sides of the border on how multiple Irish heritages might best be represented in public heritage spaces, (b) to engage an open, honest discourse on often difficult, politically sensitive issues in a safe environment, (c) to increase understanding and awareness of multiple perspectives from within a heterogeneous group, and (d) to evaluate the potential value of such exchanges for both heritage tourist attraction–visitor relations and for better informed cultural [tourism] policy formulation.

The challenges of the exercise included the mixed nature of the group in terms of origin, gender, religion and, to a lesser extent, age. The case study involved pre-visit instruction and discussion of relevant heritage and cultural policy literature, followed by a long-weekend residential programme designed to meet the research aims listed above. Practically, this included a series of lectures, workshops, guided and self-directed tours of the folk park itself, the emigration galleries and the CMS. The two groups were given the opportunity to observe and assess heritage representation at the site and were later allocated mixed workshop groups to discuss a variety of issues centred around identity, cultural representation and interpretation.

Some references to the UAFP can be found in Irish heritage literature (e.g. Brett, 1996) and this research allowed a group of mixed visitors to assess for themselves some of the ideas put forward by other writers. Brett (1996) comments that 'the mythical structure' of the UAFP as presented is a system of binary opposites that are visualised and simulated as shown in Table 3.3.

The Park, Brett suggests, presents an unproblematic migration process that deals with issues of class and religion in an implicit and taken-for-granted manner. The narrative typology of the space suggests a simple presentation of the backward versus the modern. Brett's concerns centre around the apparently neutral representation of the UAFP and the representativeness of the broader Ulster (and for some, the broader *Irish*) migratory community. The park, he comments, is not neutrally Ulster–American in a geographic sense, but Ulster–Presbyterian–American in a confessional sense (Brett, 1996). Further issues for consideration include conflicts between authenticity and myth in a public heritage space that serves both cultural–educational and entertainment (tourism) functions. Cultural representations of heritage, identity and place are produced and

Table 3.3 Ulster–American differentiation *(after Brett, 1996)*

Ulster	America
Stone	Wood
Thatch	Shingle
Shaggy	Smooth
Grazed	Planted
Dense	Cleared
Natural	Rational
Picturesque	Modern

consumed by a multiplicity of groups, even within the same bounded space (Graham *et al.*, 2000).

The student-visitor groups' activities worked at many different levels. Knowledge gain and attitude change are desirable cultural performance indicators according to much research on heritage–visitor interrelationships (e.g. Uzzell & Ballantyne, 1998). In this instance, not only were the general research aims adequately met, added learning outcomes were part of the interactive experience. These included the recognition of:

• student knowledge as legitimate,
• de-centring authority,
• deep learning (for those open to it).

There was an important pedagogic premise to the UAFP research as students were encouraged to take ownership of their own learning, deep understanding of the material content of the site, and also of their co-visitors in terms of understanding multiple perspectives. Issues of situated knowledges and positionality were important underlying principles that were raised *in situ* to help further understanding of difference and the Other. The politics of difference is an implicit issue faced daily by at least one half of the research group; the ability to assess these concerns within a safe, cultural space was a key element to the exercise.

Workshop exercises (written and verbal) and pre/post-visit questionnaires on the student visitor group (60 people) gave some interesting results on key themes of heritage representation and individual/group expectations, knowledge gain and understanding.

The following provides a selection of quotations and feedback on the exercise.

Group expectations

The group was asked what they thought they might get from such an exercise, and what their expectations were before coming to the heritage park. Responses were positive but varied and included:

• 'To listen to other people's views on migration and get a real sense of what it is all about.'
• 'A comprehensive tour of the park ... workshops and to deepen my knowledge, just for myself – and exams as well I suppose!'

Heritage representation and authenticity

Individual responses on questions about views on the content, layout and interpretation of history at the UAFP included:

- 'Some representations were valid but a lot was missing, such as the true squalor and hardship from the period.'
- 'The park described real life stories.'
- 'Presbyterianism might be relevant to Presbyterians but not to me. The predominance of this faith in this area necessitates that portrayal but to some it detracts from the museum's appeal.'
- 'I think the representation is valid and authentic, it's been researched thoroughly. It can't portray every situation, so within these limits it's very accurate...'

Overall, the responses were diverse. As expected, many from the Southern visitor group were surprised at the lack of reference to the famine, which formed a large element of their migration education and heritage, whilst the Northern group did not reference this issue as much. In certain answers, there appeared to be an element of 'wanting to say the right thing' and be politically correct, but in general, honesty and directness came through in the visitor critique of the site. The park's claim to tell the story of Irish emigrants and the choice of the Mellor family as a 'typical emigrant experience' was challenged by many members of both groups – ' in terms of a Presbyterian focus, the presentation seems valid, but not in terms of general emigration'.

Suggestions for improvements among the group included a variety of measures such as:

- 'The park should decide on a clear focus and stick to it, at the moment it appears to be trying to switch horses crossing the stream. It claims to represent emigration in general but should stick to a Presbyterian focus and openly admit to this and promote the park as such.'
- 'The park could be more inclusive and up-to-date if it provided information on emigration to other lands, and also maybe focus on return migration and modern day migration. It needs a more universal approach, encompassing all...'
- 'The park should do more live events and cross-border things, like we just got involved in; it opened my eyes a lot to how I think about things.'

Outcomes

The visit outcomes can be categorised somewhat into 'general' knowledge gain, negotiation skills, crossing borders and building bridges (Table 3.4).

Taking the concept of 'bridge-building' a little further, the group was asked also to comment on the role heritage sites such as the UAFP played in cross-border cultural education. The following responses were overwhelmingly positive and most felt the exercise they had participated in was hugely beneficial:

- 'The park helps to educate all about the perceptions people have about emigration and other issues which may not normally be addressed with regard to the North.'
- 'This place has a huge role to play and could really improve relations...'
- 'The site is an excellent provision so long as it doesn't seek to establish a superiority of North over South.'
- 'Heritage sites can bring communities together, create public awareness and help create peace in Ireland. They can educate all Irish people no matter what their religion is, but also make a statement to the world as to how the folk park is, in my opinion, making a big difference.'
- 'Sites like the UAFP can have a key role in education from primary school upwards because there is possibility for an educational setting for institutions from both sides of the border. They can really contribute to cross-cultural understanding.'

The findings of this research generally indicate that both groups had varying degrees of criticism of the UAFP, based largely around issues of representation, selectivity and diversity (or lack thereof) of historical information on Irish migration.

Plans are afoot at the UAFP to develop the park further to include a new 'National Museum of Emigration'. Despite the title 'national', correspondence on the development refers still to 'a museum [which] interprets *Ulster* emigration worldwide' and the building of 'Ulster to the world' emigrant-associated collections. This development is still in its planning stages and is heavily dependent on resources. Interestingly, one of the research workshop exercises with the cross-border groups was to discuss the possibility of developing a National Museum of Migration at the UAFP. The groups found it an exceedingly difficult exercise to assess and questioned the legitimacy of adopting the term 'national'

Table 3.4 Visitor experiences at the UAFP

Knowledge gain	'it was useful to interact with the students from the south and see their perspective'
	'the main learning outcome for me was that I learned about emigration from a different perspective – an Ulster-Presbyterian one'
	'I learned about what life was like in Ireland back then and why people wanted to leave...'
	'I saw the overall image and story of the folk park and got many views on Irish migration and Irish society as a whole'
Negotiation skills	'how important it is to be open'
	'how to communicate with the Northern students in a sensitive manner on issues raised during our stay'
	'both groups worked together and brought their own skills and resources to the questions and exercises and we worked through them together'
Crossing borders	'I suppose we were suspicious of each other, at least to begin with'
	' didn't think the southern students would be as friendly as they were'
	'I didn't think the two groups would get to know each other as well as they did'
Building bridges	'I think it might be about making connections, in the first place'
	'not to be afraid, but still sensitive... fear was there with most of us, but we all wanted to learn from each other and the work that was being carried out'

and the contentious issue of locating such a museum in the North as opposed to the South. One innovative participant suggested building an interactive museum of migration on a boat (to symbolise movement) and floating it up and down the river Shannon back and forth across the border in a politically correct effort at inclusivity and parity of location!

Conclusion

The research case study employed was simple but effective. It illustrated very clearly that different user groups can engage with heritage space on different levels yet see the perspectives of other possible interpretations. It challenged some of the pre-existing claims of the heritage park itself on issues of representation and allowed for a frank but secure exchange of views on cultural diversity and inter-pretation.

Research of this nature, although one-off, contained, and practical in nature, should be of great value to a variety of possible audiences: (1) heritage site designers/museum curators, who should welcome honest feedback of a more conceptual nature than is often the case in the typical, quantitative 'enjoyment rating' tick-box approach to feedback; (2) academics who research and teach issues of contested space, place, culture, heritage and tourism: by bringing groups of students (who may well become professionals in these sectors later in their careers) to sites of heritage difference, greater understanding of sometimes complex, aca-demic theoretical issues can be simplified and approached with practical sensitivity and pragmatism; (3) cultural policy makers and cultural tourism advisors: as new, inclusive concepts of culture emerge in Northern Ireland/Ireland, cultural departments and organisations, museums, heritage and tourism professionals will need to pay greater attention to how politically sensitive constructs of the past might best be represented.

Using a heritage tourism site to stimulate discussion of real issues of political representation and 'authentic histories' by Northern and South-ern Irish consumer groups led to valuable insights and understandings. Linking theoretical, complex issues concerning cultural identities and representation with pedagogic good practice, informed curatorship and inclusive cultural policy formulation should be enormously beneficial to cultural sector research. The role cultural tourism plays in creating contemporary cultural products should not be underestimated; the cultural tourism research agenda should openly engage with the sector on difficult discourses on the politics of heritage and its representation. Whilst considerable contemporary debate exists on the propriety of outcome-drive cultural functionality (e.g. education and social inclu-sion), in certain location-specific contexts such as Northern Ireland, cultural sites can play an important composite part of identity (re)crea-tion and representation. Such a role provides an alternative, less politically hostile form of expression than the forum of violence.

If heritage sites are to be used as contemporary spaces of leisure, cultural participation and identity formation, boundaries must shift, perhaps uncomfortably sometimes, to incorporate new ways forward. Sandell (2002) suggests, however, that despite a growing recognition that museums have often reproduced and reinforced social inequalities through their collecting and exhibitionary practices, many museum staff are uncomfortable with the notion of relinquishing their pursuit of perceived objectivity and neutrality in favour of adopting an active, political stance on equality issues. In the case of Northern Ireland, we must ask 'what obligations might be placed on heritage sites to do so, and indeed, what impacts might result from such actions?' Buckley and Kenney (1996: 145) acknowledge that these sites cannot 'heal social inequalities; they cannot remove intimidation, sectarian murder and ethnic cleansing; they cannot, by themselves, make Catholics and Protestants want to give up their preferred "social distance" from one another [but] they can provide neutral territory ... where they can learn about things which they have in common and things which divide them, in a hope to construct more harmonious relationships.' In Ireland, the jury is still out on how best to create neutral cultural spaces, or indeed, whether such an endeavour is actually possible or, indeed, always appropriate. As issues of culture, identity and heritage are challenged and played out within an emerging politicocultural policy arena in the province, should the deconstruction of culture, as Fraser (1995) proffers, aim to destabilise all fixed identities and thus create fields of multiple, debinarised, fluid, ever-shifting differences?

Acknowledgements

Special thanks to Dr Catriona Ni Laoire (formerly Queens University Belfast, now University College Cork) who co-participated in this research and to the Ireland Fund, which contributed financial aid towards the project.

References

Ashworth, G.J. and Larkham, P.J. (1994) *Building a New Heritage: Tourism, Culture and Identity in the New Europe*. London: Routledge.
Brett, D. (1996) *The Construction of Heritage*. Cork: Cork University Press.
Buckley, A. and Kenney, M. (1994) Cultural heritage in an oasis of calm: Divided identities in a museum in Ulster. In U. Kockel (ed.) *Tourism and Development: The Case of Ireland* (pp. 129–149). Liverpool: Liverpool University Press.
Centre for Migration Studies (2000) *Second Annual Report*. Omagh: CMS.

Chappell, E.A. (1989) Social responsibility and the American history museum. *Winterthur Portfolio 24* (Winter), 247–265.

Department of Culture, Arts & Leisure, Northern Ireland (DCAL) (2003) *What Culture Can Do For You*. Belfast: Government Publication.

DCAL (2001) *Guidance to District Councils on the Development of Cultural Strategies*. Belfast: Government Publication.

DCAL (2004) www.dcalni.gov.uk. Accessed 12.11.2004

Department of Environment, Heritage and Local Government, Republic of Ireland (DEHLG) (2003) *Statement of Strategy 2003–2005*. Dublin: Government Publication. (Also On WWW at www.environ.ie/DOEI.)

DCAL and DoE (2002) *Local Museum and Heritage Review. A Joint Response by the DCAL and the DoE*. Belfast: Government Publication.

Duffy, P. (1994) Conflicts in heritage and tourism. In U. Kockel (ed.) *Culture, Tourism and Development: The Case of Ireland* (pp. 77–87). Liverpool: Liverpool University Press.

Ellis, R. (1995) Museums as change agents. *Journal of Museum Education* Spring/Summer, 14–17.

Estyn Evans, E. and Evans, G. (1996) *Ireland and the Atlantic Heritage – Selected Writings*. Dublin: Lilliput Press.

Failte Ireland (2004) *Tourism Fact Card 2003*. Dublin: Government Publication.

Fraser, N. (1995) *From Redistribution to Recognition? Dilemmas of Justice in a 'Post-Socialist' Age*. London: Verso.

Graham, B. (1998) Ireland and Irishness: Place, culture and identity. In B. Graham (ed.) *In Search Of Ireland: A Cultural Geography* (pp. 1–19). London: Routledge.

Graham, B., Ashworth, G. and Tunbridge, J. (2000) *A Geography of Heritage: Power, Culture and Economy*. London: Arnold.

Harrison, J. (2000) The process of interpretation. In N. Buttimer, C. Rynne and H. Guerin (eds) *The Heritage of Ireland* (pp. 385–393). Cork: The Collins Press.

Heritage Council (1995) *The Heritage Plan*. Dublin: Government Publication. (Also on WWW at www.heritagecouncil.ie.)

Hooper-Greenhill, E. (ed.) (1995) *Museum, Media, Message*. London: Routledge.

Hooper-Greenhill, E. (2000) *Museums and Interpretation of Visual Culture*. London: Routledge.

Karp, I. (1992) On civil society and social identity. In I. Karp, C. Kreamer and S. Levine (eds) *Museums and Communities: The Politics of Public Culture* (pp. 19–34). Washington and London: Smithsonian Press.

McGovern, M. (2003) The cracked pint glass of the servant: The Irish pub, Irish identity and the tourist eye. In M. Cronin and B. O'Connor (eds) *Irish Tourism – Image, Culture and Identity* (pp. 83–104). Clevedon: Channel View Publications.

Museums and Galleries Northern Ireland (website) On WWW at www.magni.org.uk.

NITB (Northern Ireland Tourist Board) Visitor Tourism Performance (2003) (On WWW at www.discovernorthernireland.com.) Belfast: Government Publication.

O'Connor, B. (2003) Come and daunce with me in Irelande: Tourism, dance and globalisation. In M. Cronin and B. O'Connor (eds) *Irish Tourism – Image, Culture and Identity* (pp. 122–141). Clevedon: Channel View Publications.

O'Neill, S. (2003) Are national conflicts reconcilable? Discourse theory and political accommodation in Northern Ireland. *Constellations* 10 (1), 75–94.

Sandell, R. (2002) Museums and the combating of social inequality: Roles, responsibilities, resistance. In R. Sandell (ed.) *Museums, Society, Inequality*. London: Routledge.

Starrett, M. (2000) The Heritage Council. In N. Buttimer, C. Rynne and H. Guerin (eds) *The Heritage of Ireland* (pp. 534–554). Cork: The Collins Press.

Thompson, S. (2003) The politics of culture in Northern Ireland. *Constellations* 10 (1), 53–74.

Tunbridge, J. and Ashworth, G. (1996) *Dissonant Heritage: The Management of the Past as a Resource in Conflict*. Chichester: Wiley.

UAFP (website) On WWW at www.folkpark.com. Accessed April 2004.

Uzzell, D. (ed.) (1989) *Heritage Interpretation* (Vol.2). London: Belhaven.

Uzzell, D. and Ballantyne, R. (1998) *Contemporary Issues in Heritage and Environmental Interpretation: Problems and Prospects*. London: Stationery Office.

Chapter 4

Heritage Tourism and the Revitalisation of Barony Life in Norway

ARVID VIKEN

Introduction

This chapter deals with the revitalisation of the Rosendal Barony in Norway as a cultural centre, as it was in the second half of the 19th century. In the 1920s the heirs of the former barons left and the estate was handed over to the University of Oslo. Between the 1920s and the 1980s it was a low-profile museum. It is still a museum, but also a place for performing art and a tourist attraction. It is situated in Rosendal at the Hardanger Fjord (see Figure 4.1), two hours' drive from Bergen. The Rosendal Barony is the only barony Norway has ever had. The Baron was part of Danish aristocracy, as Norway was a Danish colony from 1536 until 1814. After independence from Denmark (but until 1905 in a union with Sweden) nobility was abolished in Norway (1821) and the barony lost all its privileges. However, the Rosendal Barony remained an important institution for another 80 years.

The data on which this chapter is based are drawn from an investigation into the relationship between tourist attractions and the surrounding communities. The study had no clear hypothesis concerning this relationship, but among the discussed issues was commercial tourism as a parameter for social and cultural change in the local community. The Rosendal Barony was chosen as a case due to its significant success and publicity in recent years. The method applied in the research project was focus group interviews (Morgan, 1988, 1996), supplemented by individual in-depth interviews. The focus groups were stratified, each consisting of people with a common characteristic such as gender, age or occupation. The intention of the method is to facilitate discussions of predetermined themes, with minimal interference of the researchers in the conversations. This means that 'reality' is described in the words of the interviewees, rather than those of the

Figure 4.1 Map of the southern part of Norway

researcher(s). Statistically, one cannot draw conclusions about general conditions in a community only from data collected in focus group interviews, but when there is a consensus across the groups, there is good reason to believe that whatever surfaces reflects a general trend (Macnaghten & Jacobs, 1997).

The chapter begins with a presentation of the barony and the tourism that has grown up around it, and a discussion of barony tourism as cultural heritage tourism. This is followed by a presentation of the views of the local inhabitants on the barony and how its supporters handle their relationships with the local community. The theme of tourism as a source of social distinctions comes next. In the conclusion the contemporary use of the barony is seen as a parallel to the way it was exposed almost 150 years earlier.

The Rosendal Barony

When the richest Norwegian heiress (of Scottish ancestry), Karen Mowat, married the son of a Danish noble, Ludvig Rosenkrantz, in 1658,

Figure 4.2 The Manor of Rosendal
Photographer: Håvard Sætrevik

the Hatteberg estate was a wedding present from the bride's parents (Hopstock & Madsen, 1969; Vaage, 1972). The young couple built a manor house on the estate, which was completed in 1665 (Figure 4.2). The estate was elevated to a barony in 1678. 'Barony' and 'baron' are judicial terms that designated certain rights and duties decided by the king. The title of 'Baron' allowed the holder exemption from paying taxes to the king, and also implied property rights to churches, the right to appoint vicars, and supervision of the judicial system and military conscription. Among the restrictions were that the barony's property could not be sold or mortgaged. In the 18th century the estate was classified as a hereditary property, meaning that possessions of the baron at that time would remain in his family as long as it existed. The baron was the former lector Edvard Londemann, who, to better his social position, had married the sister of the vicar of a nearby parish and subsequently purchased the title of bishop. After having bought the estate he got the title of 'baron' and added Rosencrone to his name. One of the most fascinating successors was Marcus Gerhard Hoff-Rosenkrone (spelled with 'k') who formally was not a baron, as he was born in 1823, two years after the aristocracy had been abolished. He called himself the 'estate holder', but locally he was referred to as 'the baron' (or 'the old baron'). After this the barony obviously became more and more an anachronism, also for its owners who left the place in the 1920s.

The barony has enjoyed great success as a tourist attraction after it began to market itself as such in the 1980s. The visitor count increased from a few thousand ticket-buying customers in the early 1980s to around 62,000 in 2002. The building and its surrounding rose garden and park make the place suitable for sightseeing tourism. In addition, two areas of effort have yielded dividends. Firstly, there is an extensive programme of events: concerts, theatre performances, art exhibitions, readings and lectures. These are activities for which the market is more regional than local. Secondly, there are facilities for meetings and seminars. Bed and breakfast facilities include 26 rooms in the old manor house and farm building (*Rosendal Avlsgård*), and there are also dining facilities. The manor is open to the public during the summer tourist season, but is available for closed private activities all year round.

The catering for tourism at the barony has of course changed the place. In the past, the barony manor was a home; today it is a cultural institution and a tourist attraction. Today, tourism's semiotic cover is drawn over the place: car and ticket queues, bus groups, happy guides, the gaze aimed at a common focus, ice-cream-eating and photographing people in an organisation-like frame of opening hours, ticket counter, café and souvenir shop. As an object for the tourist gaze the barony has a completely different significance than it had in the past. These signs are not especially obtrusive, but they are present, and, as in other places, do something to the spirit of the place (Hubbard & Lilley, 2000).

For most visitors the barony is an institution that lives up to the desires for a romantic and aesthetic life and provides leisure and amusement on a par with most other cultural attractions – perhaps even giving an unusually memorable experience. The barony is also a symbol of the nobility and its disappearance in Norway and it is one of the very few manor houses in the country. As such, it belongs to the spectrum of national symbols. Like many other heritage attractions, the barony provides activities for tourists, sources of income, employment for the local community and a source of financing for the further development and management of the cultural monument as it is.

The Barony as Cultural Heritage

The concept of cultural heritage can involve a variety of cultural expressions (Herbert, 1997; Lowenthal, 1997). A relatively common division is between material and immaterial cultural heritage. In its simplest form material heritage involves cultural monuments, such as stone-age settlements, Viking graves or castles, or collections of artefacts from particular cultures or periods – often in institutions named as museums and under a conservation regime. The Rosendal Barony is an example. However, in all societies there are also social remnants from the past; immaterial heritage including history, traditions, customs, legends, myths and other expressions and results of human life and relationships. History and traditions have given rise to many museums and tourist attractions. Due to its immaterial character, the narrative sides are always fundamental to such institutions. Somehow history must be told, and traditions often have to be demonstrated and explained to be understood.

Another distinction is between what Kirschenblatt-Gimlett (1998) characterises as *in situ* cultural heritage, which relates its own history because it is situated in its natural place in an original or reconstructed cultural environment, and *in context* cultural heritage, which are representations torn out of their environment, but in a professionally documented way. There are a variety of methods for presenting the context, including labels, information placards and other visual and audio aids. The *in situ–in context* distinction roughly corresponds to the difference between an ecomuseum and a traditional museum. Obviously, compromise solutions exist, and *in situ* expositions will normally use some of the informing and contextualising techniques. The most used information means, both in *in situ* and *in context* institutions, are information plaques and guides. The *in situ–in context* dimension can be combined with the material–immaterial dimension giving four different types of cultural heritage presentations (Table 4.1).

Most institutions can to some extent have elements from all four categories. The Rosendal Barony is a cultural monument that is still situated where it was first built and the building and its surrounding rose garden and park are presented just as they were when the barons' heirs left in the 1920s. But the barony also has the status of a museum. As far as traditions are concerned, there hardly exist any that have survived without interruption since the age of the barons. However, several have been revived, among them that of arranging a Christmas party for the children of the parish, bread baking and not least that of forging links

Table 4.1 The (re)presentational forms of cultural heritage

	In situ	*In context*
Material cultural heritage	Cultural monument; material objects which are conserved	Museum collection
	Cultural expressions of the past not conserved	
	Reconstructions at the locality	
Social (immaterial) cultural heritage	Living tradition	Narrative representation; text, picture and oral presentation (for instance, from a guide)
	Staged events or life forms	
	Revitalised tradition and/or life forms	

with artists. The narrative mediation is not very prominent at the barony, except for the guiding of visitors through the grounds and house. The most interesting aspect of the cultural heritage at the barony is undoubtedly the immaterial *in situ* aspect, that which in the matrix is termed revitalising life forms.

At some cultural heritage attractions guests are invited to step into simulated roles from past times, for instance by dressing in costumes from the Middle Ages, being served Viking food in Viking style, or having luxury holidays in a castle. This is not part of the offer at the Rosendal Barony. Instead, elements of the life forms such as they were 150 years ago are enacted. The model is Marcus Gerhard Hoff-Rosenkrone, the estate holder from the second part of the 1800s. He was an intellectual, took part in public affairs, contributed to the modernisation of farming and created a park around the manor. As a benefactor of artists and intellectuals, his home was like a cultural centre (Hopstock & Tschudi Madsen, 1969). The people who congregated around Hoff-Rosenkrone and who visited the barony during his time played important roles in Norwegian cultural life, and included the violinist Ole Bull and the composer Halfdan Kjerulf; painters such as Anders Askevoll and Hans Gude; and authors such as Jørgen Moe, Peter

Christian Asbjørnsen, Alexander Kielland, Bjørnstjerne Bjørnson and Knut Hamsun. They are all reckoned among the most prominent artists that Norway has fostered. Most of them also played a part in the constitution of a Norwegian national identity, and the barony was one of the places where they met and discussed such matters. Marcus Gerhard Hoff-Rosenkrone was not only the nation builders' host and benefactor, he is also said to have been fascinated by the French Republic (Sunde, 2002). This may be seen as a paradox – the barony was in fact a symbol of the system from which the young nation was about to be emancipated. On the other hand, Rosendal was an excellent site for such discussions, located as it is in the middle of rural Norway, surrounded by magnificent nature and peasant culture, both central themes in the so-called 'national romanticism' that was the ideological base for the nation builders (Sørensen, 1998).

Today the barony is again a cultural centre. Among those with which it is connected today are internationally reputed musicians such as Leif Ove Andsnes and Truls Mørch and national artists, intellectuals and celebrities. Inviting Norway's cultural elite to Rosendal to perform or exhibit has been a great success; the public have flocked to the barony, filling the till with money, and the place has attracted media attention to a degree that other places can only envy. Since the late 1990s and onwards an English theatre troop specialising in Shakespeare visited the barony every summer. Just as the artists of the 1800s did, the cultural figures of today practice their art and reside at the manor. It may be that today's artists are more extroverted than artists were in the days of Hoff-Rosenkrone, but also in the past open events were held. And the presence of celebrities not only has an artistic and a cultural dimension, but sometimes also a political one. Several of the artists have manned the barricades against the plans of the hydropower development of a river that runs through the barony area. Thus, revitalising life forms are not limited to cultural activities; as in the past the artists and intellectuals emerge as actors in contemporary society. In addition, the barony is an excellent arena for marketing the artists and their products. The place provides romantic associations and an aura of seriousness and fine arts for those who step onto this stage.

Cultural Conservation and Celebrities as Local Development Parameters

In its peak period the barony was a powerful institution and the owner of many farms and forests in its district. With the abolishment of nobility (1821), the barony lost its formal governing functions. During the 1900s the barony also lost most of its wealth as the farms were generally taken over by the tenants running them. Today, local people feel that the barony again is in the process of becoming a power factor, primarily through its position as the administrator of conservation rules and as a supporting force of various conservation authorities, especially the Directorate for Cultural Heritage.

The manor was put under a conservation order in the 1920s. Around 1990, the Cultural Heritage Act was changed and provides the basis for far more comprehensive conservation, so that the whole site may now be considered to be a cultural monument. There is a plan for an even more encompassing conservation, as an area where the cultural monument is 'part of a larger whole or context' (Cultural Heritage Act, section 2, subsection 2). The larger whole is more or less the entire village. This seems already to be the principle according to which the authorities manage the estate. Any activity in the neighbourhood that opposes the aim of the conservation can be stopped. Besides the protection of the barony decided upon by central authorities, the municipality is by law obliged to make an area regulation plan for the adjacent areas that take into account the fact that there is a cultural treasure nearby. In 2005 a National Park covering a huge glacier and the mountains behind the village was created, together with a 'landscape conservation area' between the mountain and the parish. These regimes will permanently alter the conditions for tree felling, grazing, hunting, fishing, outdoor recreation, tourism, and of course limit industrial development opportunities.

There have been several suspended local projects due to the conservation regime: a rifle range that was set to be built just above the barony, construction of houses and facilities on the farms in the neighbourhood and a planned expansion of the local graveyard. The farmers have contested a road the barony want to construct on their ground instead of the one that goes through the barony courtyard. According to a spokesman for the barony, the management has attempted to reach an amicable arrangement with the landowners, although the barony had reserved the right to construct the road when the farms bought themselves free. Relations with the farmers reached a nadir before a staging of a Shakespeare piece in the courtyard of the manor, when the police had to be called to prevent a planned demonstration with tractors that would have disrupted the show. However, the most well known conflict concerned a planned hydro-electric development of the Hatteberg watercourse (Figure 4.3).

Figure 4.3 The Hatteberg watercourse
Photographer: Willy Haraldsen

This conflict appears to have been mistakenly fought about the Hatteberg waterfall, which was visible from the manor house before the barony park grew up. If the power company and the municipality had had their way, the watercourse would have been developed for hydroelectric power, and a remote waterfall would have been channelled through pipes. However, the Hatteberg waterfall close to the barony would only have been affected in that its water level would have been dictated by rhythms other than natural ones. 'After having passed through the turbines the water had to find its way to the sea, as before', it was maintained. The barony and a number of its partners – several of them national celebrities – opposed the development and were subsequently successful in their efforts. Locally, it was felt that national singers, actors, authors and researchers appearing in the media in defence of the watercourse was provocative: 'It is irritating to listen to these people, who after a three hour visit act as spokesmen for the protectionists in media', one of the interviewees said. Another maintained: 'These people do not know the local needs and our everyday life', and: 'They [the celebrities and the media] even came up with false evidence'. As several maintained, the conservation will result in the municipality losing out on concession taxes.

As most informants saw it, conservation policies and rules are a barrier for dynamic local development. It is among other things a hinderance for agricultural revival, farming of the outlying fields and building of new housing areas in the parish. Local residents appear to have little hope that conservation and park management will provide the parish with many jobs, or result in tourism being especially strengthened, although it is recognised that the park's status may be of value in marketing terms. People feel that the brakes have been put on local development. As one respondent said: 'The areas suited for new industrial activities are occupied in the name of conservation'.

However, the conservation now in progress does not necessarily mean a 'freeze' of the current situation. Concerning the landscape, the conservation policy was looked upon as neglect and decline. As a result of the agricultural policy in recent years, there are now few cattle, sheep and goat farmers left and the outlying fields and grazing areas have become overgrown. As traditional farming is vanishing, conservation of the landscape is in the process of becoming an activity based on formal knowledge and modern technology, not local use. In the view of the farmers, traditional agriculture would have been more efficient landscape conservation. 'To preserve the landscape, it has to be utilised', it was said. Therefore, several informants thought that the conservation plans should also have included agriculture. As it now is, 'the local tradition to be creative has been perverted', it was maintained. It was also mentioned that the current development is not in the spirit of Marcus Gerhard Hoff-Rosenkrone, who 'was a creative person who established a park, a secondary school, and was a proponent of development and modernisation'. In modern times he would most likely have run experiments with deer or ostrich farming and built a golf course, and perhaps he also would have intervened over the conservation policies, it was maintained.

Cultural Heritage as a Producer of Political and Social Divisions

The public in Norway like to think of their country as an egalitarian society. However, several informants claimed that Rosendal has a long tradition of social divisions – the village has 'always been a place with both posh and ordinary people'. The revitalisation of the barony as a cultural centre has widened and intensified the division between the classy set associated with the barony – mainly people from other parts of the country – and 'ordinary' local people. 'There is a group of people that meet at the barony and sun themselves in each other's admiration', it was maintained. The classy set that uses the barony as their playground comprises cultural managers, artists, academics and fund donors – often well-off business people – and they build alliances and networks in which the barony forms a hub, and where the managers of the barony are included. It is perhaps unsurprising, therefore, that in local parlance the present manager of the barony and her allies are spoken of as 'the baroness and her court'. Although the barony no longer has formal authority over people in the district, it seems as if the ongoing 're-baronisation' has reawoken old ill will in the local community, and created conceptions about a sociocultural division. This could be termed negative reminiscence (Urry, 1996), a process in which the problematic aspects of the social life of the past are reawoken, a life which appears perhaps even more problematic today than it was for the group of people it affected in the past. A milieu where it is suspected that the wine flows and decadence rules will always provide fertile ground for public indignation and envy. Justified or not, the people of Rosendal feel that a division exists between people on the inside of the barony and those on the outside. According to a specialist in the history of the barony interviewed in the project, 'the local people of Rosendal often seem to feel excluded from rights which they have never had'. And one should not completely dismiss the idea that the managers of the barony are victims of the tall poppy syndrome, as the transformation of the barony over the last 10–15 years has undoubtedly been very successful.

The informants are not only negative towards the development. The majority recognise the amount of work done by the manager of the barony, and what has been achieved: the barony has been transformed from an abandoned manor into today's active, well known, dynamic cultural institution and tourist attraction. People are proud of being from the place with the barony. However, even the rich cultural programme offered by the barony has a problematic side; for decades cultural activities among people were very high. Popular culture is currently much weaker. 'Whereas we used to entertain, we now expect to be entertained', it was maintained.

The disapproval and ambivalence referred to above can be linked to the manner in which today's management has worked to establish the barony as a national cultural institution rather than a local or regional one. The strategies used in connection with this have been to establish strong alliances with the national conservation authorities, and with national artists and celebrities. In the eyes of most informants the barony and the national authorities have formed an alliance in which the local community is not included. Formally speaking, the alliance acts correctly in relation to the municipal authorities that champion local interests. The people's complaint is about the degree and manner in which the public is included in matters. Several informants said that they had been informed about the enlarged conservation – amongst other things – at popular meetings, but felt nevertheless they had not been asked for their opinion on the matter. There was a widespread perception among informants that, as one of them expressed it: 'The alliance does not communicate, it informs; and they do not negotiate, just act'. Several of the informants felt that if matters had been handled with more flexibility and diplomacy, the relationship could have been much improved.

Although many of the barons have a posthumous reputation bestowed by posterity for having taken good care of their subjects, the Rosendal of the past was not without its antagonisms. But it was a different historical period, in which it probably was more readily accepted that people held positions according to their social class and other hierarchical social systems. In contrast, the prevailing ideology in Norway today may be considered to be an egalitarian and democratic one. It therefore arouses reaction when the barony or the conservation authorities are felt to be intractable or acting on the basis of their imputed higher position. The barony can probably be considered to be an actor in the local community to an even smaller degree than during the period of the barons; today's managers have national and international, professional and conservation interests as their frame of reference, and feel that their primary responsibility is to these milieus. However, the negative attitudes may also be explained by the fact that the barons in the old days took care of the local inhabitants and other people with connections to the barony, whereas the barony of today is governed in accordance with interests that are perceived not to benefit the local community.

Within the academy there is a tendency to consider experienced reality more or less as a social construction – a kind of agreed-on description. This may be applied to the informants' ideas about the celebrity lifestyle associated with the barony, social divisions between the 'posh people' and the others, the perception that these divisions are reinforced by the way the barony is run, and the importance of the conservation policies and measures. Whether this is true or not is not the question; the constructions are the 'reality' on which people's feeling, actions and reactions are based. The local people may also be provoked by the fact that the spirit of Marcus Gerhard Hoff-Rosenkrone and what he represented is now being revitalised. He was an intellectual who was interested in the fine arts and who mingled with the cultural elite – an elitist. The fact that he is now brought to the fore may be because his spirit seems to suit today's postmodern society, in which aesthetics and intellectual snobbery have experienced a renaissance. However, this culture is far removed from the daily life of ordinary people in Rosendal.

Conclusion

The conclusion of this chapter is that the Rosendal Barony is a thriving cultural heritage institution that brings with it a new dimension to the field, the revitalisation of life forms. The model of today's management is the life of Marcus Gerhard Hoff-Rosenkrone, the most renowned estate holder of the 1800s. There are many similarities, but also interesting differences between now and then. Some of them are summarised in Table 4.2.

It is by no means unproblematic to manage a cultural heritage establishment in a small place like Rosendal. It results in a number of cases where consideration of national cultural importance comes into conflict with local interests and – in the eyes of many – with prospects for local development. It often seems like a battle for power, a question of who is going to have the last word, the nation or the local community, or as it is probably seen locally, the barony's administrator or the local landowners and municipal authorities.

As a consequence of the attraction's national profiling and association with intellectuals and celebrities, the local population feels that the historical social divisions between the 'posh people' associated with the barony and the ordinary people are in the process of being reawoken. Thus, for the time being even social divisions seem to be revitalised and cultivated in the name of cultural heritage. Cultural heritage management is not just a tableau of another period, but part of today's everyday life at the location, albeit a modern one adapted to today's society. Both cultural heritage as a life form based on social division between those who are inside and those who are outside the circle of the barony, and cultural heritage that fights for its special conservation interests, are much more difficult for local inhabitants to digest than are conservation-worthy buildings and objects, tableaux and other recreations of the past.

Table 4.2 The barony past and present

	The barony during the period of the Hoff-Rosenkrone	The barony as a contemporary culture centre and tourist attraction
Power and authority	Estate and manor	National cultural monument
	Well-off estate	State-owned through the University of Oslo
	Innovator in the development of agriculture, industry and banking	Cultural conservation limits local political room for action
	Estate holder interested in society	Politically active administrator and guests
	Participated in the debate on the development of the Norwegian national state	The barony as a national symbol, and a national tourist attraction
Social and cultural aspects	Social distance from the majority of people in a hierarchical society	Cultural distance from the majority of people in an egalitarian society
	Cultural centre, benefactor/patron of artists, support to students	Cultural centre, promotion of artists, support to students
	Power centre: with a tradition based legitimacy	Power centre: provoking resistance, many tensions with the local inhabitants
	Care for its subjects	Perceived by many to be a political opponent

References

Herbert, D.T. (ed.) (1997) *Heritage, Tourism and Society*. London: Pinter.
Hopstock, C. and Tschudi Madsen, S. (1969) *Baroniet i Rosendal*. Oslo: Universitetsforlaget.
Hubbard, P. and Lilley, K. (2000) Setting the past: Heritage-tourism and place identity in Stratford-upon-Avon. *Geography* 85 (3), 221–232.
Kirschenblatt-Gimblett, B. (1998) *Destination Culture: Tourism, Museums and Heritage*. Berkeley: University of California Press.
Lowenthal, D. (1997) *The Heritage Crusade and the Spoils of History*. London: Viking.

Macnaghten, P. and Jacobs, M. (1997) Public identification with sustainable development. *Global Environment* 7 (1), 5–24.

Morgan, D.L. (1988) *Focus Groups as Qualitative Research.* Thousand Oaks: Sage.

Morgan, D.L. (1996) Focus groups. *Annual Review of Sociology* 22, 129–152.

Sørensen, Ø. (ed.) (1998) *Jakten på det norske: perspektiver på utviklingen av en norsk nasjonal identitet på 1800-tallet.* Oslo: Ad notam Gyldendal.

Sunde, J.Ø. (2002) 'Den duftende lavendel'. Baroniet Rosendal og konstruksjonen av Noreg og det norske. *Syn og Segn* 108 (3), 26–37.

Urry, J. (1996) How societies remember the past. In S. Macdonald and G. Fyfe (ed.) *Theorizing Museums* (pp. 45–65). Oxford: Blackwell.

Vaage, E. (1972) *Kvinnherad. Bygdesoge.* Rosendal: Kvinnherad Bygdeboknemnd.

Chapter 5

Cultural Tourism and Socioeconomic Development in Poland 社会经济学

BARBARA MARCISZEWSKA

Introduction

Tourism has always been linked with the commodification of culture, landscape, recreation and indigenous people (Marciszewska, 2000). There has recently been fresh concern about the role of tourism as a force for cultural commodification and socioeconomic development both in postmodern societies and in societies undergoing transformation.

This chapter is divided into two sections. In the first I focus on the place of cultural tourism in national/regional tourism development strategy in Poland. Selected data will be presented from national research carried out in this field from an international perspective.

In the second part the relationship between culture and tourism and their impact on socioeconomic development will be analysed. An attempt is made to present cultural tourism as a people-based activity, which can be seen as a factor influencing national and regional identity.

On the other hand, the impact of globalisation upon labour issues in the sector of culture and tourism markets can be simply stated as follows: to cope with the international intensity of competition brought about by globalisation a knowledge-based economy has emerged to replace the previously dominant national culture. The knowledge-based economy utilises the skills of the workforce in culture and creates new responses to the management of human resources by the organisations (Marciszewska, 2004: 28). This new organisational behaviour is characterised by innovation, diversity and flexibility, and requires meaningful changes in cultural policy to influence tourism.

Cultural tourism development in Poland faces a number of barriers that have to be recognised by both the national tourism administration and the sector of culture. The process of globalisation partly reduces borders and barriers for culture exchange between nations, but it also creates new directions for national policy. 'Some assert that globalisation goes beyond the idea of permeating boundaries between nations and organisations, but also crosses the traditional borders of time, space, scope, geography, function, thought and cultural assumptions' (Knowles *et al.*, 2001: 176). This, in turn, demands a new political approach to both culture and tourism, which are shaped by market economy from one side and social needs from the other. It means that culture, because of its 'sensitive' nature, requires long-term policy at national, regional and local levels (Marciszewska & Fache, 2004: 248). Cultural consumption in Poland is shifting from high culture to popular culture and this necessitates providing the opportunity to develop a new infrastructure. Religious sites, historical properties, galleries, museums and theatres are constant elements of the tourist package but they are particularly significant factors influencing demand among young scholars and foreign tourists. These cultural attractions are partly being replaced by small cultural festivals and sport events – 'popular culture' – and performing arts attractions are also becoming important for young people and families with children. Therefore, regional and local development strategies include tasks to build a new infrastructure (e.g. theme parks, leisure centres) and adapt existing buildings for cultural activities. Such tasks could be supported by indirect investment, but this kind of financing is lacking in Poland at the present stage of socioeconomic development.

Many approaches are taken in the literature on the subject of measuring the economic impacts of tourism. Traditional approaches have concentrated upon the multiplier effects on national economic variables such as GDP or employment (Mules, 2001: 312), while those of other authors are based on an input–output model (Archer, 1996) in order to compare in general terms the costs incurred and the benefits created by tourism for the economy. The number of tourists and the amount of tourist spending are used as basic economic indicators to gauge the economic impact of tourism.

Traditional quantitative approaches have prevented the role of culture through tourism in socioeconomic development from being fully identified. Mules (2001: 313–314) indirectly suggests that the input–output model does not, for example, serve to highlight environmental and social costs, feedback effects via links with other branches of economy, or other impacts which can only be assessed outside the multiplier process.

Such quantitative indicators do not show the full influence of cultural tourism on the economy and social environment because culture itself is by nature complicated and requires a qualitative approach. In this context it is possible to use as a basis the approach of Dann and Philips (2001: 251) that '...to a large extent, the decision whether to opt for quantitative or qualitative methods (or maybe a mixture of both) is generally predicated on the nature of the topic at hand and the type of medium through which it is normally accessed'.

Cultural tourism can probably be analysed on the basis of both qualitative and quantitative methods. It can also be confirmed by numbers that culture is '...a major determinant of the growth of tourism and leisure consumption' (Richards, 2001: 8). There is, however, no way of identifying all the aspects of such growth without using qualitative methods. Socioeconomic development requires a qualitative approach in order to assess its diverse characterisation, and therefore cultural tourism should also be analysed in this fashion.

The Role of Government in the Development of Cultural Tourism in Poland

Cultural tourism consists of two different words and two different types of human activity, 'tourism' and 'culture'. The characteristics of these areas are as different as the meanings of the words. In combining them into one field of human activity (for tourists) and also one managerial field, problems are created in interpreting government intervention, which is based on both the commercial and social functions of the products with regard to the customer. Cuts in public expenditure on culture, the privatisation of the cultural infrastructure and the necessity of generating demand for visits to exhibitions, museums and galleries give rise to a particular conflict within the managerial branch operating under the banner of cultural tourism. Tourist enterprises expect short-term economic profit. The same is true of cultural institutions, but these have to keep in mind their social and educational role. Such conflict can only be resolved by government intervention, as the market economy is too weak and unstable in Poland to influence prices in culture to the extent that they are acceptable to all social groups. In this context it is obvious that '...the state should fall back on its core tasks needed to run today's market economy' (Wanhill, 2001: 224).

Cultural Consumption: Selected Aspects Identified on the Basis of an ATLAS Questionnaire Survey in Northern Poland

The national approach to cultural tourism in Poland has aimed to broaden knowledge about the role of Polish culture in tourism development on the one hand and in socioeconomic conditions on the other. This would appear useful for the purpose of further comparative studies of cultural tourism developments and trends across Europe. While it is true that '...cultural [...] tourism covers not just the consumption of the cultural products of the past, but also of the contemporary culture or the 'way of life' of a people or region' (Richards, 2001: 7), this does not apply to Poland as much as to more developed European countries, as the range of cultural offerings is not the same and the lower level of disposable income of the population holds back the growth of a framework of cultural consumption, particularly in the field of high culture.

Some features of cultural consumption in Poland related to the visiting of cultural attractions have been identified in the relevant literature (Marciszewska, 2001: 224):

- Cultural tourism in Poland can be defined as a professional and well educated market.
- 'Popular culture' attractions may cater mainly for local people but the attractions surveyed in 1997 also attracted a reasonable number of tourists.
- The high occupational standard of respondents does not relate to a high level of income.
- Cultural attractions are visited principally by young people and by people over the age of 40.
- Cultural visitors are motivated by the opportunity to learn new things, to experience new things, to accompany other people and to relax.

Other aspects, including the relationship of cultural tourism to the socioeconomic environment, have also been discussed in recent Polish publications (Karczewska, 2002; Marciszewska, 2002; Sikorska-Wolak, 2002). These are mainly based on secondary data and focus on the role of tangible and intangible culture for tourism development. Little attention has been given to the interrelationships between cultural tourism and socioeconomic development, which should mainly be analysed from a qualitative perspective.

It is recognised that heritage and cultural tourism have featured prominently in the development of tourism in cities in Poland as consumers search for new types of visitor experience that are focused on the value of culture in a wider sense. However, over the last decade the public and private sectors in Poland have identified niches in the market for new recreational products, which should not be separated from

Table 5.1 Motivation for visiting the attractions

Motivation	Respondents who agreed with the reason given (%)	
	1997	*2001*
To learn something new	28.1	46.3
To experience something novel or unique	34.2	44.4
To relax	32.9	62.7
To learn about the history of a place	–	45.5
To experience the atmosphere of a place	–	43.3
To find out more about local culture	–	45.0

cultural tourism products. Their complementary nature can be seen as a new opportunity for a higher standard of service and new tourist experience.

The importance of a new experience for tourists when it comes to decision-making regarding holidays is shown by data collected during a survey in Northern Poland. The research was carried out using a standard Association for Tourism and Leisure Education (ATLAS) questionnaire translated into Polish.[1] A total of 2195 respondents visiting 13 types of cultural tourism attractions were interviewed in 1997; in 2001, 561 respondents were asked at six cultural sites. Selected data are shown in Table 5.1.

The data in Table 5.1 indicate that respondents visit cultural attractions mainly to relax, to learn something new or to discover a unique experience. The findings, both from 1997 and 2001, demonstrate that participation in cultural tourism is often linked to the aspirations of consumers to learn and/or experience something new. This implies that tourism managers must be proactive and innovative if long-term revenue growth is to be expected. Innovative and proactive approaches require a sound economic basis both inside the enterprise and in its environment. Unfortunately, this is not yet the case in Poland. Small- and medium-sized tourism enterprises have to find the optimal market strategy from an economic point of view

---

[1] ATLAS has been carrying out regular cultural tourism surveys using a standardised questionnaire since 1992. These have been translated into a range of European languages and are distributed nationally, regionally or locally, usually by native speakers.

and so tend to promote the sale of holidays abroad (to America, the Mediterranean and Asia, for example) rather than attract people to their own region. Lack of economic stability on the tourism market itself, together with an unsatisfactory standard of living as a consequence of Poland's slow socioeconomic development, have an adverse influence on domestic tourism in Poland and can, in the long term, be to the detriment of the peoples' engagement with national culture.

The economic situation of Poles also determines their spending on holiday travel and accommodation (Table 5.2). These data are not

Table 5.2 Cultural tourist spending in relation to purpose

Purpose of expenditure	Answers (%)	Predominant level of spending (in PLN)[a]
Travel	10.8	50.00
	10.6	100.00
	6.1	150.00
	9.9	200.00
	6.1	300.00
Accommodation	6.1	20.00
	5.4	50.00
	12.9	100.00
	9.3	150.00
	8.2	200.00
	5.0	300.00
	4.7	500.00
Food and drink	56.4	Less than 100.00
Shopping	65.2	Less than 100.00
Attractions and admissions	67.8	Less than 100.00
Total expenditure	57.3	> 500.00

[a]Polish złotych. €1 = 4.75 PLN (13.3.04)
Source: ATLAS questionnaire survey, Poland, 2001

surprising: more than half of Polish tourists spend less then 500 zł on a trip, as 43.2% of respondents belonged to the lowest household income bracket (€0–5000), which is typical for an average Polish family. In 2001 an average monthly salary amounted to approximately 2045.11 zł (Statistical Yearbook, 2002: 190) and an average monthly disposable income (for 1 person) to 620.44 zł (Statistical Yearbook, 2002: 190). These numbers bring into sharp focus the economic situation of the average Polish cultural tourist.

Relationships Between Cultural Tourism and the Economic Environment

Taking into account that cultural activities and heritage sites can be combined with other forms of leisure activity in a holiday, it may be assumed that cultural consumption is based on a low household budget and is restricted by slow economic growth.

Cultural tourism could be a subject of interest to tourist destinations with cultural amenities, heritage sites, arts centres, historical museums and natural resources, if these destinations could combine culture and leisure in the tourist product. Unfortunately, this requires the development of various leisure facilities (such as sports and entertainment venues) and long-term investment. Thus the low economic growth highlighted here acts as a constraint on cultural consumption. The proposition that 'Today, the growth of tourism around cultural themes has the potential to bring benefits to economically peripheral regions' (Butcher, 2001: 11) can only partially be applied in Poland. Culture itself and cultural tourism, particularly those offerings that are based on historical sites, require constant or periodic investment. The intervention of government and regional authorities, at least at some stages during the transition period, would appear crucial for socioeconomic development.

To analyse cultural tourism as connected with economic factors or as an economic factor in itself, it is necessary to take into account not only the social construction of identities in postmodern society but also the potential means of conceptualising people's desires and their links with social processes. This is true within the framework of developed capitalism and in countries such as Poland, which joined the European Union recently. In this context an attempt to identify the most important features of the relationship between cultural tourism and socioeconomic development should stress the following:

- There is a need for governmental intervention and/or public–private partnership ventures to provide long-term development

(Marciszewska, 2001: 217; Marciszewska & Miecznikowski, 2003: 86).

- Cultural attractions, along with live culture such as festivals, can become a meaningful factor in economic development in order to be able to raise incomes, stabilise the labour market and sustain cultural heritage.
- National and regional/local cultural identity should be seen as a factor in terms of competitiveness on the global tourism market.
- Culture as a function (Butcher, 2001: 12) of society can also be seen as a prerequisite for social and political creativity, which depend on the creativity of individuals. In looking at the development of Polish tourism, it is possible to find some positive examples where culture in its intangible sense does influence socioeconomic development as a stimulating factor.
- Potential conflicts between mass tourism and the need to create new packages in the field of cultural tourism that provide a 'special' unique experience for consumers should be resolved by proactive behaviour on the part of managers.
- The importance of culture as an area for policy development has been recognised at the national level. This development needs to be implemented at all levels of authority to provide a creative role for culture, as consumed by both local people and tourists, in socio-economic development.

As a result of its influence on levels of cultural consumption, cultural tourism has been seen as a means of supporting culture itself. This implies that it indirectly stimulates a society's development, providing an opportunity for greater cultural participation on the one hand and the financing of culture on the other. The present stage of the market economy in Poland can be characterised by the indicators of cultural participation shown in Table 5.3.

The data in Table 5.3 do not show as rapid a growth in cultural facilities as in cultural participation, which relates to people's disposable incomes. Theatre audiences per 1000 of the population remained nearly the same in 2002 as in 1995 (about 130 persons). This kind of cultural activity seems to appeal less to Poles, but the picture is similar to that in other European Union countries. According to Eurostat (Europeans' Participation in Cultural Activities, 2002: 9), European citizens, when asked how many times in the last 12 months they had participated in cultural activities, gave theatre as 1.33 on a scale from 1 to 5 (where 1

Table 5.3 Participation in culture

Specification	1995	2000	2001	2002	1995	2000	2001	2002
	Performances (in thousands)				Visitors (in thousands)			
Theatres and musical institutions	47.9	50.1	48.5	46.7	10,197	10,533	10,143	9800
Concert halls, orchestras and choirs	17.6	17.4	16.9	15.9	3325	3167	3189	3302
Entertainment enterprises	4.6	4.4	5.2	4.5	1149	2047	1495	1252
	Number of amenities (in thousands)				Visitors (in thousands)			
Art galleries	0.209	0.253	0.266	0.268	2318	2644	2667	2685
Exhibitions	2.6	3.0	3.4	3.3	a	a	a	a
Museums	0.6	0.6	0.7	0.7	17,060	16,612	15,137	15,259
Students visiting museums	a	a	a	a	6547	6537	5908	5541
Cinemas	0.7	0.7	0.7	0.6				
Cinema audiences (in millions)					22.6	20.9	27.6	27.1

Source: GUS

corresponds to 'never' and 5 corresponds to 'over 12 times' and the mid position is 3, corresponding to 4–6 visits).

Taking into account the difficulties of a time of transformation in Poland, it can be said that the fact that cultural participation did not decline in the 1990s indicates that the lifestyle of some social groups has remained relatively stable, despite cuts in subsidies for culture and price increases for these services.

The annual figures for borrowing from public libraries are analogous. These are nearly the same for 2002 as in 1995, standing at approximately 7.0–7.5 million books, which, when averaged, would mean every fifth Polish citizen reads books. Europeans give a rating of 1.67 on a scale of 1–5 for going to a library in the last 12 months, putting this activity in second place after going to the cinema (Eurostat, 2002: 9).

There has been insufficient research in Poland to explain why people prefer one kind of cultural activity above another, but the preference for the cinema can be partly explained by the relatively low prices for entrance tickets compared with those for the theatre or concert hall. When the low dynamic of household incomes is taken into account, the explanation might lie in economic factors and, additionally, fashion. Young people, in particular, choose the cinema as an attractive leisure activity. There has been some research showing that Poles changed their cultural preferences between 1972 and the 1990s (Jung, 1996: 185–186): cinema, the theatre, opera, museums, concerts and exhibitions have lost their popularity to mass culture. This situation is influenced by:

• Television, video and other forms of media used in leisure time.
• A decrease in the role of those cultural activities that had been subsidised before the market economy was implemented. The new socioeconomic conditions (which saw cuts in subsidies for culture, rising competition from foreign companies offering new attractive cultural products and a decrease in mass cultural consumption as a result of changes to the system of social provision) have led to greater emphasis on home-based cultural activities.

These changes are, to some degree, typical for nearly all social groups, even those that are professionally connected with culture.

New opportunities for sustaining culture as a main component of leisure time and tourism products will be shaped in the immediate future by the following factors:

• the promotion of the educational function of culture and historical heritage;

- the promotion of learning as a component of cultural tourism;
- the development of an infrastructure for culture;
- the creation of interesting tailor-made tourism packages;
- a marketing approach directed at the tourism services market;
- physical and economic access to culture for all social groups;
- differentiation of cultural tourism products according to the criteria of leisure-time budgets on the one hand and disposable incomes on the other;
- the recognition of culture as an experience-creating factor, both based on emotions and at the same time serving as a source of emotions for visitors.

The degree to which these factors influence cultural consumption in present-day Poland will depend on the way activities are planned and arranged, not only within a tourism or cultural organisation but also with regard to the markets and the socioeconomic and political conditions in which the organisation operates. The major challenges in the management of culture in Poland include increasing and diversifying the demand for cultural services. Those who participate in culture expect more from programmers than the supply of cultural activities. They want to see a high level of organisation of the events in order to have an opportunity to rest and relax. Participants whose work is related to culture expect to enjoy a good experience, which would provide them with a new opportunity to tailor their own work to the demands of the employment market. These factors influence the allocation of existing financial resources on the central and regional level and managers have to be more flexible and proactive (Marciszewska, 2003). Managers can no longer rely on traditional sources of funding for culture. The new economic climate, in which the field is dominated by the market economy, new fiscal policy and fierce competition on the labour market, is forcing managers to become more innovative and resourceful in securing the financial support required for cultural development. The interaction and impact of these forces upon cultural policy require creative approaches to marketing in culture and to the staging of cultural activities so as to result in a favourable image, financial benefits for cultural organisations and a satisfying experience for participants.

Employees must be prepared to see their job as requiring a solid background in promotion and marketing skills. The benefits of training in the field of marketing in culture can be viewed as opportunities (Marciszewska, 2003):

(1) to clarify the vision of managers as to why, how and for what they are operating;
(2) to identify participants' cultural needs, expectations and desires and to meet these;
(3) to identify the level of available human, physical and financial recourses that can be available for commercial and/or non-profit-making cultural organisations;
(4) to develop a standard for cultural services with an emphasis on quality;
(5) to improve the accessibility of cultural facilities to satisfy participants and create profits for the organisation;
(6) to develop innovative strategies for maintaining the desired level of customer service.

With regard to the potential contribution of the so-called 'cultural industries' (Smith, 2001: 229) to the process of tourism development in Poland, it has to be pointed out that there has been some attempt to forge a relationship between cultural policy and tourism policy. Some events have two aspects: the commercial and the cultural (such as the Amber Fair 'Amberif'), the historical and the cultural (the Exhibition *Roads to Freedom*, a history of Solidarity being an example), the cultural and the issue of postindustrial environmental regeneration (in the performing arts and The Campus for Young Artists, *Mlode Miasto*, on the site of the former Gdańsk shipyard), and tourism and culture (tourist fairs and the performing arts, including music, *Jarmark Dominikanski* and cultural festivals). Along with these events, other 'branches' of cultural industries have been developing, such as advertising, the photographic industry, printing and video. Such combinations of events provide an opportunity to develop unique live cultural attractions and contribute to local or/and regional budgets. It should be noted that the majority of these attractions have long traditions and are one of the main reasons for visiting a place. An example of this is the *Jarmark Dominikanski* in the city of Gdansk, which is held in the first half of August and always attracts a large number of tourists.

There is no doubt that cultural events stimulate consumption of various products and positively influence socioeconomic development. They can be seen as long-term new employment, and investment factors and core components of tourism itself. In addition, national and regional identity is highlighted by such 'mixed' events and can create a particular tourism demand.

Cultural tourism is becoming a socioeconomic activity with the potential to contribute to the development of the destination and is referred to in all regionally accepted strategies for socioeconomic development and in most local ones as well. This is because most tourist destinations in Poland not only have many tourism attractions but are creating the conditions for a higher level of consumption and improving the quantity and quality of leisure services.

With respect to demand, it can be said that individuals' needs and wants constitute the main reasons for consumption. These are changeable and it will always be unclear how far it is possible to intervene in personal preferences by means of marketing and promotion in order to stimulate economic development.

In the context of globalisation the importance of strong national identity needs to be stressed as a factor in tourist appeal, which has a bearing on consumption in different groups of goods. Identity, innovation, positive experience (both of tourists and local communities) and a knowledge-based society create the best opportunities for qualitative socioeconomic development.

Conclusions

Considering the particular nature of the Polish economy, which is at yet insufficiently stable, and also the multifaceted character of the tourism product and its relation to culture (heritage, entertainment, high culture, lifestyle and pop culture), it may be supposed that cultural tourism can become one of the major economic drivers of the present century, if the government and public sector 'control' or coordinate the market processes in keeping with principles of sustainable development. The Polish government should run a market economy with parallel intervention in the sector of culture. In the light of all this the following government tasks can be identified:

- the provision of macroeconomic stability;
- the provision of financial resources for cultural development in the state budget;
- the establishment of a strong public–private partnership to sustain cultural heritage (both tangible and intangible) and to create new cultural events, which will provide a strong impulse for dynamic socioeconomic development;
- the provision of access to cultural services and cultural education for all social groups;

• the adjustment of policy in relation to the market economy. The government should make institutional arrangements to support both public and private cultural organisations.

It is, however, clear that government intervention has to be seen as action that is differentiated at particular stages of socioeconomic development. At the present stage, the central planning model no longer operates and information, knowledge and, particularly, cultural values are not under the planners' control. This situation has not yet provided stimulus to the development of culture. New production-consumption instruments, flexible institutions and policy makers at all levels are required to exert an influence on the cultural environment. In the current Polish tourism development model such instruments are assigned to regional and local strategies for tourism development.

References

Archer D.H. (1996) Economic impact analysis. *Annals of Tourism Research* 23 (4), 704–707.

Butcher J. (2001) Cultural baggage and cultural tourism. In J. Butcher (ed.) *Innovations in Cultural Tourism* (pp. 11–18). Tilburg: Association for Tourism and Leisure Education.

Dann, G. and Philips, J. (2001) Qualitative tourism research in the late twentieth century and beyond. In B. Faulkner, G. Moscardo and G. Laws (eds) *Tourism in the 21st Century. Lessons from Experience* (pp. 247–265). London and New York: Continuum.

Eurostat (2002) European's participation in cultural activities. A Eurobarometer survey carried out at the request of the European Commission. Brussels: European Commission.

GUS. On WWW at http://www.stat.gov.pl/servis/polska/2003/rocznik11/teat. htm. Accessed 15.3.04.

Jung, B. (1996) Leisure statistics during the period of reforms in Poland. In J. Cushman, A.J. Veal and J. Zuzanek (eds) *World Leisure Participation* (pp. 262–276). Wallingford: CAB International.

Karczewska, M. (2002) Udział społeczności lokalnych w ochronie i popularyzacji dziedzictwa kulturowego wsi jako elementu rozwoju turystyki. *Problemy Turystyki i Hotelarstwa* 4, 35–39.

Knowles, T., Diamantis, D. and El-Mourhabi, J.B. (2001) *The Globalisation of Tourism and Hospitality: A Strategic Perspective.* London: Continuum.

Marciszewska, B. (2000) Turystyka kulturowa a rozwój społeczno-gospodarczy. *Teoria Ekonomii.* Gdansk: Wyd. Uniwersytetu Gdanskiego, 5/6 (21/22), 77–87.

Marciszewska, B. (2001) Consumption of cultural tourism in Poland. In G. Richards (ed.) *Cultural Attractions and European Tourism.* Wallingford Oxon: CABI Publishing.

Marciszewska, B. (2002) Społeczno-ekonomiczne uwarunkowania rozwoju turystyki kulturowej. *Problemy Turystyki i Hotelarstwa* 3, 5–9.

Marciszewska, B. (2003) Marketing of culture: The Polish perspective. Paper presented at the Annual IFEA Conference, Vienna, March.

Marciszewska, B. (2004) Kreowanie wiedzy warunkiem racjonalnego wykorzystania potencjału turystycznego Pomorza. In B. Marciszewska and S. Miecznikowski (eds) *Usługi a rozwój gospodarczo-społeczny* (pp. 24–31). Gdansk: AWFiS &GTN.

Marciszewska, B. and Miecznikowski, S. (2003) Partnerstwo publiczno-prywatne a rozwój turystyki w regionie. In *Unia Europejska a przyszłość polskiej turystyki* (pp.75–88). Warszawa: Szkoła Główna Handlowa.

Marciszewska, B. and Fache, W. (2004) Europejskie trendy wpływajace na funkcjonowanie sektora kultury. In B. Marciszewska and J. Ozdziński (eds) *Rekreacja, turystyka, kultura. Współczesne problemy i perspektywy wykorzystania czasu wolnego* (pp. 239–249). Gdansk: Wyd. AWFiS.

Mules, T. (2001) Globalization and the economic impacts of tourism. In B. Faulkner, G. Moscardo and G. Laws (eds) *Tourism in the 21st Century. Lessons from Experience* (pp. 312–327). London and New York: Continuum.

Richards, G. (2001) Development of cultural tourism in Europe. In G. Richards (ed.) *Cultural Attractions and European Tourism* (pp. 3–29). Wallingford Oxon: CABI Publishing.

Sikorska-Wolak, I. (2002) Popularyzacja dziedzictwa kulturowego regionu i jej znaczenie w rozwoju turystyki (na przykładzie Beskidu Śląskiego). *Problemy Turystyki i Hotelarstwa* 4, 17–23.

Smith, M. (2001) Bridging the gap through cultural regeneration: The future of London's north/south divide. In *North–South: Contrasts and Connections in Global Tourism*, Proceedings of 7th ATLAS International Conference (pp. 227–338). Savonlinna: ATLAS and Finnish University Network for Tourism Studies.

Statistical Yearbook of the Republic of Poland (2002) Year LXII. Warsaw: Central Statistical Office.

Wanhill, S. (2001) Issues in public sector involvement. In B. Faulkner, G. Moscardo and G. Laws (eds) *Tourism in the 21st Century. Lessons from Experience.* London and New York: Continuum.

Part 2

Community Participation and Empowerment

Chapter 6

Cultural Tourism, Community Participation and Empowerment

STROMA COLE

Introduction

Following an examination of cultural and ethnic tourism and the false divide between the two, this section examines how communities balance socioeconomic integration and cultural distinction, how aspects of culture are used and sold or are commodified. This process is not seen as negative or positive but the processes involved are discussed. Cultural commodification has stimulated preservation, community consciousness and an appreciation of local traditions. Identity affirmation and pride are examined as integral aspects of the cultural commodification process.

This section also examines a widely accepted criterion of sustainable tourism: community participation. It unpicks the overused notion of community, to examine the flaws that exist: the heterogeneous nature of communities, how as some members of communities are ruled in, others are necessarily ruled out; the complex and fluid nature of community make-up; as well as how political and psychological factors are as important as geographical, sociological and territorial aspects in considering notions of community.

While it is noted that 'participation' is open to a variety of interpretations, the chapters in this section examine active participation for empowerment. While active participation in tourism development initiatives would seem to empower community members, in many instances this is not necessarily the case. A number of factors are identified that both increase empowerment, for example esteem, pride, confidence and external contacts; and that restrict empowerment, for example a lack of knowledge about tourism, lack of self-belief or a lack of skills.

This section includes four case studies that illustrate many of these issues and more. These focus on craft tourism development in Lapland, place-making and community participation in Kiltimagh, Ireland,

89

township tourism in Soweto, South Africa and Maasai tourism in Kenya and Tanzania.

Cultural Tourism

The term *'cultural tourism'* is subject to many definitions (Sofield & Birtles, 1996) and much confusion (Hughes, 1996) and is symptomatic of Tribe's (1997) 'indiscipline' of tourism. In her seminal book, *Hosts and Guests*, Valene Smith (1978: 4) differentiates between ethnic and cultural tourism: 'ethnic tourism is marketed to the public in terms of quaint customs of indigenous often exotic peoples'. Wood (1984: 361) further defined ethnic tourism by its focus on people living out a cultural identity, whose uniqueness is being marketed to tourists. The focus of tourists' visits is on cultural practices according to Wood, and on 'native homes and villages, observations of dances and ceremonies and shopping for curios' (Smith, 1978: 4).

Firstly, both Wood (1984) and Smith (1978) differentiate between ethnic and cultural tourism, whereas in fact a continuum exists (Cole, 1997). Secondly, the use of the term ethnic is problematic. The popular use of the term ethnic implies a minority, a framing of the 'other'. '. . .The nostalgic longing for untouched primitive peoples' (Mowforth & Munt, 1998: 69) in the minds of the tourists is part of the process of 'othering' (MacCannell, 1984). 'Othering' is thus a prerequisite aspect and consequence of tourism (Cole & Viken, 1998). Most tourists have an ethnocentric view of the societies and cultures they visit (Laxson, 1991). Selwyn (1996: 21) asserts that 'it is widely accepted by anthropologists of tourism that much of contemporary tourism is founded on the 'Quest for the Other''. The Other belongs to a premodern, precommodified, imagined world and is authentically social (Selwyn, 1996: 21).

Tourism transforms difference into the global discourse of consumerism, a process by which 'otherness' becomes a commodity to be consumed. This is 'a kind of institutional racism that celebrates primitiveness' (Munt & Mowforth, 1998: 270) as suffering and poverty have become aestheticised by tourists' accumulation of images of the poor. Human practices are redefined as commodities as tourists are exposed to cultural differences and local cultural variation is confirmed. This leads to differentiation and a revival of culture and ethnicity (Walters, 1995).

The dichotomy between ethnic and cultural tourism, where the former is used for the 'primitive other' and the latter for the high arts in developed nations (as Richards, 1996, for example, uses it), serves to entrench inequalities between the rich and poor. MacIntosh and Goeldner (1990) use the concept of 'cultural distance' to refer to the extent a tourist's home culture differs from that of the area being visited. At present, Western academics use the term 'ethnic tourism' when the cultural differences are great and 'cultural tourism' when they are less so. All communities have culture; the further removed that culture is from the tourist, the more exotic it will appear. It would be interesting to ask those who see a difference whether they would consider tourism in Lapland (see Miettinen's chapter in this volume), on the fringe of Europe, as ethnic or cultural tourism. A similar question could be asked about township tourism that includes visits to the homes of some of Africa's poorest communities and at the same time an understanding of the burgeoning middle-class Black communities living in townships (see Briedenhann & Ramchander's case study in this volume) – certainly no single ethnic group is being represented as the term ethnic would suggest.

Furthermore, the term ethnic group is usually used to define a specified racial or linguistic group (see for example Hitchcock's (1993: 307) use in reference to the Ata Modo). If ethnicity and identity are seen as processional, contested and changing, it is inappropriate for the groups and their ethnonyms to be reified by tourism. Local groups creatively use well known ethnonyms for their benefit. As van der Duim *et al.* report in this volume, only four out of the eighteen cultural tourism projects in Tanzania are on Maasai land. This powerful ethnonym is used, as Chagga, Juhundi or Ujaama do not have the same marketing advantage.

MacCannell's (1984: 386) analysis of ethnic tourism suggests that 'touristified ethnic groups are often weakened by a history of exploitation, limited in resources and power, and they have no big buildings, machines, monuments or natural wonders to deflect the tourists' attention away from the intimate details of their daily lives'. Furthermore, the economic structure of ethnic tourism is such that most of the money involved does not change hands at the site, resulting in little economic advantage for such groups. Cohen's more recent analysis also stresses that underdevelopment is a group's resource. However, he makes a number of further important points: it is a group's marginality that is their major source of attractiveness, and preservation of their distinctiveness is a crucial precondition of the sustainability of their tourism. Their representation tends towards essentialisation as homogenous entities, marked by distinct, easily recognisable traits (Cohen, 2001: 28).

In considering the evolution of ethnic tourism, Cohen (2001) suggests that the tourees become active agents, achieving a degree of empowerment while gaining little financial reward, mainly through the sale of crafts. He goes on to suggest that, as tourism matures, some inhabitants accumulate some capital and gain familiarity with the tourists' tastes and increasingly gain a share of tourists' expenditure. Hospitality, performance and the arts then become commodified or at least reorientated towards outsiders. MacCannell (1984) suggests that when a group sees itself as an ethnic attraction the group members begin to think of themselves as representatives of an ethnic way of life, and any change has economic and political implications for the whole group. The 'group is frozen in an image of itself or *museumized*' (MacCannell, 1984: 388). As Butcher (2001) discusses, cultural tourism can create a straightjacket for communities. Their culture becomes cast in stone. Furthermore, when levels of economic development are seen as part of culture and inequality becomes reinterpreted as 'cultural diversity', tourism can preserve poverty.

The Challenge of Balancing Socioeconomic Integration with Cultural Distinction

There is a paradox central to cultural tourism development in peripheral areas. To develop is to modernise; if a remote cultural tourist destination modernises, it is no longer 'primitive' and it loses its appeal. The challenge of balancing socioeconomic integration with cultural distinction (Li & Butler, 1997) is a challenge fraught with conflict. As cultural assets are refined as consumerables for tourists, culture becomes commodified. As the destination modernises, a process, many suspect, of becoming more like the Western tourist's society, it becomes less different and distinct. The destination appears less authentic and so the value of the tourism product is reduced (Dearden & Harron, 1992; Go, 1997; Swain, 1989).

While cultural globalisation results in the homogenisation of cultures around the world, it simultaneously brings about increasing cultural differentiation. People can use cultural commodification as a way of affirming their identity, of telling their own story and establishing the significance of local experiences (McDonald, 1997). Far from rendering culture superficial and meaningless, commodification can be seen as ery positive process by which people are beginning to re-eir history and shake off the shame of peasantry' (Abram, in the case of the Lappish community described by Miettinen (this volume), a village museum stimulated the collection of historic objects and stories. The villagers not only preserved their local culture and heritage but also created a feeling of togetherness and an appreciation of local traditions. In Kiltimagh, Western Ireland, improving the town's appearance and recreating the 19th century market town was an important aspect of creating a sense of 'pride of place', a vital part of the community's empowerment according to McGettigan *et al.* (this volume). In Soweto, tourism has been liberating for the residents who have had an opportunity to share visions of their past oppression, and the role residents played in the struggle for freedom. The residents have become proud of their 'struggle' heritage and want visitors to understand and share it (Briedenhann & Ramchander, this volume).

In order to grasp how culture is changed as a result of globalising forces including tourism, it is helpful to recognise that traditions are creations in the present, socially constructed in an on-going process (Wood, 1993). Culture is a tool kit or a template (Wikam, 1990) that is used by people to suit their requirements. The questions that need to be asked are not about how tourism impacts on a culture but how tourism is used and how the facets of culture are articulated in the face of increased tourism. As Wood discusses, 'the central questions to be asked are about process, and about the complex ways tourism enters and becomes part of an already on-going process of symbolic meaning and appropriation' (Wood, 1993: 66).

For many commentators, globalisation generates ambivalence and uncertainty and leads individuals to emphasise their identity and security of their location (e.g. O'Riordan & Church, 2001). This emphasis on the local or localisation is considered 'inextricably bound together' (Featherstone, 1996: 47) with globalisation. They are two sides of the same coin. The search for identity is pursued in terms of ideas about tradition, history, locality and community (Robertson, 1992). The link between identity, locality, community and tradition and how these can be promoted to bring pride and hope to a community and their development is analysed in McGettigan *et al.*'s chapter.

The affirmation of local identity and the creation of ethnicity can be a response to and consequence of difference and 'otherness' becoming consumable tourist commodities. By understanding ethnicity as 'a set of social relationships and processes by which cultural differences are communicated' (Hitchcock, 2000: 210), ethnicity can be understood as a resource to be mobilised. Tourism thus has important consequences for identity and ethnicity. 'A distinct cultural identity is a marketable resource for a tourism destination' (Scott, 1995: 385). Elements of culture may be commodified through tourism, but self-conscious awareness of traditional culture as something local people possess, that attracts tourists, can bring political legitimacy (where traditional culture and the identity associated with it has hitherto been debased). Tourism can thus provide marginalised communities with political capital to manipulate (de Burlo, 1996).

Community Participation

An important early work that emphasised the community's role was Murphy's (1985) *Tourism a Community Approach*. The purpose of his book was 'to examine tourism development issues and planning options in industrial nations' (Murphy, 1985: 118). Murphy focuses on the host community, identifying their goals and desires for, and capacity to absorb, tourism. Using an ecosystem approach or ecological community model and the notion of social carrying capacity, he emphasised that the planning system must extend down to the microlevel, to the community. A consensus of opinion now exists to suggest that community participation is essential in development (Botes & van Rensburg, 2000; Porritt, 1998), and that the public have a right to participate in planning (Simmons, 1994).

The reasons for community participation in tourism development are well rehearsed in the tourism literature and it is widely accepted as a criterion of sustainable tourism. As a service industry tourism is highly dependent on the good will and cooperation of host communities. Service is the key to the hospitality atmosphere (Murphy, 1985: 120) and community participation can result in an increased social carrying capacity (D'Amore, 1983). Virtually all tourism surveys show that the friendliness of the local people rates high on the list of positive features about a destination (Sweeny & Wanhill, 1996: 159). Support and pride in tourism development are especially the case in cultural tourism where the community is part of the product. Furthermore, involvement in planning is likely to result in more appropriate decisions and greater motivation on the part of the local people (Hitchcock, 1993) and protection of the environment is more likely to be supported (Tourism Concern, 1992). Not only does local community participation look good on paper (Mowforth & Munt, 1998; Kadir Din, 1997); it is often essential in securing funding. Community participation is considered necessary to get community support and acceptance of tourism development projects and to ensure that benefits relate to the local community needs. Tosun and Timothy (2003) further argue that the local community is more likely to know what will work and what will not in local conditions; and that community participation can add to the democratisation process and has the potential to increase awareness and interest in local and regional issues. Furthermore, they suggest that democracy incorporates the rights of the individual, which often encourage various forms of equity and empowerment.

While the reasons for community participation in tourism are many, the paradigm is subject to great debate (Mitchell, 2001). Some debates surround how to define 'the community' and 'participation', while many researchers question how community participation can work in practice considering the heterogeneous nature of communities (e.g. Braden & Mayo, 1999; Harrison, 1996; Joppe, 1996; Warburton, 1998). The heterogeneous nature of communities involved in East African cultural tourism is a key theme in van der Duim *et al.*'s chapter.

The approach to defining the community that should participate or have control is subject to a number of interpretations. Murphy's ecological model is one of four basic interpretations of the community (Pearce *et al.*, 1996). By identifying the community as synonymous with place, this approach fails to focus on decision-making and control. It assumes that all parties have equal opportunities to participate in the political process. Such notions of community, defined by territory, are fixed, discrete and relatively stable. However, communities need to be seen as more complex and fluid. Consideration needs to be given to power and decision making between and within community groups. While the heterogeneous nature of communities is frequently referred to, few analysts unpick how communities are fractured along lines of kinship, gender, age, ethnicity and existing levels of wealth (Crehan, 1997). As van der Duim *et al.* discuss in relation to the African communities, the interconnectedness between identity, space and place leads to a dynamic and fluid notion of community.

Definitions of who in the community should be involved in community participation involves ruling some people in and some people out; who is local and who is included are vital considerations as conflict over limited resources can result in tourism being a divisive force. The case study about township tourism in Soweto illustrates how resentment has developed due to nonresidents acting as tour leaders. In the case of Kiltimagh 'sense of place' and participation was extended to emigrants to foster economic rejuvenation and empowerment. The case clearly shows how community is far more than an environmental or geographical territory and that our understanding of community needs to extend to psychological and intangible aspects as well as the political.

Notions of 'community spirit', for example, may be grounded originally in 'place' but values are shared and negotiated between evolving groups of people.

Participation is also open to a variety of interpretations. As has been identified by Arnstein (1969), Pretty (1995) and France (1998), a ladder of participation exists, ranging from 'being consulted' (often only being told of a *fait accompli*) to being able to determine every aspect of the development process. While all communities participate to a certain degree, sharing a despoiled environment, receiving menial jobs or getting a percentage of gate fees to a National Park, community participation in the chapters in this section have taken a more inclusive understanding: active participation for empowerment. As Warburton (1998) points out, the need for participation is not doubted but the empowerment end of the ladder has received little attention in the tourism development literature.

The case studies here examine how different communities have actively participated in tourism development initiatives. In Finland women were empowered through their participation in a craft cooperative. In Ireland voluntary contributions from the community both in terms of funds and efforts were crucial for the initiative leading to commitment and sense of ownership. The voluntary input gave the community a sense of being involved, which, combined with a strong sense of place, led to pride and community empowerment.

The examples from Africa paint a less glowing and more complex picture, with some members of the communities participating while others are marginalised. Local elites in both Tanzania and Kenya have tended to monopolise power, dividing rather than uniting communities, and leading van der Duim *et al.* to conclude that local participation and involvement itself does not automatically lead to the empowerment of individuals.

Even if definitions were easier, and communities less complex, there are a number of reasons why active community participation is hard to achieve in practice. Lack of ownership, capital, skills, knowledge and resources all constrain the ability of communities to fully control their participation in tourism development (Scheyvens, 2003). Furthermore, in urban tourism destinations in the West a lack of interest on the part of residents would also appear to constrain participation (Goodson, 2003). Both Cole (1999) and Sofield (2003) discuss how a lack of knowledge is the constraining factor in marginalised communities in the world. Van der Duim *et al.* discuss how differential access to knowledge has affected participation in Tanzania. Tourism-specific and project management knowledge is not equally spread and those with better access have more opportunities. As Cole (1999) discusses, participation beyond lip service and rhetoric cannot be achieved without elucidation. Knowledge of tourism must be a precursor for those who want to participate in decisions about tourism planning and management. Many communities lack any real understanding of what it is they are supposed to be making decisions about (Sofield, 2003). Kadir Din (1996: 79) considers ignorance as the greatest barrier to participation, but that the ignorance is not restricted to residents but 'also affects the planning machinery and bureaucracy vested with implementation'.

Cultural Tourism and Empowerment

Empowerment is the capacity of individuals or groups to determine their own affairs. It is a process to help people to exert control over factors that affect their lives. It represents the top end of the participation ladder where members of a community are active agents of change and they have the ability to find solutions to their problems, make decisions, implement actions and evaluate their solutions. While a body of literature exists in relation to empowerment and employment (cf. Lashley, 2001; Wynne, 1993), there are few studies 'that focus specifically on empowerment and tourism development outside the business sector' (Sofield, 2003: 96).

In South Africa, Black economic empowerment (BEE) is advanced at many levels in order to integrate historically disadvantaged persons into the economic mainstream. The South African government en-courages corporations to consider empowerment as part of their strategic management through a number of mechanisms including ownership, operational controls, employment, staff development and corporate social responsibility. While some success has been noted, research suggests more monitoring and disclosure is necessary, possibly though the use of audits and reports, to further encourage the empowerment strategy (The Cluster Consortium, 1999). Concerns of transparency and accountability with regard to the equitable distribution of tourism benefits and the impacts on the empowerment of communities through tourism in both Kenya and Tanzania are discussed in van der Duim *et al.*'s chapter.

Scheyvens (2003) builds a framework around the four dimensions of empowerment. The economic gains of tourism that are well documented in the tourism literature are signs of economic empowerment. Psycho-logical empowerment comes from self-esteem and pride in cultural traditions. The ability of tourism to bring pride has been widely discussed (Adams, 1997; Boissevain, 1996; Cole, 1997; Crystal, 1978; Erb, 1998; Mansperger, 1992; Van den Berghe, 1992). Outside recognition of tourism initiatives adds to the self-esteem brought to individuals and communities. In Ireland a number of enterprise development awards added to the communities pride (McGettigan *et al.*, this volume). Similarly, in Tanzania, the TO DO! prize contributed to increased confidence (van der Duim *et al.* this volume).

Social empowerment results from increased community cohesion when members of a community are bought together through a tourism initiative. The enhancement of community cohesion is discussed by Sanger (1988) in relation to Bali, by Cole (2003) in relation to Ngada, by Ashley *et al.* (2001) and also in this volume by McGettigan *et al*. Not only can festivals provide an opportunity for celebrating local identity, but they can also bring the community together, enhancing community empowerment (cf. Razaq, 2003).

Scheyven's (2003) fourth dimension is political empowerment and can be regarded as empowerment in the sense Sofield (2003) discussed it. According to Sofield (2003), empowerment is about a change of power balance between actors; it is about a shift in balance between the powerful and the powerless, between the dominant and the dependent. It can be:

> regarded as a multidimensional process that provides the community with a consultative process often characterised by outside expertise; the opportunity to choose; the ability to make decisions; the capacity to implement/apply those decisions; acceptance of responsibility for those decisions and actions and their consequences; and outcomes directly benefiting the community and its members, not directed or channelled into other communities and/or their members. (Sofield, 2003: 112)

As Scheyvens (2003) points out in the conclusion to her book, empowerment should be promoted as a precursor to community involvement. Communities need access to a wide range of information about tourism. As discussed, information provision is an essential first step; meaningful participation cannot take place before a community understands what they are to make decisions about (Cole, 2007; Sofield, 2003). In addition to the need for information is the confidence to take part in the decision-making process. In many marginal communities, especially where there has been a long history of colonisation and/or authoritarian rule, communities lack the confidence to take part in decision making (Cole, 2007; Timothy, 1999). Tourism can be important in increasing a community's access to information and external contacts (Ashley, 2001), as well as new language skills and globalised media (Williams, 1998). In Ngada contacts in distant places and information from the 'outside world' were key reasons that villagers identified for liking tourists (Cole, 1997). Tourism can be important in giving individuals and communities confidence and strengthening their identity (Johnston, 1992; Swain, 1990), thus encouraging the self-belief necessary to be active in decision-making forums. These are at once signs of empowerment and part of the process by which a community can challenge outside and elitist interests in tourist destinations. As Kalisch (2000: 2) suggests, in a destination where the community has organised itself into a strong and knowledgeable force for social and economic empowerment, transnational corporations and governments will think twice before they displace people or take away their land and resources.

In order to bring about the confidence for meaningful participation and empowerment, many researchers have recognised the need for and value of considerable public education (for example Connell, 1997; Pearce, 1994; Simmons, 1994). As Ashley *et al.* (2001) have examined, the poor[1] have a weak capacity in the general understanding of tourists and how the industry works. An understanding of tourists and tourism is the first stage of empowering local communities to make informed and appropriate decisions about their tourism development. Di Castri (2003) emphasises the importance of access to electronic information – the Internet and email – and the freedom of communication it brings, for the empowerment of remote island communities. As Ashley *et al.* (2001), Timothy (1999) and Hampton (1999) report, further help is required in skills training and capacity building. As Miettinen discusses, the crafts people in Lapland lacked business and marketing skills. Considerable investments are required in communication and building trust between actors. Beyond the need for capacity building in the form of education, there is, as Sofield (2003) discusses, a need for legal and institutional change to allow for the genuine reallocation of power.

---

[1] In Ashley *et al.*'s report on pro-poor tourism, the poor are defined according to these prevailing socioeconomic characteristics: widespread unemployment, low per capita incomes or extreme remoteness.

References

Abram, S. (1996) Reactions to tourism: A view from the deep green heart of France. In J. Boissevain (ed.) *Coping with Tourists. European Reactions to Mass Tourism* (pp. 174–203). Oxford: Berghahn Books.

Adams, K. (1997) Touting touristic 'primadonas': Tourism ethnicity and national integration in Sulawesi, Indonesia. In M. Picard and R. Wood (eds) *Tourism Ethnicity and the State in Asian and Pacific Societies* (pp. 155–180). Honolulu: University of Hawaii Press.

Arnstein, S.R. (1969) A ladder of citizen participation. *Journal of the American Planning Association* 35 (4), 216–224.

Ashley, C., Roe, D. and Goodwin, H. (2001) *Pro-poor Tourism Strategies: Making Tourism Work for the Poor. A Review of Experience*. London: Overseas Development Institute.

Boissevain, J. (1996) Introduction. In J. Boissevain (ed.) *Coping with Tourists. European Reactions to Mass Tourism* (pp. 1–26). Oxford: Berghahn Books.

Botes, L. and Van Rensburg, D. (2000) Community participation in development: Nine plagues and twelve commandments. *Community Development Journal* 35 (1), 40–57.

Braden, S. and Mayo, M. (1999) Culture, community development and representation. *Community Development Journal* 34 (3), 191–204.

Butcher, J. (2001) Cultural baggage and cultural tourism. In J. Butcher (ed.) *Innovations in Cultural Tourism*. Proceedings to the 5th ATLAS International Conference (pp. 11–17). Tilburg: ATLAS.

Cohen, E. (2001) Ethnic tourism in Southeast Asia. In T. Chee-Beng, S.C.H. Cheung and H. Yang (eds) *Tourism, Anthropology and China* (pp. 27–53). Singapore: White Lotus Press.

Cole, S. (1997) Cultural heritage tourism: The villagers' perspective. A case study from Ngada, Flores. In W. Nuryanti (ed.) *Tourism and Heritage Management* (pp. 468–481). Yogyakarta: Gadjah Mada University Press.

Cole, S. (1999) Education for participation: The villagers' perspective. Case study from Ngada, Flores, Indonesia. In K. Bras, H. Dahles, M. Gunawan and G. Richards (eds) *Entrepreneurship and Education in Tourism*. ATLAS Asia Conference Proceedings, Bandung, Indonesia (pp. 173–184).

Cole, S. (2003) Cultural tourism development in Ngada, Flores, Indonesia. Unpublished PhD thesis, London Metropolitan University.

Cole, S. (2007) Information and empowerment: The keys to achieving sustainable tourism. *Journal of Sustainable Tourism*. 15, to appear.

Cole, S. and Viken, A. (1998) Tourism: On holiday from ethics? In *8th Nordic Tourism Symposium*, 18–21 November, Alta, Norway.

Connell, D. (1997) Participatory development: An approach sensitive to class and gender. *Development in Practice* 7 (3), 249–259.

Crehan, K. (1997) *The Fractured Community. Landscape of Power and Gender in Rural Zambia*. Berkeley: University of California Press. On WWW at http://ark.cdlib.org/ark:/13030/ft0779n6dt/. Accessed 11.4.06.

Crystal, E. (1978) Tourism in Toraja (Sulawesi Indonesia). In V. Smith (ed.) *Hosts and Guests: The Anthropology of Tourism* (pp. 109–126). Oxford: Basil Blackwell.

D'Amore, L. (1983) Guidelines to planning harmony with the host community. In P.E. Murphy (ed.) *Tourism in Canada: Selected Issues and Options* (pp. 135–159). Victoria, BC, Canada: University of Victoria, Western Geographical Series 21.

Dearden, P. and Harron, S. (1992) Case study: Tourism and the Hill tribes of Thailand. In B. Weiler and C.M. Hall (eds) *Special Interest Tourism* (pp. 95–104). London: Belhaven Press.

De Burlo, C. (1996) Cultural resistance and ethnic tourism on South Pentecost, Vanuatu. In R. Butler and T. Hinch (eds) *Tourism and Indigenous Peoples* (pp. 255–275). London: Routledge.

Di Castri, F. (2003) Sustainable tourism in small Islands local: Empowerment as a key factor. On WWW at www.biodiv.org/doc/ref/island/insula-tour-em. Accessed 5.7.04.

Erb, M. (1998) Tourism space in Manggarai, Western Flores, Indonesia: The house as a contested place. *Singapore Journal of Tropical Geography* 19 (2), 177–192.

Featherstone, M. (1996) *Undoing Culture: Globalization, Postmodernism and Identity*. New York: Sage.

France, L. (1998) Local participation in tourism in the West Indian Islands. In E. Laws, B. Faulkner and G. Moscardo (eds) *Embracing and Managing Change in Tourism: International Case Studies* (pp. 222–234). London: Routledge.

Go, F. (1997) Entrepreneurs and the tourism industry in developing countries. In H. Dahles (ed.) *Tourism, Small Entrepreneurs and Sustainable Development* (pp. 5–22) Tilburg: ATLAS.

Goodson, L.J. (2003) Social impacts, community participation and gender: An exploratory study of residents' perceptions in the City of Bath. Unpublished PhD thesis, Brunel University, Uxbridge.

Hampton, M. (1999) Cracks in the honey pot? Tourist attractions, local communities and economic development in Indonesia. In W. Nuryanti (ed.) *Heritage, Tourism and Local communities* (pp. 365–380). Yogyakarta: Gadja Mada University Press.

Harrison, D. (1996) Sustainability and tourism: Reflections from a Muddy Pool. In L. Briguglio, B. Archer, J. Jafari and G. Wall (eds) *Sustainable Tourism in Small Island States: Issues and Policies* (pp. 69–89). London: Pinter.

Hitchcock, M. (1993) Dragon tourism in Komodo eastern Indonesia. In M. Hitchcock, V. King and M. Parnwell (eds) *Tourism in South East Asia* (pp. 303–315). London: Routledge.

Hitchcock, M. (2000) Introduction. In M. Hitchcock and K. Teague (eds) *Souvenirs: The Material Culture of Tourism* (pp 223–237). Aldershot: Ashgate.

Hughes, H. (1996) Redefining cultural tourism. *Annals of Tourism Research* 23 (3), 707–709.

Johnston, B. (1992) Anthropology's role in stimulating responsible tourism. *Practicing Anthropology* 14 (2), 35–38.

Joppe, M. (1996) Sustainable community tourism development revisited. *Tourism Management* 17 (7), 475–479.

Kadir, D. (1997a) Indigenization of tourism development: Some constraints and possibilities. In M. Oppermann (ed.) *Pacific Rim Tourism* (pp. 77–81). Oxford: CAB International.

Kadir D. (1997b) Tourism development: Still in search of an equitable mode of local involvement. In C. Cooper and S. Wanhill (eds) *Tourism Development Environment and Community Issues* (pp. 153–162). Chichester: Wiley.

Kalisch, A. (2000) Fair trade in tourism. *Tourism Concern Bulletin* 1. On WWW at www.tourismconcern.org.uk/pdfs/fairtrade%20. Accessed 5.7.04.

Lashley, C. (2001) *Empowerment: HR Strategies for Service Excellence.* Oxford: Butterworth-Heinemann.

Laxson, J. (1991) How 'we' see 'them': Tourism and native Americans. *Annals of Tourism Research* 18 (3), 365– 391.

Li, Y. and Butler, R. (1997) Sustainable tourism and cultural attractions: A comparative experience. In M. Oppermann (ed.) *Pacific Rim Tourism* (pp.107– 116). Oxford: CAB International.

MacCannell, D. (1984) Reconstructed ethnicity: Tourism and cultural identity in third world communities. *Annals of Tourism Research* 11, 375– 391.

MacIntosh, R. and Goeldner, C. (1990) *Tourism Principles, Practices and Philosophies* (6th edn). New York: John Wiley and Sons.

Mansperger, M. (1992) Yap: A case of benevolent tourism. *Practicing Anthropology* 14 (2), 10– 14.

Mitchell, R. (2001) Community perspectives in sustainable tourism: Lessons from Peru. In S. McCool and N. Moisey (ed.) *Tourism, Recreation and Sustainability: Linking Culture and the Environment* (pp. 137– 162). Oxford: CABI.

Mowforth, M. and Munt, I. (1998) *Tourism and Sustainability: New Tourism in the Third World.* London and New York: Routledge.

Murphy, P. (1985) *Tourism: A Community Approach.* London and New York: Routledge.

O'Riordan, T. and Church, C. (2001) Synthesis and context. In T. O'Riordan (ed.) *Globalism, Localism and Identity.* London: Earthscan.

Pearce, P. (1994) Tourism-resident impacts: Examples, explanations and emerging solutions. In W. Theobald (ed.) *Global Tourism* (pp. 103– 123). Oxford: Butterworth-Heinemann.

Pearce, P., Moscardo, G. and Ross, G. (1996) *Tourism Community Relationships.* Oxford: Pergamon.

Porritt, J. (1998) Foreword. In D. Warburton (ed.) *Community and Sustainable Development.* London: Earthscan.

Pretty, J. (1995) The many interpretations of participation. *In Focus* 16, 4– 5.

Razaq, R. (2003) The impact of festivals on cultural tourism. Conference paper, The 2nd de Haan Tourism Management Conference, Nottingham, UK.

Richards, G. (1996) *Cultural Tourism in Europe.* Oxon: CABI.

Robertson, R. (1992) *Globalisation: Social Theory and Global Culture.* London: Sage Publications.

Sanger, A. (1988) Blessing or blight? The effects of touristic dance drama on village life in Singapadu. In *The Impact of Tourism on Traditional Music* (pp. 79– 104). Kingston, Jamaica: Memory Bank.

Scheyvens, R. (2003) *Tourism for Development: Empowering Communities.* London: Prentice Hall.

Scott, J. (1995) Sexual and national boundaries in tourism. *Annals of Tourism Research* 22 (2), 385– 403.

Selwyn, T. (1996) Introduction. In T. Selwyn (ed.) *The Tourist Image. Myths and Myth Making in Tourism* (pp. 1– 32). Chichester: John Wiley and Sons.

Simmons, D. (1994) Community participation in tourism planning. *Tourism Management* 15 (2), 98– 108.

Smith, V. (1978) Introduction. In V. Smith (ed.) *Hosts and Guests: The Anthropology of Tourism* (pp. 3–14). Oxford: Blackwell.

Sofield, T. (2003) *Empowerment and Sustainable Tourism Development*. Oxford: Pergamon.

Sofield, T. and Birtles, A. (1996) Indigenous Peoples' Cultural Opportunity Spectrum for Tourism (IPCOST)'. In R. Butler and T. Hinch (eds) *Tourism and Indigenous Peoples* (pp. 396–432). London: Routledge.

Swain, M. (1989) Developing ethnic tourism in Yunan China: Shalin Sani. *Tourism Recreation Research* 14 (1), 33–40.

Swain, M. (1990) Commoditizing ethnicity in Southwest China. *Cultural Survival Quarterly* 14 (1), 26–29.

Sweeney, A. and Wanhill, S. (1996) Hosting the guest: Changing local attitudes and behaviour. In L. Briguglio, B. Archer, J. Jafari and G. Wall (eds) *Sustainable Tourism in Islands & Small States: Issues and Policies* (pp. 148–159). London: Pinter.

The Cluster Consortium (1999) *Strategy in Action*. Black Economic Empowerment and Tourism. On WWW at Memory Bank, www.nedlac.org.za/research/fridge/satourrep/chpt6.pdf. Accessed 11.4.06.

Timothy, D. (1999) Participatory planning: A view of tourism in Indonesia. *Annals of Tourism Research* 26 (2), 371–391.

Tosun, C. and Timothy, D. (2003) Arguments for community participation in the tourism development process. *The Journal of Tourism Studies* 14 (2), 2–15.

Tourism Concern (1992) *Beyond the Green Horizon*. Surrey, UK: World Wildlife Fund.

Tribe, J. (1997) The indiscipline of tourism. *Annals of Tourism Research* 24 (3), 638–657.

Van den Berghe, P. (1992) Tourism and the ethnic division of labour. *Annals of Tourism Research* 19, 234–249.

Warburton, D. (1998) A passive dialogue: Community and sustainable development. In D. Warburton (ed.) *Community and Sustainable Development*. London: Earthscan.

Walters, M. (1995) *Globalisation*. London: Routledge.

Wikam, U. (1990) *Managing Turbulent Hearts: A Balinese Formula for Living*. Chicago: University of Chicago Press.

Williams, S. (1998) *Tourism Geography*. London: Routledge.

Wood, R. (1984) Ethnic tourism, the state and cultural change in Southeast Asia. *Annals of Tourism Research* 11, 353–374.

Wood, R. (1993) Tourism, culture and the sociology of development. In M. Hitchcock, V.T. King and M.J.G. Parnwell (eds) *Tourism in South East Asia* (pp. 48–70). London: Routledge.

Wood, R. (1997) Tourism and the state: Ethnic options and the construction of otherness. In M. Picard and R. Wood (eds) *Tourism, Ethnicity and the State in Asian and Pacific Societies* (pp. 1–34). Honolulu: University of Hawaii Press.

Wynne, J. (1993) Power relations and empowerment in hotels. *Employee Relations* 15 (2).

Chapter 7

Cultural Tourism in African Communities: A Comparison Between Cultural Manyattas in Kenya and the Cultural Tourism Project in Tanzania[1]

RENE VAN DER DUIM, KARIN PETERS and JOHN AKAMA

Introduction

This chapter uses case studies of community tourism projects in Kenya and Tanzania (Eastern Africa) to illustrate how communities in Third World countries have, over the years, embraced tourism and have eventually become part of the already on-going practices and processes of tourism development in the global arena. Community tourism projects are currently being undertaken among the Maasai people of Eastern Africa. The Maasai, as an ethnic community, are widely dispersed in the two East African countries of Kenya and Tanzania. The chapter examines existing linkages and power relations between the tourism industry and host communities. The cultural tourism projects are: a conglomerate of cultural manyattas, special Maasai homesteads where tourists come to visit, hear and experience Maasai culture, that are situated in areas adjacent to Amboseli National Park in Southern Kenya, and the Cultural Tourism Project (CTP) near Arusha in Northern Tanzania.

The chapter is based on premises of complexity and heterogeneity of communities. In this regard, communities in the Third World are not seen as possessing common elements of self-contained characteristics (Meethan, 2001: 15); neither are they seen as passive 'victims' of the global tourism industry, but are instead perceived as dynamic and interactive systems. Thus, the chapter deals with the concept of community as a complex and sometimes fluid notion that keeps evolving and changing over time (Crehan, 1997; Liepins, 2000a,b). The chapter also discusses existing interactive space between tourism and communities, the continuous processes within which different social practices and values interact, and where new meanings are created (Wearing *et al.*, 2002). It also examines the consequences of omnipresent power relations in a community (Cheong *et al.*, 2000) and the division of power between and/ or within communities, tourism entrepreneurs and intermediary organisations.

The Cultural Tourism Projects in Tanzania and Cultural Manyattas in Kenya: A Comparative Analysis

Although the development of tourism in the African continent is lagging seriously behind, countries such as Kenya and Tanzania are currently well 'plugged' into the global flow of tourism. Particularly, communities around important tourism nodes such as Amboseli National Park and Maasai Mara Game Reserve in Kenya, and the Arusha region in Northern Tanzania have become, in recent years, part of the global tourism industry. The communities have taken advantage of existing transport infrastructure and communication systems, the abundance of tourists visiting adjacent wildlife parks and existing tourist agencies in the tourism nodes, as well as powerful, albeit stereotypical images of the Maasai to promote and enhance their involvement in tourism.

In conventional tourism circles, the Maasai have, over the years, been represented, stereotypically, as a unique and esoteric community that represents the essence of real Africa; people who have managed to resist Western influence and have retained their exotic culture. As a consequence, overseas tour operators and travel agents most often market the Maasai as one of those extraordinary, mysterious indigenous African communities that have managed to remain untouched by Western influence and other forces of modernisation. These forms of touristic images are usually represented as ideal for tourists, particularly Western tourists, keen for exoticism and adventure 'in the manner of the early European explorer'. In most instances, international tourists, particularly tourists from North America and Europe, want to see the Africans and the African landscape in the same way as they were taught during the formative years of image-moulding; where examples of Africa were usually based on information that dated back to the colonial period (Wels, 2001: 64). Therefore, Europeans long for pristine African landscapes with picturesque huts that are made of grass-thatched roofs that dot and blend into the natural African landscape. They also expect to hear the sound of drums the minute they arrive in Africa, with African natives, rhythmically, dancing to the ongoing cadence representing real and quintessential Africa (Norton, 1996).

The establishment of cultural manyattas in areas adjacent to Amboseli National Park and other parts of Maasailand is closely linked to the establishment of wildlife parks and the development of safari tourism in Eastern Africa at the turn of the 20th century. The National Parks and Reserves were established in areas that were traditional grazing lands of the Maasai pastoral community (Akama, 2002). Initially, at the start of colonial rule in Eastern Africa in 1897, the Maasai pastoralists were moved from their expansive pastoral lands in Central and Northern Kenya and were eventually confined in selective Native Reserves in Southern Kenya. After this spatial relocation, the colonial government went a step further and declared the whole of southern Kenya (an area covering 27,700 km^2) as a protected game reserve. As a consequence the Maasai were lumped together with wildlife and were supposed to share their land with the diverse array of savannah wildlife. Further, with the aim of providing the requisite protection to the wildlife and promotion of organised safari tourism, the government enacted legislations for the establishment of specific wildlife parks in Maasailand in the 1950s, such as Maasai Mara and Amboseli. As a consequence, the establishment of the cultural manyattas, therefore, came as an off-shoot of the creation of the wildlife parks. Due to displacement from their grazing lands and diminishing livestock numbers, the Maasai people in various group ranches joined hands to establish cultural manyattas in areas adjacent to wildlife parks, as an alternative source of livelihood. Currently there are several cultural manyattas that are adjacent to Amboseli National Park including Olgulului, Lolavashi, Kimana and Tikondo.

The manyattas stereotypically reproduce the image of dome-shaped mud houses encircling a cattle enclosure, 'where women plaster their roofs with dung, while the elders wait for the cattle to come home. Tourists see the herdsman leaning "one-legged" on his staff. They hear the sound of tinkling cowbells and watch girls and warriors' dance bedecked in red ochre and coloured beads' (Berger, 1996: 178). As Ongaro and Ritsma (2001: 131) further explain, the procedures for receiving tourists are more or less the same among the existing Maasai cultural manyattas. Community representatives visit lodge owners or talk with local guides and drivers in order to attract tourists. Guides and/or drivers receive commission (around 10% of the entrance fee paid by tourists) if they bring tourists to a particular cultural manyatta (Ritsma, personal communication). Upon arrival, each tourist pays an entrance fee of around $10. Upon entering, the tourists are welcomed with song and dance by Maasai women. A community representative talks about the Maasai culture and the manyatta set-up and takes them around the manyatta. The tourists are also exposed to demonstrations of several aspects of Maasai lifestyle such as warriors making fire by rubbing a stick against a small log, and women making bracelets or necklaces and plastering a sun-bales mud hut with cow dung. Towards the end of the visit, the warriors stage a dance and during the dance visitors are permitted to join them and even take pictures together. In the end the tourists are led to a designated market place within the cultural manyatta where Maasai beadwork and other handicrafts are sold to tourists as souvenirs (Ongaro & Ritsma, 2001).

Compared to the cultural manyattas in Kenya, the village tourism project in Northern Tanzania is relatively recent. In 1994 the Netherlands Development Organization SNV and Maasai initiated commercial activities around Amboseli. A group of young Maasai asked SNV also to assist in developing tourism activities in the region. A pilot project in 1994 near Loliondo showed the possibilities for local people to benefit from tourism. With limited resources and inputs an income of about $10,000 was generated (Leijzer, personal communication). Based on these experiences, in 1995 the Cultural Tourism Program (CTP) started. SNV seconded an expert, took over the financing of the operating costs for the coordination office in Arusha and provided a few vehicles on loan. The concept for the CTP has been developed, propagated and implemented by a six-member project team in close cooperation with the national Tanzanian Tourist Board (TTB) and with the local population, until it reached the present stage, which now involves 18 projects. Every village offers a package of different possible visits. A half-day trip in the Ilkiding'a village, for instance, typically begins with the provision of lunch consisting of local cuisine, a walk through the village, a visit to the traditional craftsman and/or the traditional medicine man, buying of local souvenirs, sightseeing at the local waterfall and finally a traditional dance performed by local dancers. In 1995 the tourism projects attracted 50 tourists, and five years later the number had increased to over 5000 tourists. In 2001 the number of visitors had gone up to 7500, mainly consisting of backpackers, organised travellers as well as expatriates (Verburg, 2004). Although more villages and communities tried to be connected to the CTP, others had to withdraw. For example, Syikilili (2002) documents the 'rise and fall' of Gezaulole, one of the CTP projects. Successes amongst projects differ: whereas the project in Machame only received 80 tourists between December 2000 and May 2003, the project in Longido received around 1500 (Verburg, 2004).

SNV controlled the expenditure and made sure that the budget provided was strictly used for the earmarked purposes. Its staff in Arusha saw to it that the quality of the product was continually assessed. Moreover, they opened up contacts with local agencies to propagate the programme, and they took pains to open up additional communities for tourism and to continuously improve the products offered. SNV also supported the training of the guides by the Professional Tourguide School (PROTS) in Arusha and it coordinated all organisational tasks in connection with the arrival of tourists, apart from the product-marketing component, which was coordinated by the TTB (Adler, 1999; SNV, 1999). In 2002 SNV handed over the projects to local coordinators, with the TTB remaining the custodian of the CTP.

Comparing the cultural tourism projects in Kenya and Tanzania reveals existing similarities as well as distinct differences. In both cases relatively well developed transport infrastructure and communication networks existed, enabling the development of the projects. Also, from the 1960s, the utilisation of jet planes for efficient transportation of international tourists to Nairobi and/or Arusha and the use of relatively luxurious mini-buses to take visitors on tour around Amboseli or Arusha was decisive for the development of tourism in these regions. Furthermore, the recent introduction of mobile phones has enabled proactive project coordinators to use the facility to linkup up with tour operators and international tourists arriving in Arusha; this has enabled the projects to flourish and attract more tourists compared to projects that don't have this communication facility. For instance, the Gezaulole community project, which is located in a relatively remote area, and does not have any communication facility linking it to the outside world, has tended to lag behind, with only a few tourists visiting the project.

Moreover, most of the cultural manyattas in Kenya and the CTPs in Tanzania have, in essence, tended to link up with and/or are connected to existing nature-based/wildlife safari tourism activities. Consequently, they form part of a well developed tourism complex that combines specific nature-based attractions (Amboseli, Serengeti, Ngorogoro Crater, Kilimanjaro and Mount Meru National Parks), the existing relatively well developed tourist facilities (lodges, camp sites) and the unique Maasai cultural attractions. In this regard, the existing mega wildlife attractions, Maasai culture and the famous Kilimanjaro are icons for international tourists 'looking for exoticism and adventure in the African wilderness' (Akama, 2002: 43). In reality, however, the cultural manyattas in Kenya are more like a museum, as most of the activities are simulated and the villages are recent reconstructions. It can therefore be argued that the cultural manyattas fit in and they also exemplify the shift from a cattle-based subsistence and transition towards a profit-oriented diversified economy, based on new forms of land tenure and utilisation of resources (Berger, 1996).

However, in contrast, although similar transformation processes are currently taking place in the various Tanzanian villages where the cultural tourism projects are being undertaken, it should be stated that the initiation of various tourism activities is more or less embedded in the daily life of the local people, and they appear to be less 'stage managed' (although the degree of staging varies from village to village). Consequently, in Tanzania tourism activities are integrated with already existing socioeconomic and cultural activities. Furthermore, some of the villages are not only inhabited by the Maasai, but are also inhabited by people from other tribes. For instance, although most of the CTPs are often marketed and promoted using the powerful Maasai images, the villages of Gezaulole, Machame and Mto wa Mbu are inhabited by predominantly non-Maasai communities. Other tribes such as the Chagga, Juhundi and Ujaama have, in recent years, established their own settlements in many parts of Northern and Central Tanzania. As a matter of fact, of the 18 cultural tourism projects, only 4 projects are located in areas that can be said to be original Maasai land (Leijzer, personal communication).

In addition, compared to the CTP, cultural manyattas in Kenya have tended to mushroom in an uncontrolled manner and, as a consequence, most settlements near parks have grown into unplanned trading centres that are surrounded by zones of increasingly denuded landscapes (Berger, 1996: 183). In Tanzania, the initiation of various tourism activities was properly planned within the CTP framework. In this regard, the cultural manyattas in Kenya lack a well coordinated marketing and tourist distribution network, whereas the TTB coordinates the marketing and also facilitates the flow and distribution of tourists in the various cultural tourism projects. However, it should be stated that the situation doesn't always remain static. New attempts to coordinate tourism activities in cultural manyattas are currently underway, with the creation of the *Association for Cultural Centers in Amboseli Ecosystem* (ACCA) as a coordinating body responsible for joint marketing and promotion (Ongaro & Ritsma, 2002). Inversely, in Tanzania currently the coordination of various CTP initiatives appears to be weakening after the withdrawal of SNV support. For instance, in February 2002 a local daily newspaper, the *Arusha Times*, reported that the level of cooperation between various projects was noticeably going down (*Arusha Times*, 2003). Furthermore, recent attempts to establish a new body, the *Tanzania Cultural Tourism Organization* (TACTO), to be in charge of coordination of CTP activities has failed to take off due to disagreement on the functions that are to be undertaken by the organisation.

Discussion: Fractured Communities and the Development of Tourism

Since the 1970s, the concept of 'community participation' in tourism has become an umbrella term for a supposedly new genre of tourism development strategy (Tosun, 2000). However, the concept of community participation is still not easy to define or easy to accomplish in real world situations (Tosun, 2000: 616). Furthermore, there has been a belief that problems with 'community participation' only exist in terms of the methods and techniques that are employed in the development process (Mowforth & Munt, 2003: 213-214). However, this contention fails to acknowledge that in real world situations there exist various structures of 'power' both within and between communities. As a consequence, the main problem of this concept originates from the existing notion of perceiving *a* community as *the* '"natural" social entity' that has identifiable reality. Existing heterogeneity and unequal access to power in a community are therefore assumed away (p. 214).

In this regard, over the years most studies have taken 'community' as a discrete, relatively stable and homogenous object that can be defined by territoriality or place. Also these approaches have perceived communities as relatively fixed objects that exist in specific spatial locations (Liepins, 2000a). However, recent studies perceive 'community' as a more complex and fluid notion. Moreover, to think of communities as homogenous entities is to assume that everyone in a specific locality will have the same wants, needs and expectations. It should therefore be stated that although in any community set-up some people may have a clear sense of attachment, others don't have it (Meethan, 201: 140). Furthermore, communities are also *fractured* along lines of gender, age, kinship, ethnicity and existing levels of wealth (Crehan, 1997). The cultural manyattas in Kenya and the CTP in Tanzania should not be perceived as having distinct, homogeneous sociopolitical elements and/ or have collections of self-contained essential characteristics. Instead, most of the local people living in the various villages are usually caught up in a whole range of different groupings which are, themselves, socially different, and which impact on one another in various different ways; as a consequence, they are very much *fractured* communities.

Liepins (2000a,b) has proposed a framework of perceiving communities in both their material and imagined forms. This framework starts with the acknowledgement that neither territorial nor imagined communities exist in a vacuum, but rather occur within specific contexts, which must be considered. Communities consist of people and things that are perpetually being reproduced, sustained, undermined and reconfigured by cultural, political-economic and socioecological processes that occurred in the past and are still occurring in the present (van der Duim, 2004; Urry, 2003). As a consequence, communities are peculiar to both time and place (Crehan, 1997; Liepins, 2000b). Therefore, a robust and dynamic understanding of 'community' should amalgamate and include aspects of community as a series of meanings, the diversity and heterogeneity in social life, the interconnections (and struggles) between identity, space and place, and the notion of fluidity and change. Thus, according to Liepins (2000a), communities should be discerned in four dimensions: *people*, *meanings*, *practices* and *spaces*. The four dimensions of community are going to be used to illustrate existing complexity and diversity in the cultural manyattas in Kenya and the CTP in Tanzania.

First, the collective action and enactment of 'community' by *people* predicate community as a social construct. People can therefore live within a community, but may also be multiply located in a range of positions, groups and networks that are situated beyond the community in question. For example, members of the cultural manyattas interlink with members of other Maasai villages and/or group ranches, with various government departments, ministries, the Kenyan Wildlife Service, NGOs and the predominantly foreign-owned tour operators. Similarly, the CTPs in Tanzania are also made up of people who live and work in their respective villages and who also have contacts with 'outsiders' including intermediary organisations such as the TTB, TACTO and SNV, and with more than 120 tour operators that are based in Arusha and beyond (which include CTPs in their various itineraries). As a consequence, the Maasai people in both Kenya and Tanzania are linked to various groups and institutions within and outside their community, and they may also be involved in different roles, functions and activities. As Berger (1996: 176) asserts (at least in the case of Kenyan Maasai), for many Maasai, their values and practices, currently, have more in common with the culture and way of life of Kenya as a nation. They are intermarrying, adopting the languages and livelihoods of neighbouring communities, and participate in various national development activities. In the case of Tanzania, Honey (1999: 220) lucidly illustrates these changing roles and functions of the Maasai:

> It was a classic African scene: A Maasai elder, caught in a time warp, entering his kraal, as his ancestors had done for hundreds of years. But there was a twist to this photo-perfect panorama. The Maasai was Moringe Parkipuny, former Member of Parliament, former college professor, and social activist, and his compound was a newly built Maasai secondary boarding school.

The diverse functions, roles, positions, performances and relationships are, therefore, usually visible in a variety of identities that are mobilised by people within any given community (Liepins, 2001a). In any given situation and/or location, the same individuals may perform different and sometimes conflicting roles as locals, brokers and, also, even as tourists. Perceived relationships and existing power therefore work in many different ways, and usually take different forms and directions. These conflicting roles and functions performed by the same individuals in a given community defy the binary way of perceiving existing social structures as consisting of solely 'dominators' (i.e. tourism investors and tourists) on one side and 'dominated' (i.e. host community) on the other side.

Local coordinators of CTPs in Tanzania can, for instance, simultaneously participate in the 'community' (i.e. local network of interaction) whilst at the same time they are also connected to various stretched-out tourism networks that have linkages extending to far-off external groups and international organisations (i.e. global network of interaction). As a consequence, local project coordinators or local brokers greatly influence the tourism development process because they act as agents transmitting various distinctions of the tourism products and tourist experiences. They influence what tourists can and cannot do, where they can and cannot go, and what they select and reject to see in a given location. It can therefore be argued that, as agents, the local coordinators not only focus the tourist gaze, but they also determine what is *not* to be seen or experienced by the tourists (Cheong *et al.*, 2000). However, also, the external groups that have linkages with various villages where the tourism projects are situated may also be very powerful in raising and/ or constricting the manner in which the community is perceived; as is often the case with the construction of the Maasai, and other forms of African tourism, images.

Second, people will develop shared or contested *meanings* concerning their connectedness with their community and other neighbouring communities via local discourses and activities. Various tourism studies and other narratives have provided information that shows if, how and when given beliefs and values have changed through the influence of connectedness with tourism. The underlying process is that tourism, arguably, encourages the 'commodification of uniqueness' (Meethan, 2001: 65). Peculiar cultural objects and practices (guiding, souvenirs, dances, food) are given a *monetary* exchange value (see also Crehan, 1997). However, according to Meethan (2001: 65), the nature of commodities cannot be reduced to production of exchange value only, but is grounded in the social context from which they derive their symbolic value. As a consequence, inclusion of communities in tourism networks also leads to the reassertion of more localised forms of culture, and the emergence of new 'hybrid' forms of culture that are created for both domestic as well as for tourism consumption (p. 115). For example, the rich material culture of the Maasai reflects the life and natural landscape of the community and simultaneously provides required income and tourism-related employment for the local people. As Berger (1996: 184–185) puts it, 'Maasai decoration is a rich tradition that can be recognized and encouraged to strengthen an appreciation of culture, develop local and national artistic talent, but also generates income from tourism. Maasai crafts are already a popular aspect of cultural tourism and enable Maasai women, in particular, to earn income directly from tourists'.

Third, people will enact community relations and, discursively, construct their meanings about community based on a range of processes and *practices* that connect people with key activities, institutions and spaces. However, such practices will include both those exchanges that are commonly accepted as well as those that are contested. Akama (2002: 48) particularly illustrates the latter aspect, pointing out various forms of unwanted behaviour and vices of mass tourism in cultural manyattas in Kenya, including incidents of prostitution, alcoholism, smoking and drug taking.

Fourth, communities will be embodied through specific *spaces and structures* and in this way the people, meanings and practices that construct a given community will take a material and political shape in the form of key sites and organisational spaces. For instance, by interlocking communities with tourism, local landscapes, and even herbs and plants that are inspected by tourists, become part of the symbolic space by which and through which people create and recreate values, and hence the communities themselves (Meethan, 2001: 117). Tourist regions and communities therefore can be understood as multiplex, and as a set of spaces where a range of relational networks and flows coalesce, interconnect and fragment. Any such place can be viewed as the particular nexus between, on the one hand, propinquity characterised by intensely thick co-present interaction, and on the other hand, fast-flowing webs and networks stretched corporeally, virtually and imaginatively across distances. These nearby and extensive networks come together to enable performances in, and of, particular places (Urry, 2000: 140).

Interlocking communities with tourism also maintains, defends or contests key institutions that are established in communities. For instance, *Ilmoran* (young Maasai warriors) never used to stay in cultural manyattas. Traditional customary practices stipulated that they should live separately from the rest of the community in temporary encampments in surrounding areas (Ongaro & Ritsma, 2002: 132). However, the advent of cultural manyattas attracted the warriors, who stage cultural dances for tourists, to integrate and become part and parcel of a sedentary community. Secondly, local management committees (consisting of a chairman, secretary, treasurer and committee members) manage the cultural manyattas in Kenya. These committees are registered separately from existing group ranch committees. This administrative arrangement has introduced a new level of governance in the Maasai villages and leadership crisis among the Maasai (Knegt, 1998).

Community Tourism and Empowerment

Tourism and communities link up in various *interactive spaces* that are continuous processes where different social values interact and new meanings are formed (Wearing *et al.*, 2002). In these interactive spaces new forms of *power* are created, as different social groupings and individuals are placed in distinct positions of power in relation to various aspects of tourism developments. However in most tourism studies power is usually conceived as something that is either invisible or its existence is based on the assumption of the continual oppression of the local versus powerful external interest groups; it then follows that local people should be empowered in order for them to take charge of their destiny. In this line of thought, therefore, the usual stance is that the local community *needs to be empowered* to decide what forms of tourism facilities and wildlife conservation programmes they want to be developed in their respective communities, and how the tourism costs and benefits are to be shared among different stakeholders (see Akama, 1996: 573; Scheyvens, 1999). However, as the case studies of Kenya and Tanzania indicate, the real situation of power is quite complex and may not conform to the tourism development paths so often conveyed by the centre–periphery concept or dependency theories. Although not denying the history of displacement of the Maasai as a people (see also Mowforth & Munt, 2003: 238), it should be recognised that through the initiation of various tourism activities the Maasai have also, over the years, acted as 'agents' (Cheong *et al.*, 2000) with distinct power to influence the path of tourism development as an important source of livelihood within their respective communities. In other words, power is always *omnipresent* and *relational*, and host communities should not always be perceived as victims in predetermined global development processes. This line of thought therefore provides a contrast to the conceptualisation that sees power as being a resource that can be obtained and can be utilised to achieve specific objectives. As Wearing *et al.* (2002) states, power should therefore be perceived as a specific kind of social relation, which only exists through people's actions. Consequently, this understanding of 'relations of power' regards power not as possessed, or as a structure or a force (see also Boomars *et al.*, 2002), but as always being a negotiated and contested notion. The fluidity and relational character of power relations is illustrated by the continuous negotiations taking place between tourists and locals when buying souvenirs, and negotiations between tour guides/drivers and local representatives of the cultural manyattas in Kenya. Furthermore, there is also monopolisation of power by local elites at the expense of the majority of people in the community, as exemplified by the current struggle over the legacy and ownership of the CTP in Tanzania since the withdrawal of SNV (Verburg, 2004), leading to a new situation where certain local people are becoming brokers and intermediaries.

The binary classification of the host community on the one hand and guests on the other, in current tourism discourse, should therefore be discarded and instead the global tourism process should be perceived as a *tripartite system* consisting of tourists, locals and brokers (Cheong *et al.*, 2000; Wearing *et al.*, 2002). As existing power relations in tourism are always dynamic and are constantly changing, the qualitative and quantitative relations between tourists, local and brokers continuously change as well (Cheong *et al.*, 2000). Moreover, in any community there are several categories of brokers that originate in the public sector (i.e. the TTB in Tanzania and KWS in Kenya), and the private sector (i.e. tour operators and hoteliers). In these interactions there are also NGOs, such as SNV, tourism media brokers and advertising agents. For example, in the cultural manyattas the KWS, local NGOs, staff working in hotels, campsites or lodges, and driver/guides play a significant role in determining the quality of the overall tourism product and the forms of tourism development in the community. In the CTPs in Tanzania, the TTB, local tour operators, project coordinators and SNV have all played a role in determining the nature of tourism development. It can therefore be argued that the success or failure of community-based tourism projects, particularly as regards to project sustainability, usually depends more on the power of brokers and locals project coordinators than on the power of tourists and other external interest groups.

It can also be stated that differential access to knowledge is one of the constituent factors of this particular reality and, to a large extent, the exercise of power is usually determined by the level of *knowledge* that various individuals and groups in the tourism relationship are able to utilise. Knowledge lays the foundation for new strategies and actions, which in turn create new knowledge, as individuals obtain new experiences in the process (Wearing *et al.*, 2002). As a consequence, members of a community do not cease to have power because their way of governing is inspired by new forms of knowledge but, rather, power is exercised in relation to the knowledge that is being obtained and transmitted. For instance, as specific tourism-related knowledge is not usually available and/or is not spread around adequately, most of the cultural tourism projects in Tanzania are gradually becoming reduced to small enterprises that are managed by one coordinator or a small interest group within the community. Thus it can be argued that with the departure of SNV, increasingly, existing knowledge on project management is currently not being shared equitably within and between the various villages, and this has tended to enhance the power base of certain coordinators vis-à-vis other members of the community. As a consequence, the ownership of various tourism projects, and even the ownership and coordination of the CTP as a whole, is increasingly being disputed, as illustrated by the failure to institutionalise TACTO as the overall coordinating body that should take over the management of the various projects after the withdrawal of SNV. Successful implementation and management of the CTP therefore to a large extent depends on the existence of a proper communication network, sharing of new ideas and information between project coordinators and the other community members, and the promotion of transparency and accountability, particularly with regards to the management of financial resources.

Similarly, in the cultural manyattas in Kenya, increasing conflicts among various interest groups and the emergence of local elites are critical issues that are at the heart of the current problems that are confronting the projects (see also Buysrogge, 2001; Tosun, 2000). The local elites tend to monopolise leadership and thwart democratic processes. As a consequence, the monopoly of power and knowledge by the local elites has tended to divide the community, and it is therefore not easy for the local people to unite, organise and claim what is rightfully theirs. In this regard, it is critical that for community-based tourism projects to succeed, development agents and other intermediaries should always be aware of existing and emerging conflicts within the communities, as lack of understanding of existing social and power structures has greatly impacted on the success of community participatory processes.

Acknowledging the fluidity and relational character of power relations implies that empowerment is not the start but the *effect* of dynamic processes in which (parts of) communities, tourists, tourist organisations and governmental as well as development agencies interact. Local participation and involvement itself does not therefore lead automatically to empowerment of individuals. In this regard, it can be asked: what forms of empowerment initiatives have evolved in the cultural manyattas in Kenya and the CTP in Tanzania?

First, the development of community tourism has the potential to bring economic gains to local people and tourism can directly contribute to overall socioeconomic development. For instance, in most of the cultural manyattas in Kenya, the tourism revenue has been used in the improvement of supply of piped water, and the construction of primary schools and dispensaries. In the CTP in Tanzania a compulsory Village Development Fee (VDF) is levied in all the projects. This has enabled the entire community to benefit from tourism revenue. A substantial amount of the tourism revenue is allocated to community development projects such as the construction of local schools and cattle dips. For instance, between 1996 and 2001 the CTP generated a total income of approximately $260,000 of which over $90,000 was allocated to various local community projects. In addition, it was estimated in 1999 that over 100 local people received employment from the CTP (SNV, 1999). Similarly, it has been estimated that in only three cultural manyattas in Kenya, close to 1500 Maasai people receive direct or indirect income (Knegt, 1998).

Second, in terms of psychological empowerment, self-esteem of some community and CTP members is enhanced because of the outside recognition of the uniqueness and value of their culture, natural resources and traditional knowledge (Scheyvens, 1999). The award to the CTP of the prestigious TO DO! 1999 prize (Adler, 1999) and the training of disadvantaged young people by PROTS definitely contributed to increasing confidence and access to employment and cash. Particular factions (for example local project coordinators and guides) from within the community became empowered as a result of establishing relations with tourists, drivers, tour operators and NGOs (i.e. SNV). However, in this process other factions were left behind. Both in the Kenyan and the Tanzanian case studies, there is serious concern as regards to inequity in the distribution of the benefits and tourism revenue. There is also concern over issues of transparency and accountability in the management of the projects (Buysrogge, 2001; Knegt, 1998; Syikilili, 2002; Verburg, 2004). As a consequence, as many people have not (equally) shared in the benefits of the projects, there is also confusion and disinterest or even disillusionment with the initiatives (Scheyvens, 1999).

Third, and related, empowerment of women is a principle ingredient in sustainable local community development. In most instances there is inequitable power relations as regards to gender. For instance, in most of the cultural manyattas in Kenya the Maasai men tend to receive most of the tourism revenue compared to women. This is despite the fact that in most of the cultural manyattas women are the main providers of services. Furthermore, due to increasing competition and rivalry among leaders (who tend to be predominantly male) there are frequent disagreements and fallout. This has led to increasing divisions and fragmentations, as dissatisfied members move way from existing cultural manyattas to establish new projects. As a consequence, there is rapid mushrooming of cultural manyattas resulting in the reduction of the quality of cultural attractions, degradation of the local habitats and increasing impoverishment of women.

Similarly, in the CTP in Tanzania there is also inequitable distribution of the tourism revenue between men and women. Thus, for instance, although it has been estimated that a significant 40% of the people who provide services in the various CTP are women, only 25% of the revenue goes directly to women. Furthermore, empowerment of women and gender parity should not only be based on the amount of revenue that goes to a particular group but should also be based on overall participation in decision-making processes. In this regard, it should be stated that although both in the Kenyan and Tanzanian projects women play an important role in the delivery of various services, there are few women who serve as brokers and are actually involved in the decision-making processes.

Fourth, in terms of political empowerment, the cultural manyattas and the CTP have introduced new political structures in the communities as well as between the communities. As already stated, in most of the cultural manyattas a management committee (consisting of a chairman, secretary, treasurer and committee members) was established to manage the projects. Before starting a cultural manyatta, local project initiators have to consult with leaders of group ranches and also the local chief. However, the management committees are usually registered separately from existing group ranch committees. As a consequence, this form of arrangement usually introduces a new level of governance in the local community. In addition, the recent establishment of the ACCA (jointly by the African Wildlife Society, Kenyan Wildlife Society and the Ministry of Culture and Social Services) has new political implications that will affect local governance. Apart from involvement in marketing and revenue distribution, the ACCA also aims at relocating the cultural manyattas that are situated on critical wildlife corridors and dispersal areas. In other words, through ACCA the government and other interest groups are trying to control and reduce haphazard development of cultural manyattas in areas adjacent to Amboseli National Park.

Similarly, the recent establishment of TACTO to coordinate the activities of the CTP also has political implications. The main aim of TACTO is to coordinate various CTP initiatives after the withdrawal of SNV. However since its establishment TACTO has become a source of conflict among various community projects. Although personal and financial disputes were immediate sources of the conflict, in essence the main cause of conflict centres around the issue of ownership of the CTP. In this regard, most of the local people in the various villages do not see TACTO as *their* organisation. A lack of trust and cooperation among stakeholders remains. Successful projects within the CTP do not feel responsible for less successful ones and the variety of organisational forms within the 18 projects also impede cooperative action. As one of the stakeholders observes: 'TACTO is like a house hit by a storm. And sometimes it is easier to build a new one in stead of rebuilding it' (Verburg, 2004). As SNV pulled out and the TTB only feels responsible for the marketing of the projects, the CTP is about to fall apart into different projects; some very successful, others almost out of businesses.

Conclusion

This chapter provides a comparative analysis of community-based tourism projects using case studies of cultural manyattas in Kenya and the CTP in Tanzania. The study illustrates the various complex ways in which tourism enters communities and how communities become entangled in the global tourism industry. It is also argued that we cannot understand various contexts of community-based tourism unless we grapple with this complexity and various ways in which key stakeholders (i.e. locals, tourists, intermediaries, communities) interact both within and between multiple interlocked scales (van der Duim *et al.*, 2005). In unravelling this complexity, some issues seem to prevail.

Of particular importance, studies on community-based tourism needs to move away from the static concepts of tourism that reduce complexity into a binary situation of either 'good' or 'bad' (i.e. modernity versus primitive, authentic versus inauthentic, global versus local) (see also Meethan, 2001: 15). We need to be prepared to undertake the laborious work of unscrambling the complicated interconnections of the local and the global, as well as the ways in which communities are fractured along lines of modernity and tradition, ethnicity or gender.

Hence, neither tourism nor communities should be dealt with as homogenous entities; on the contrary, they are complex, open, fluid and heterogeneous and their relations are even more intricate. Therefore, studies on community-based tourism may commence with critical investigation of the diversity of people, meanings, practices and spaces that are (at least temporarily) indicative of a particular community. In doing so, it is also important to consider the processes by which these elements are simultaneously constituting, translating and at times shaping or challenging each other (Liepins, 2000a). Different groups and institutions will therefore influence and be affected by the meanings, practices and spaces of the community. Likewise, these meanings, practices and spaces will mutually legitimate, circulate, embody, materialise and shape each other (Liepins, 2000b: 330).

Finally, in interlocking tourism and communities, power should be dealt with as omnipresent, relational and productive (Cheong *et al.*, 2000). However, although subsequent realities may not be to everybody's liking, they are a genuine evaluation of complex processes. The understanding of power underlies rethinking community-based tourism, as 'power in tourism can be negotiated, even mediated, but it cannot be denied' (Cheong *et al.*, 2000).

Note

1.   This chapter is based on a paper presented at the ATLAS conference 'Quality of life: Competing value perspectives in leisure and tourism', Leeuwarden, 19 June 2003. We would like to thank Marcel Leijzer and Nanda Ritsma for their valuable contributions.

References

Adler, Chr. (1999) *Rationale for the Award TO DO! 99 Contest Socially Responsible Tourism*. On WWW at http://www.studienkreis.org/eng⌐/wettbewerbe/todo/99tansania.html.

Akama, J.S. (1996) Western environmental values and nature-based tourism in Kenya. *Tourism Management* 17 (8), 567–574.

Akama, J.S. (2002) The creation of the Maasai image and tourism development in Kenya. In J. Akama and P. Sterry (eds) *Cultural Tourism in Africa: Strategies for the New Millennium*. Proceedings of the ATLAS Africa International Conference, December 2000, Mombasa. Arnhem: ATLAS.

Arusha Times (2003) Lack of cooperation threatens cultural tourism programme. *Arusha Times* 15 (2).

Ashworth, G.J. and Dietvorst, A.G.J. (1995) *Tourism and Spatial Transformations. Implications for Policy and Planning*. Oxon: CAB International.

Berger, D.J. (1996) The challenge of integrating Maasai tradition with tourism. In M.F. Price (ed.) *People and Tourism in Fragile Environments*. Wiley, Chichester.

Boomars, L. and Philipsen, J. (2002) Communicating meanings of tourist landscapes: A discourse approach. Paper presented at the World Leisure Conference in Malaysia, 2002.

Buysrogge, W. (2001) Sustainable safaris? Participation of the Masaai in tourism development on Kimana Group Ranch, adjacent to Amboseli National Park. MSc thesis, Wageningen University, Wageningen.

Cheong, S. and Millar, M. (2000) Power and tourism: A Foucauldian observation. *Annals of Tourism Research* 27 (2), 371–390.

Crehan, K. (1997) *The Fractured Community. Landscape of Power and Gender in Rural Zambia*. Berkeley: University of California Press. On WWW at http://ark.cdlib.org/ark:/13030/ft0779n6dt/.

CTP (2002) Price Quotation for Cultural Tourism Activities 2002. Arusha: Cultural Tourism Program.

Harvey, D. (2000) *Spaces of Hope*. Edinburgh: Edinburgh University Press.

Honey, M. (1999) *Ecotourism and Sustainable Development. Who Owns Paradise?* Washington: Island Press.

Knegt, H.P. (1998) Whose (wild)life. Local participation in wildlife-based tourism related activities under the Kenya Wildlife Service's Partnership Programme. MSc thesis, Catholic University, Nijmegen.

Liepins, R. (2000a) New energies for an old idea: Reworking approaches to community in contemporary rural studies. *Journal of Rural Studies* 16 (1), 23–35.

Liepins, R. (2000b) Exploring rurality through 'community': Discourses, practices and spaces shaping Australian and New Zealand rural 'communities'. *Journal of Rural Studies* 16 (1), 23–35.

Lukes, S. (1974) *Power: A Radical View. Studies in Sociology*. London: Macmillan Press.

Meethan, K. (2001) *Tourism in Global Society. Place, Culture and Consumption*. New York: Palgrave.

Milne, S. and Ateljevic, I. (2001) Tourism, economic development and the global–local nexus: Theory-embracing complexity. *Tourism Geographies* 3 (4), 369–393.

Mowforth, M. and Munt, I. (2003) *Tourism and Sustainability. Development and New Tourism in the Third World*. London: Routledge.

Nelson, F. (2003) Community-based tourism in Northern Tanzania. Increasing opportunities, escalating conflicts, and an uncertain future. Paper presented to the Association for Tourism and Leisure Education Africa Conference, 'Community Tourism: Options for the Future', February, 2003, Arusha.

Norton, A. (1996) Experiencing nature: The reproduction of environmental discourse through safari tourism in East Africa. *Geoforum* 27 (3), 355–373.

Ongaro, S. and Ritsma, N. (2002) The commodification and commercialization of the Masaai culture: Will cultural manyattas withstand the 21st century? In J. Akama and P. Sterry (eds) *Cultural Tourism in Africa: Strategies for the New Millennium. Proceedings of the ATLAS Africa International Conference, December 2000, Mombassa.* Arnhem: ATLAS.

Reid, D., Sindiga, I., Evans, N. and Ongaro, S. (1999) Tourism, bio-diversity and community development. In D. Reid (ed.) *Ecotourism Development in Eastern and Southern Africa.* Harare: Weaver Press.

Reid, D. (2002) Cultural tourism: Learning from the past. In J. Akama and P. Sterry (eds) *Cultural Tourism in Africa: Strategies for the New Millennium.* Proceedings of the ATLAS Africa International Conference, December 2000, Mombasa. Arnhem: ATLAS.

Rutten, M. (2002) Park beyond parks. Genuine community-based wildlife eco-tourism or just another loss of land for Maasai pastoralists in Kenya. London: International Institute for Environment and Development, Issue Paper 111.

Scheyvens (1999) Ecotourism and the empowerment of local communities. *Tourism Management* 20, 245–249.

Syikilili, U. (2002) The development of cultural tourism in Gezaulole Tanzania: A critical analysis. MSc thesis, Wageningen University, Wageningen.

SNV (1999) *Cultural Tourism in Tanzania. Experiences of a Tourism Development Project.* The Hague: SNV Netherlands Development Organization.

Tosun, C. (2001) Limits to community participation in the tourism development process in developing countries. *Tourism Management* 21, 613–633.

Urry, J. (2000) *Sociology Beyond Societies: Mobilities for the Twenty-first Century.* London: Routledge.

Urry, J. (2003) *Global Complexity.* Cambridge: Polity Press.

van der Duim, V.R. (2002) The 'culture' of sustainable tourism: A quest for innovation. In J. Akama and P. Sterry (eds) *Cultural Tourism in Africa: Strategies for the New Millennium.* Proceedings of the ATLAS Africa International Conference in Mombasa, Kenya. Arnhem: ATLAS.

van der Duim, V.R. (2003) 'Tourismscapes'. An essay on tourism, globalization and sustainability. To be presented to the Research Conference 'Managing on the Edge: Shifts in the Relationship between Responsibility, Governance and Sustainability', University of Nijmegen, 25–26 September 2003.

van der Duim, V.R., Peters, K.B.M. and Wearing, S.L. (2005) Planning host and guest interactions: Moving beyond the empty meeting ground in African encounters. *Current Issues in Tourism* 8(4), 286–305.

Verburg, D. (2004) Cultural tourism as an arena: A case study from Tanzania. MSc thesis, Wageningen University, Wageningen.

Wearing, S.L. and McDonald, M. (2002) The development of community-based tourism: Re-thinking the relationship between tour operators and development agents as intermediaries in rural and isolated area communities. *Journal of Sustainable Tourism* 10 (2), 31–45.

Wels, H. (2002) A critical reflection on cultural tourism in Africa: The power of European imagery. In J. Akama and P. Sterry (eds) *Cultural Tourism in Africa: Strategies for the New Millennium. Proceedings of the ATLAS Africa International Conference, December 2000, Mombasa.* Arnhem: ATLAS.

Chapter 8

Township Tourism: Blessing or Blight? The Case of Soweto in South Africa

JENNIFER BRIEDENHANN and PRANILL RAMCHANDER

Introduction

Prior to the 1994 democratic elections, urban tourism in South Africa was strictly confined to so-called 'White areas'. The reasons for this were twofold. Firstly, apartheid legislation prohibited visits by members of the 'White' community into areas designated by law as 'Black' townships. Secondly, such townships were widely regarded as 'no-go' areas due to perceivably high levels of crime and violence. The urban Black townships in South Africa differ from other deprived areas predominantly as a result of circumstances that prevailed during the apartheid regime. Barred from constituting an integral part of 'White' cities, the townships were developed as dormitory towns, far removed from central business districts and White urban areas. Whilst these townships facilitated the exploitation of Black labour, the lives of the 'rulers' and the 'ruled' were kept strictly segregated. Soweto, the focus of this study, is a sprawling urban conurbation constructed with the specific purpose of housing African people who were then living in areas designated by the government for White settlement. With a population of over two million, it remains an overwhelmingly Black-dominated city.

Soweto, which has a rich political history, first captured world attention when it became the centre of political campaigns aimed at overthrowing the apartheid regime. The 1976 uprising, during which students protested against the introduction of Afrikaans as the medium of instruction at the racially segregated Black high schools, and the political strife of the 1980s, turned the eyes of the world on the city. Today, Soweto has come to symbolise the political freedom of the new South Africa. The legacy of repression, pain and violence makes this township an unlikely tourist destination. Yet, whilst there is a dearth of reliable data, the Provincial Tourism Board (GTA, 2001) estimates that

124

some 800 visitors, seeking to experience the political history and culture of South Africa's Black urban communities, are exposed to the renewed vitality of township life daily. The choice of Soweto as a case study was motivated by the fact that it has characteristics, such as socioeconomic status, political/historical orientation and informal settlements, that are common to other South African townships. Findings from this case study are thus analogous to circumstances prevailing in townships in all South Africa's provinces. In addition it is the largest and best known of South Africa's townships.

Defining Township Tourism

Burgeoning tourist interest in visiting South Africa's Black townships can be ascribed to three primary factors. Firstly, township visits are meant to provide a more authentic and nonperformative experience, depicting 'real' history, 'real' people and the 'real' South Africa (Witz *et al.*, 1999: 17). Tourists are motivated by interest in the ethnic diversity and rich cultural heritage, which manifests itself in the daily lives and practices of township residents. Tourists generally visit Soweto by air-conditioned minibuses from luxurious accommodation in more affluent areas of the city. The experience ranges from visits to traditional African beermakers and healers (sangomas), to enjoyment of African dance and cuisine, and stopovers at squatter settlements, new housing projects, soup kitchens and recycling depots (Witz, 2001). Visits to a few carefully selected people in homes ranging from small wood and iron houses to hostel rooms and newly developed bed and breakfast establishments are also included. A short walk through designated streets, under the watchful eye of a guide, is intended to impart a 'feel' of the township. At a craft centre tourists are able to make the 'feel-good' gesture of purchasing what appear to be hand-made memories of an African experience. Social interaction is played out in a 'safe shebeen' (tavern) where tourists can observe and participate in township life but will not be harassed by drunken and disorderly clientele. Shebeens, formerly illegal drinking houses that owe their existence to erstwhile government policies of restricting Blacks from formal economic activity, epitomise the pulse of township life. In order to earn a living, township mamas or shebeen queens (female proprietors) sold a variety of home-brewed concoctions. A new cultural expression was spawned and shebeens became a popular social rendezvous. Many people turned their houses into venues for a drink, a date, a chat or beautiful music. Thanks to an eclectic mix of clientele, shebeens became a place where subjects ranging from philosophy and politics to soccer and music were discussed. Police raids were a common occurrence. Undeterred, the shebeen queens went back to their trade.

Secondly, township tourism offers visitors visual evidence of the deprivation wrought by the apartheid regime. Poverty is ubiquitous, a factor that makes the lives and indomitable spirit of township dwellers even more admirable. Squatter camps, or informal settlements, are home to many of the escalating number of unemployed who use corrugated iron sheets, or any other available material, to build shelters. Lacking basic amenities such as running water and electricity, these shelters, which are extremely hot in summer and freezing cold in winter, make for hazardous living. Despite their poverty, the shack dwellers have built a strong sense of community. Other manifestations of apartheid include the original dwellings, sardonically known as 'matchbox houses', constructed to accommodate the first Black migrants to Johannesburg. By contrast there are suburbs that display the homes of the newly emerging Black middle class. These suburbs boast beautiful houses, good roads and playgrounds and schools for resident's children.

Finally, Soweto offers tourists the opportunity to share its resistance heritage. These memorials include the tomb of Hector Peterson, the first victim of the 1976 riots. Other buildings of political significance include the Regina Mundi Catholic church, which served as the venue of many protest meetings; the house that Nelson Mandela occupied before his imprisonment, and the home of Desmond Tutu prior to his move to the archbishop's house in Cape Town. This is the only street in the world where two Nobel Peace Prizewinners have lived. Tourists also have the opportunity to peek into the infamous hostels and visit Freedom Square, which commemorates the struggle for liberty and where the Freedom Charter, which espouses that 'all shall be equal before the law', was adopted as the guiding document of the African National Congress.

Tourists express surprise that townships are not, as people have been led to believe, deprived areas steeped in violent crime. By contrast they are vibrant centres brimming with friendly people and overwhelmingly inspirational stories. Township tours have proved themselves cultural eye-openers not only for foreign tourists but also for many White South Africans venturing into these areas for the first time. Most tourists leave with an impression far different from the one with which they arrived. However, as a new and unique tourism phenomenon, little research has been undertaken into the development or planning of township tourism, or of its impact on the resident community. This study seeks to ascertain the degree of meaningful community participation and concomitant empowerment that has resulted from township tourism and to gain an insight into residents' perceptions of its social and cultural impacts.

Authenticity and Community Issues

Interaction between tourists and local residents takes place in a variety of contexts. Aronsson (1994: 86) refers to 'authentic meeting-places' as those in which tourists and residents meet in areas that form part of the everyday culture and practice of local people and are an integral part of community life. De Kadt (1992: 51), however, argues that what comprises authenticity for the tourist is highly subjective. 'Authenticity...is wholly focused on the tourist...it concerns his or her perceptions of the reality encountered in the tourist experience.' Whilst the general perception is that township tourism offers visitors the opportunity to experience 'real' people and the 'real' South Africa (Witz *et al.*, 1999: 17), there is a distinction between situations that involve a purely visual spectacle such as arts, crafts and political landmarks, and those situations that involve visitors in an interactive context, such as visits to people's homes, attendance at traditional healers (Moscardo & Peace, 1999) or, in the case of South Africa's townships, visits to the local shebeen.

De Villiers (2003: 4) highlights that one of Africa's primary short-comings is the assumption that 'in order to be successful we must emulate the West'. In South Africa indigenous culture has undergone deep-seated change as the vast majority of the population have adopted Western norms, religions, customs, dress and language. On the one hand tourism is alleged to further distort, commodify and ultimately destroy indigenous culture (Greenwood, 1989; MacCannell, 1976) and to accelerate social and cultural value change, particularly amongst the young (Harrison, 1992). On the other hand it is argued that tourism can act as a catalyst in renewing community pride (Esman, 1984) and 'contribute to the protection and enhancement of traditions, customs and heritage, which would otherwise disappear' (Hashimoto, 2002: 215). Dyer *et al.* (2003: 93) cite the potential of tourism in reducing stereotypical images and enhancing cross-cultural understanding. There is anecdotal evidence in Cape Town's Langa township that 'homestays' are serving as a conduit in helping people overcome prejudices and through positive interaction between hosts and guests generating new understanding that helps to bridge the racial divide (Tavener, 2003). It is significant that the original antipathy and suspicion evinced by Langa residents of the motives of White tourists in visiting townships has been overcome and that these same residents now vie for the opportunity for host/guest interaction and feel pride in the fact that tourists show an interest in learning more about township life, customs and heritage. What is noteworthy, however, is that it is by virtue of the intervention of one dynamic township resident that positive interaction between hosts and guests has been encouraged, rather than a result of statutory agencies or tour operators recognising the benefits and empowerment potential of widespread community participation in tourism. Nonetheless, one of the most fundamental changes since the advent of the country's democracy has been the recognition that African culture and political history are valid and sought-after components of South African tourism offerings (Briedenhann & Wickens, 2003).

Countless studies have been conducted to ascertain community attitudes to tourism and its impacts. The findings of this study, however, underpin Lankford and Howard's (1994) argument that attitudes are influenced by residents' perceptions of their level of control over tourism planning and development, and the level of economic activity generated (Johnson *et al.*, 1994). There is also evidence that whilst those residents with greater dependency on tourism view its development more favourably (Lankford & Howard, 1994), they also recognise that the industry has brought in its wake both positive and negative impacts (King *et al*., 1993). What is fundamental is the extent to which tourism is benefiting township residents by virtue of employment and entrepreneurial opportunity. Tourism scholars (Koh, 2000; Timothy, 2002) emphasise that an increase in small entrepreneurial enterprises and activities functions as an impetus for local economic growth and the stimulation of employment opportunity. It is also argued that equity and 'ecological and cultural integrity' are more easily entrenched when communities affected by the impacts of tourism participate in its planning and development (Timothy & Tosun, 2003: 181) and when local people retain ownership of their culture and the power of decision-making with regard to what elements they wish to portray and those they wish to conceal (Crouch, 1994). However, in the South African context, where the vast majority of the population have had no previous exposure to tourism, support and guidance enabling communities to empower themselves with the skills needed to take decisions pertaining to tourism are imperative. Southgate and Sharpley's (2002: 262) assertion that the future of tourism will be largely dependent on adoption of the principles of 'community empowerment, participatory development planning and the value of local indigenous knowledge' is particularly pertinent to tourism in South Africa's Black townships.

The Study

The study, which adopted a combined qualitative/quantitative methodology, utilised a five-point Likert scale questionnaire and in-depth interviews as instruments of data collection. The first section of the questionnaire elicited the demographic characteristics of respondents and their relationship, if any, to tourism activities. The second section consisted of 57 attitudinal statements, constructed from a pool of variables drawn from the literature, designed to measure respondents' level of agreement or disagreement with factors relating to the perceived impacts of tourism. The third section provided for additional respondent comment regarding the development and planning of township tourism. The research sample comprised 350 households, identified by systematic random sampling, in the 14 main tourist hubs of Soweto. Fieldworkers, fluent in local languages, conducted the surveys and interviews. Respondents were generally well spread across gender, age, income levels and education. Forty-one percent of the respondents earned an income from tourism. Eighty percent had a monthly income below R5000 (£385).

Calculation of frequency distribution and the mean and standard deviation provided descriptive statistical analysis of quantitative data.[1] Chi-square tests were conducted to determine the statistical significance of cross-tabulated variables. Findings of quantitative data, arising from questionnaires, are reinforced by the results of qualitative data emanating from respondent comments and interviews. Qualitative data were coded, repeated themes recorded and categories identified as they emerged. Direct quotes gave voice to respondents in their own terms. Table 8.1 and Figure 8.1 in the next section depicts the most positively perceived impacts of township tourism development.

Discussion of Principal Findings

Respondent comments underscored Dyer *et al.*'s (2003) assertion that beneficial cross-cultural exchange can result from tourism. Respondents alleged that 'township tourism has allowed Black and White people the opportunity to interact. The stereotypical views of townships as no-go areas, dangerous and a haven for criminals and hijackers are being

---

[1] Although inferential statistics were calculated, these are not reported in this paper. Multivariate and ANOVA tests were carried out between independent variables (for example: gender, income from tourism, years of residence) to check for significant relationships.

Table 8.1 Most positively perceived impacts of tourism development

Attitudinal statement	Respondents with household income derived from tourism		Respondents with no income derived from tourism	
	Mean	Standard deviation	Mean	Standard deviation
Township tourism has resulted in a greater demand for female labour	3.56	1.20	3.30	1.32
Tourism increases the development of recreational facilities and amenities for residents	4.01	0.79	3.89	0.94
Township tourism has made residents more conscious of the need to maintain and improve the appearance of the area	3.93	0.94	3.58	1.15
The development of township tourism has generally improved the appearance of Soweto	3.75	0.99	3.46	1.29
Tourist interest in culture has resulted in a strengthening of traditional activities and cultural pride	4.07	0.81	3.99	0.94
Township tourism has stimulated the locals' interest in participating in traditional art forms	3.86	0.76	3.92	0.90
Local culture is being renewed as a result of township tourism	3.67	0.98	3.64	1.18
Township tourists show respect for the cultural lifestyle of the local people	4.14	0.82	3.82	1.03

Table 8.1 (*Continued*)

Attitudinal statement	Respondents with household income derived from tourism		Respondents with no income derived from tourism	
	Mean	*Standard deviation*	*Mean*	*Standard deviation*
Tourism encourages a variety of cultural activities by the local population	4.00	0.59	3.90	0.86
Township tourism helps to conserve the cultural identity and heritage of the host population	4.08	0.73	3.85	1.05
Meeting tourists promotes cross-cultural exchange (greater mutual understanding and respect one another's culture)	3.90	0.98	3.84	1.15
By creating jobs and generating income, township tourism promotes an increase in the social well-being of residents	4.02	0.72	3.72	1.11
Township tourism has led to more people leaving their former jobs for new opportunities in tourism	3.10	1.15	2.68	1.22
Township tourism provides many worthwhile employment opportunities for Soweto residents	3.79	0.88	3.28	1.25
Township tourism holds great promise for Soweto's economic future	4.08	0.71	3.65	1.14

Statements rated on a five-point Likert scale: 1, strongly disagree; 2, disagree; 3, undecided; 4, agree; 5, strongly agree

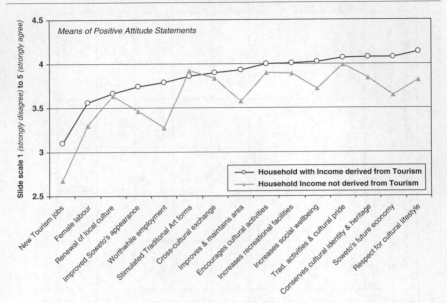

Figure 8.1 Most positively perceived impacts of tourism development. Statements rated on a five-point Likert scale: 1, strongly disagree; 2, disagree; 3, undecided; 4, agree; 5, strongly agree

destroyed.' Respondents perceived the opportunity to expand their horizons as empowering and claimed that locals had 'increased awareness of tourism and hospitality. They are beginning to broaden their knowledge about international tourism, foreign places and people due to the cross-cultural exchange of learning taking place.'

Other respondents argued that 'township tourism has certainly fostered a renewed interest in local art, craft and traditions. Locals have been instilled with a sense of pride about their heritage and culture.' The majority of respondents similarly believed that township tourism would lead to conservation of cultural practices and political landmarks/monuments. This perception is congruent with the contention that tourism can serve as a catalyst leading to a renewed sense of identity and enhanced cultural and ethnic pride (Esman, 1984; Hashimoto, 2002). In the South African context, where indigenous culture has suffered a century of debasement, a renewal of self-belief and ethnic pride is particularly significant. De Villiers (2003: 4) frames this succinctly: 'you and I know that people need to feel good about themselves; to be proud of who and what we are – otherwise nothing goes right.' Affirmation of tourism's ability to catalyse such rejuvenation of pride and self-confidence came from a participant in route development designed to encourage tourism to South Africa's historic mission stations. Her impoverished community had always, she claimed, been known by the derogatory term 'patatvreters' (potato guzzlers), signifying that, even amongst other destitute communities, they were looked down upon. Participation in the tourism route had, however, brought about a mind-change. 'I and my fellow community members have always been ashamed of the Patatvreter label, always felt that we are inferior, but as of today we are going to turn this into a positive factor; going to carry it with pride as a banner of our resilience and a mark of our character' (de Villiers, 2003: 5).

Respondents showed appreciation of the employment benefits generated by tourism. 'Township tourism has resulted in new opportunities for careers in tourism as more people are taking up employment in tourism. The youth have a new area to develop their interests in. This type of tourism has created opportunities for the locals to enter the tourism industry, find jobs as tour guides, tour operators and entrepreneurs.' It is, however, predominantly women who have been empowered by access to new careers in tourism, most especially as owners and managers of township 'bed and breakfasts' and homestays. This has resulted in increasing numbers of township women applying to undergo courses in tourism and hospitality. This factor is particularly significant in view of the fact that Black women have traditionally been the most marginalised sector of South African society. Respondents further believed that the creation of employment through tourism would gradually improve the local economy. Previous research conducted in South Africa similarly provided evidence that employment was amongst the most sought-after benefits of tourism development (Briedenhann & Wickens, 2003). Others argued that tourism had encouraged the entrepreneurial spirit amongst the community. 'Shebeens, restaurants and bed and breakfasts have developed. Many hawkers are selling arts and crafts at tourism hubs.' This finding is analogous to Koh's (2000) assertion that tourism growth is driven by entrepreneurial development. Respondents in favour of tourism alleged that the appearance and image of the township was improving, and that the economy of Soweto would soon be well developed. The benefits of tourism to residents in terms of the upkeep and development of infrastructure, and new facilities and amenities catering to both locals and tourists, were similarly acknowledged. Despite an overall positive attitude, Sowetan residents, however, also recognised that negative impacts were occurring as a consequence of the development of 'township' tourism (Table 8.2 and Figure 8.2).

Table 8.2 Most negatively perceived impacts of tourism development

Attitudinal statement	Respondents with household income derived from tourism		Respondents with no income derived from tourism	
	Mean	Standard deviation	Mean	Standard deviation
Township tourism will gradually result in an increase in municipal rates and taxes	3.10	1.01	3.26	1.25
Traditional African culture in Soweto is being commercialised for the sake of tourists	3.29	1.02	3.35	1.36
Locals often respond to tourist needs by adapting traditional practices to enhance their commercial value	3.79	0.72	3.84	0.94
Township tourism causes changes in the traditional culture of local residents	2.82	0.98	3.30	1.25
Only a small minority of Soweto residents benefit economically from tourism	3.59	1.04	4.16	0.96
The development of township tourism in Soweto benefits the visitors more than the locals	2.99	1.13	3.54	1.21
Township tourism in Soweto is in the hands of a few operators only	3.83	1.01	4.04	1.07

Statements rated on a five-point Likert scale: 1, strongly disagree; 2, disagree; 3, undecided; 4, agree; 5, strongly agree

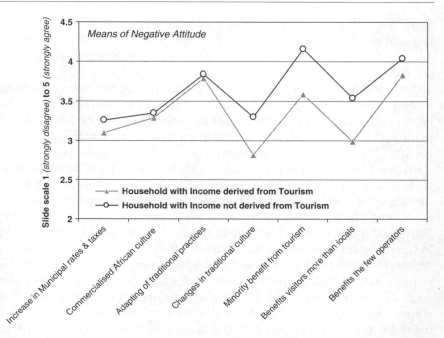

Figure 8.2 Most negatively perceived impacts of tourism development. Statements rated on a five-point Likert scale: 1, strongly disagree; 2, disagree; 3, undecided; 4, agree; 5, strongly agree

In particular, older respondents voiced concern that traditional African culture was being commercialised and claimed that 'certain locals sell or trivialise their culture to tourists to make a profit.' An entrepreneur explained resident antipathy this way: 'you have to understand that township people do not always like the tours that now pass regularly through this place. Some of these give them the feeling that they are living in a zoo.' She has thus been 'educating' her neighbours to welcome her guests, ensuring that they understand that the more visitors she receives, the more they, as local suppliers, will benefit. The allegations of these respondents are, however, congruent with arguments that, as tourism cannot take place in isolation from the host community, residents, their culture and resources inevitably become part of the product consumed by tourists (McKercher, 1993). This has led Craik (1995: 93) to argue that in order to 'maximise the benefits of tourism and minimise adverse changes and impacts, social and cultural issues must be defined as part of the tourist resource and incorporated in the planning, development and management processes of tourism'. In

Soweto, many respondent misgivings can, however, be attributed to the fact that residents have, in general, not been afforded the opportunity to participate in planning for tourism nor in decision-making with regard to the nature of cultural tourism offerings.

Lack of interest by tourists in cross-cultural interaction was considered disempowering and spawned feelings of inferiority amongst residents. 'Some tourists appear to feel superior to locals. They don't make an effort to interact with the locals and simply listen to the commentary of the tour guides.' The behaviour of tourists was occasionally seen as rude and intrusive. 'Tourists often take photographs of the locals without permission. Locals should be compensated if they are asked to pose for photographs and have the right to know what the photos will be used for. Locals find tourists who don't seek permission very intrusive. Tourists should be briefed on how to behave.' A tour guide, embarrassed by guests who demanded that local children dance for their cameras, agrees. Evans (1994) has observed that whilst some tourists will abide by requests not to photograph local people or their ceremonies, others insist on doing so, expressing it as their right. Tour operators point to a lack of respect by tourists for local people as a significant factor in the breakdown of relationships between hosts and guests (Tearfund, 2001). One respondent claims she saw a tour bus stop in the township whilst tourists threw money at the people standing below. Such behaviour has led to an increase in the number of beggars and street children along main tourist routes. Concern was expressed that crime in tourist hubs had escalated. 'Wherever there are tourists carrying expensive cameras and money, criminals loiter. Security should be improved as both tourists and the local community are at risk.' In South Africa, the high incidence of poverty provides fertile breeding ground for crime against tourists, a factor that would be discouraged by the more equitable spread of tourism benefits amongst South Africa's population (George, 2003).

Tour guides insist that tours are not an attempt to make a voyeuristic theme park out of poverty, and profess that they do brief tourists on acceptable behaviour and offer them an opportunity to interact with residents. They lay the blame for the lack of cross-cultural interaction on tour operators who run 'safari-style' drive-through tours, where tourists snap photographs and peer at the surrounding poverty from air-conditioned buses. Having bought their postcards and African masks, most tourists leave with only the most fleeting contacts with the local people. There are some enlightened operators who allow tourists to meet locals in the township taverns, jazz clubs and restaurants, and encourage them to support local artists and community projects. Those fortunate enough to be involved in the industry profess that they are being exposed to the world through tourists. A local bed and breakfast entrepreneur reports: 'some days, I have two buses full of people. There's no room to sit down, so I have people in my kitchen and everywhere, just talking about everything. They come from Germany, Ireland, Florida, Michigan, Denmark. Because of apartheid, we never had the opportunity to share our cultures before.' Respondents find the opportunity to share visions of their past oppression, and the role played by Soweto residents in the struggle for freedom, both liberating and empowering. They are proud of their 'struggle' heritage and want their visitors to understand and share it.

The most negative comments pertained to the lack of opportunity for participation in tourism with the concurrent inequality in the distribution of economic and employment benefits. Residents feel disempowered by their lack of control over tour operators and the opportunities for participation in tourism. 'Local people are unhappy about the tour guides and operators presently conducting tours in Soweto. They don't ask permission to bring tourists into their areas and seem to control where the tourists go and spend their money. Some locals believe that tour guides are receiving kickbacks. They believe that the majority of the guides live outside Soweto. Locals who know their area better should be given preference to conduct tours.' Another respondent phrased the problem in these terms: 'tour companies bring tourists on short fleeting trips. This does not provide the opportunity for tourists to interact enough with locals and for them to spend money at the local craft centres. Some tourists don't spend their money in Soweto and actually buy their crafts outside the township.' Tourism benefits are perceived to be in the hands of only a few. 'It seems like tourism benefits only those living close to the hot spots such as the struggle/political route or the homes of prominent ANC activists and other high profile people of Soweto. If you do not live close to these hubs you are completely left out.' Many residents endorse Dogan's (1989) allegation that the benefits of tourism do not accrue equitably to the host population. They claim that there is insufficient evidence of the espoused tourism benefits and that whilst there is much talk around tourism, and tourists are in evidence in the township, the majority of local residents do not see the rewards. Eadington and Smith (1992: 9), however, argue that it is not uncommon that 'tourism development creates winners and losers among the local residents. . .many of the winners might be outsiders who are then viewed as exploiters of the native population.'

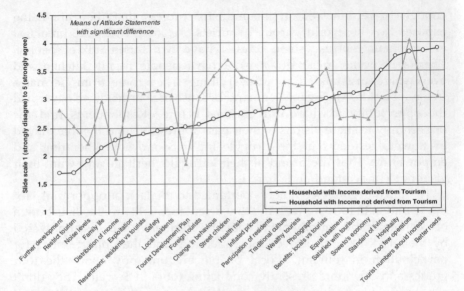

Figure 8.3 Differences of perception between respondents who do and do not receive an income from tourism. Statements rated on a five-point Likert scale: 1, strongly disagree; 2, disagree; 3, undecided; 4, agree; 5, strongly agree

Figure 8.3 highlights significant differences of perception between respondents who earn an income from tourism as opposed to those who do not. Respondents who have a direct business relationship with tourism exhibit more positive attitudes than those with no direct business relationship to the industry. In addition, respondents with immediate family members working in tourism-related business or services tended to have more positive attitudes towards tourism than those who did not.

Many of the shortcomings of township tourism are laid at the feet of government. Residents believe that public sector support for Soweto as a tourist destination is called for and that funds and grants should be made available to assist local people in starting businesses. The lack of opportunity for participation is a major bone of contention. Residents argue that they have not been adequately consulted about the development and planning of tourism. This has led to resentment between local people who have started tourism businesses and those who have not, and antipathy between residents not benefiting from tourism and tourists. Residents are now demanding the right to be consulted with regard to both present and future tourism planning and development and its associated costs and benefits. They believe that government should assist in enabling local people to empower themselves to participate in tourism by providing workshops and training in tourism awareness, establishing small businesses and entrepreneurial skills. Tourism theorists agree that, in order for tourism to sustain itself, local communities must be willing partners whose participation from the early stages of the planning process is imperative (Gunn, 1988; Haywood, 1988; Murphy, 1985). It is also argued that in new tourism destinations awareness programmes should be conducted to manage expectations and increase community understanding of the potential rewards and opportunities that tourism will generate (Din, 1996). Government promotion of tourism as panacea to the ills of unemployment and economic marginalisation has, however, led to expectations of the economic benefits of tourism running unrealistically high amongst previously disadvantaged communities.

Concluding Points

The tourism industry in post-apartheid South Africa has given the responsibility of constructing, packaging and transmitting images and representations of the 'new' society and its tumultuous past to a limited number of stakeholders within the public and private sector. Government perceives tourism as the catalyst through which economic and modernising benefits can trickle down to previously marginalised communities. In climates of economic hardship people look to exploitable resources, such as the natural and cultural environment, for potential economic benefit. As a result, host communities find their culture and traditions under threat from the purchasing power of the tourism industry. There is little consistency in the way cultural tourism in South Africa is interpreted and implemented. Black alienation and exclusion from mainstream tourism has meant that most township residents have lacked control over the way in which their diverse cultures are portrayed.

Wider consultation and collaboration in developing a brand of sustainable township tourism that will benefit the greater Sowetan community is crucial. Whilst tourism is perceived as a substantial and attractive economic sector, residents have voiced their dissatisfaction with regard to inequitable participation by the township community. In many developing countries tourism policymakers tend to conceal the negative impacts of tourism from host communities and attempt to develop the industry at all costs to solve chronic macroeconomic problems and maximise interests for a small number of local people.

Whilst outside forces generally determine the speed and direction of tourism development, and local people are seldom consulted, issues such as the equitable redistribution of tourism revenue and the need to involve the host community in ownership and management roles must be addressed. False expectations are raised amongst local people who are promised that the arrival of tourists will bring new wealth to the community. They soon discover that the real economic gain from tourism goes to the organisers and a select few entrepreneurs.

Facilitating community empowerment through tourism, however, extends beyond merely supplying the funding with which to start businesses. Fetterman (2001) argues that processes aimed at empowerment are those that help people to develop the skills needed to solve their own problems and take their own decisions. Taylor (2000: 4) agrees, asserting that empowerment processes are those 'which result in people exercising more control over the decisions and resources that directly affect the quality of their lives'. Townships are becoming high-growth areas for the South African tourism industry. Tourist numbers will grow and pressures on local cultures will increase. Whilst locals may be antagonistic to the tourist invasion, an ethos of disempowerment makes it extremely difficult for them to raise their concerns and take action. Township residents argue that their consent to tourism development can only be fully informed if they are in possession of all the facts, including the long-term negative impacts of any proposed tourism project. South Africa faces many challenges in transforming her tourism industry. Empowering local people to take decisions, which promote a type and scale of tourism development that allows them to uphold, respect and nurture their cultures and share in the economic benefits of tourism development is, however, key to the sustainability of township tourism.

References

Ap, J. (1992) Residents perceptions on tourism impacts. *Annals of Tourism Research* 19 (4), 665–690.

Aronsson, L. (1994) Sustainable tourism systems: The example of sustainable rural tourism in Sweden. *Journal of Sustainable Tourism* 2, 77–92.

Boyd, S.W. and Singh, S. (2003) Destination communities: Structures, resources and types. In S. Singh, D.J. Timothy and R.K. Dowling (eds) *Tourism in Destination Communities* (pp. 19–34). Wallingford: CABI Publishing.

Briedenhann, J. and Wickens, E. (2003a) Community involvement in tourism development white elephant or empowerment? In S. Weber and R. Tomljenović (eds) *Reinventing a Tourism Destination* (in press).

Briedenhann, J. and Wickens, E. (2003b) Developing cultural tourism in South Africa: potential and pitfalls. Paper Presented at the ATLAS Expert Cultural

Tourism Group Conference *Cultural Tourism: Globalising the Local – Localising the Global*. Barcelona, November 2003.

Brunt, P. and Courtney, P. (1999) Host perceptions of sociocultural impacts. *Annals of Tourism Research* 26 (3), 493–515.

Butler, R.W. (1980) The concept of a tourism area cycle of evolution: Implications for management of resources. *Canadian Geographer* 24 (1), 5–12.

Craik, J. (1995) Are there cultural limits to tourism? *Journal of Sustainable Development* 3 (2), 87–98.

Crouch, D. (1994) Home, escape and identity: Rural cultures and sustainable tourism, In B. Bramwell and B. Lane (eds) *Rural Tourism and Sustainable Rural Development* (pp. 93–101). Clevedon: Channel View Publications.

De Kadt, E. (1992) Making the alternative sustainable: Lessons from development for tourism. In V. Smith and W. Eadington (eds) *Tourism Alternatives* (pp. 47–75). New York: John Wiley.

De Villiers, N. (2003) Address delivered at the *Corporate Social Responsibility Conference*, Johannesburg, 14 February.

Din, K. (1996) Tourism development: Still in search of a more equitable mode of local involvement. *Progress in Tourism and Hospitality Research* 2, 273–281.

Dogan, H.Z. (1989) Forms of adjustment: Sociocultural impacts of tourism. *Annals of Tourism Research* 16 (2), 216–236.

Doxey, G. (1975) A causation theory of visitor–resident irritants, methodology and research inferences. The impact of tourism. In *Proceedings of the Sixth Annual Conference of the Travel and Tourism Research Association*, San Diego (pp. 195–198).

Dyer, P., Aberdeen, L. and Schuler, S. (2003) Tourism impacts on an Australian indigenous community: A Djabugay case study. *Tourism Management* 24 (1), 83–95.

Eadington, W.R. and Smith, V.L. (1992) Introduction: The emergence of alternative forms of tourism. In V.L. Smith and W.R. Eadington (eds) *Tourism Alternatives: Potentials and Problems in the Development of Tourism* (pp. 1–12). Philadelphia: University of Pennsylvania Press.

Esman, M. (1984) Tourism as ethnic preservation: The Cajuns of Louisiana. *Annals of Tourism Research* 11, 451–467.

Evans, G. (1994) Whose culture is it anyway? Tourism in Greater Mexico and the Indigena. In A. Seaton, C.L. Jenkins, R. Wood, P.U.C. Dieke, M.M. Bennett, L.R. MacLellan and R. Smith (eds) *Tourism: The State of the Art* (pp. 836–847). London: Wiley.

Fetterman, D.M. (2001) *Foundations of Empowerment Evaluation*. Thousand Oaks, CA: Sage Publications Inc.

Gauteng Tourism Authority (GTA) (2001) *Soweto Tourism 2000 – Developing Tourism in Soweto*. Johannesburg: Gauteng Tourism Authority.

George, R. (2003) Tourist's perceptions of safety and security while visiting Cape Town. *Tourism Management* 24 (5), 575–585.

Greenwood, D. (1989) Culture by the pound: An anthropological perspective of tourism as cultural commoditisation. In V.L. Smith (ed.) *Hosts and Guests: The Anthropology of Tourism* (pp. 171–186). Philadelphia: University of Pennsylvania Press.

Gunn, C.A. (1988) *Tourism Policy and Planning* (2nd edn). Philadelphia: University of Pennsylvania Press.

Harrison, D. (1992) Tradition, modernity and tourism in Swaziland. In D. Harrison (ed.) *Tourism and the Less Developed Countries* (pp. 148–162). London: Belhaven Press.

Hashimoto, A. (2002) Tourism and sociocultural development issues. In R. Sharpley and D. Telfer (eds) *Tourism and Development: Concepts and Issues* (pp. 202–230). Clevedon: Channel View Publications.

Haywood, K.M. (1988) Responsible and responsive tourism planning in the community. *Tourism Management* 9 (2), 105–107.

Johnson, D., Snepenger, J. and Akis, S. (1994) Residents' perceptions of tourism development. *Annals of Tourism Research* 21 (3), 629–642.

King, B., Pizam, A. and Milman, A. (1993) Social impacts of tourism: Host perceptions. *Annals of Tourism Research* 20 (4), 650–665.

Koh, K.Y. (2000) Understanding community tourism entrepreneurism: Some evidence from Texas. In G. Richards and D. Hall (eds) *Tourism and Sustainable Community Development* (pp. 205–217). London: Routledge.

Lankford, S.V. and Howard, D.R. (1994) Developing a tourism impact attitude scale. *Annals of Tourism Research* 21 (1), 121–139.

MacCannell, D. (1976) *The Tourist: A New Theory of the Leisure Class*. London: Macmillan.

McCarthy, J. (1994) *Are Sweet Dreams Made of This? Tourism in Bali and Eastern Indonesia*. Northcote, Australia: Indonesia Resources and Information Programme.

McKercher, B. (1993) The unrecognized threat to tourism: Can tourism survive sustainability? *Tourism Management* 14, 131–136.

Moscardo, G. and Pearce, P.L. (1999) Understanding ethnic tourists. *Annals of Tourism Research* 26 (2), 416–434.

Murphy, P.E. (1985) *Tourism: A Community Approach*. New York and London: Methuen.

Southgate, C. and Sharpley, R. (2002) Tourism, development and the environment. In R. Sharpley and D.J. Telfer (eds) *Tourism and Development: Concepts and Issues* (pp. 231–264). Clevedon: Channel View Publications.

Tavener, T. (2003) A life in the day. *The Sunday Times Magazine* London, 19 January, 86.

Taylor, J. (2000) *So Now They Are Going To Measure Empowerment*. Woodstock: The Community Development Resource Association.

Tearfund (2001) *Tourism: Putting Ethics into Practice*. Teddington, Middlesex: Tearfund.

Timothy, D.J. (2002) Tourism and community development issues. In R. Sharpley and D.J. Telfer (eds) *Tourism and Development: Concepts and Issues* (pp. 149–164). Clevedon: Channel View Publications.

Timothy, D.J. and Tosun, C. (2003) Appropriate planning for tourism in destination communities: Participation, incremental growth and collaboration. In S. Singh, D.J. Timothy and R.K. Dowling (eds) *Tourism in Destination Communities* (pp. 181–204). Wallingford: CABI Publishing.

Witz, L. (2001) Repackaging the past for S.A tourism. *Daedalus* 130 (1), 277–296.

Witz, L., Rassool, C. and Minkley, G. (1999) *Tourism in African Renaissance*. Paper presented at Public History, Forgotten History Conference, Windhoek, University of Namibia, 22–23 August, 1999.

Chapter 9

Community Empowerment through Voluntary Input: A Case Study of Kiltimagh Integrated Resource Development (IRD)

FRANCES MCGETTIGAN, KEVIN BURNS and FIONA CANDON

Introduction

In Ireland the promotion of development at a local level has been the focus of a number of policy initiatives over the last decade. This facilitated an area-based approach for economic and social development. The 1994–1999 European Union (EU) Community Support Framework placed particular emphasis on the regeneration of local communities, particularly urban and rural areas blighted by high levels of unemployment and social exclusion, areas that Nolan *et al*. (1998) argue are located in geographically confined 'blackspots', including several peripheral rural areas. The decision to emphasise the local dimension of development stemmed from an understanding that disadvantage and social exclusion had to be tackled at a local level within the urban and rural communities. It reflected and promoted the explosion of community initiative and innovation in Ireland in the 1990s. Local development initiatives followed the partnership model promoted by the European Commission throughout Europe. The approach was to empower local communities to tackle their problems and improve the quality of life. The basis of the alternative 'bottom-up' approach is the recognition that it is the people of rural areas who are responsible for their own futures. Therefore, a vital aspect of this approach is the inclusion of the local community in their own development process. Local community development is a complex process as it integrates the economic, social, cultural and environmental development of an area with the involvement of the community, public and private sectors.

In the past the approach taken by government in Ireland to local development was essentially a 'top-down' approach. This approach was rarely developmental as it relied on trying to attract multinational companies and other local industries into disadvantaged areas within Ireland. The intention was that this would lead to positive spin-off effects, which would benefit the local economy of these areas. This chapter aims to explore these implications further through a case study of local development in the small town of Kiltimagh, County Mayo, Ireland. The chapter identifies how a 'stage of readiness' and 'community tourism empowerment' can deliver emigrant tourism projects.

Background

The town of Kiltimagh is located in the centre of East Mayo (Figure 9.1). One of the main disadvantages of the town of Kiltimagh is that it is the only inland town in County Mayo with a population of circa 1400 that has neither a national primary or secondary route passing through it to provide the economic boost normally associated with these through-ways. In 1986 a regional airport opened 35 km from Kiltimagh, but has had little impact on the region. Whilst tourism has developed rapidly around the honey-pot of Westport in the south of the county, the north is less well known and it was for this reason that the area was chosen as the site for the case study.

Like many other areas in rural Ireland, economic stagnation and business decline in Kiltimagh grew gradually throughout the 1970s and

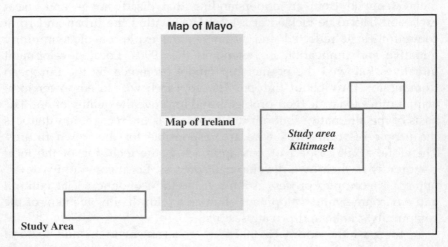

Figure 9.1 Study area

Table 9.1 Comparison of % changes in population from 1971 to 1996

Area	1971–1981	1981–1986	1986–1991	1991–1996
Kiltimagh District Electoral Division	+ 13%	− 11%	− 6.2%	− 5.3%
West region	+ 7.5%	− 0.9%	− 0.9%	+ 2.4%
State excluding Dublin	+ 15.7%	+ 3.4%	− 0.7%	+ 0.04%

Source: Census of Population: Small Area Population Statistics 1971–1996

1980s with the sharp decline in the population (see Table 9.1). In the period 1981–1986 Kiltimagh experienced a greater decrease in population than the West region or the state.

The decrease in population in Kiltimagh can be linked directly to emigration trends from the area, which was mainly due to lack of local employment opportunities. The Kiltimagh Diaspora Survey of the population migration in the Kiltimagh area was carried out in 1988 and showed that 75% of the youth (17–25 age group) of the area were forced to emigrate in order to find employment. The figure in absolute terms was estimated as being about half of the overall emigration from the area. This survey only confirmed what the locals knew – that this area was dying. *Irish Times* columnist, Ms Caroline Walsh, reported on the Diaspora Survey in the *Irish Times* in January 1989. She portrayed the town as 'decimated with no hope' and described heart-breaking scenes at Knock Airport as children said goodbye to their parents and wives to their husbands. Emigration brought with it a huge loss of services to the area. Not alone had no new businesses been established for many years, it was nearly a weekly feature that a business closed. From the results of an interview by Ms Walsh, she writes, 'Tom Higgins Chairman of the district community council lists some of the 50 businesses he reckons that have gone from Kiltimagh' (*Irish Times* 21.1.89). The decaying, derelict and overgrown houses and farmyards were clearly visible in the countryside. In the town the problem was equally apparent. Over 40% of the buildings in the town were derelict, with the other 60% not far behind. There was evidence of the collapse of the social fabric of the community, as there was a shortage of youths to play on sporting teams. The people of Kiltimagh have a strong tradition of voluntary community activity, particularly in the arts, charitable organisations and sport. In summary, the area had lost its productive and economic population, most with no hope of ever returning. It was a picture that would not entice or encourage investment. The conventional 'top-down' system had failed the Kiltimagh area and reliance on it had to change in the future. The local community had to come out of a denial phase and acknowledge the problem. The report on the Diaspora survey in 1988 activated the following characteristics in the community:

- a deep sense of community spirit and pride of place;
- a hunger for change given that many parents had watched their offspring emigrate;
- a harness-able bank of leadership, vision and innovation.

In rural areas the human resource is regarded as being of special importance and successful tourism development is seen as dependent on the active engagement of local people. This participation in turn is viewed as a means of regenerating crumbling senses of place identity and providing communities with 'the occasion for a new self-reflection: a cultural examination of conscience' (Feehan, 1992: 21).

The Formation of Integrated Resource Development Kiltimagh Ltd: A Community-Led Initiative

The results of the Diaspora Survey and the *Irish Times* articles were regarded by many as 'the spark that lit the fire' (Higgins, 1996: 49). In 1988 ten independent individuals approached the local priest about their fears for the area. A group was formed to attempt to initiate some form of economic development in the area and a model for development was adopted from Portugal where local community representation came together with state agencies and employers to form an entity that would prepare and implement an action plan for the area. Increased commercial and local community involvement would be sought through a 'bottom-up approach' that would be funded by public subscription. Initially Integrated Resource Development (IRD) would depend on subscriptions but its aim was to become self-sufficient, promote small businesses and work in close collaboration with both the community and various state agencies. The company prepared a prospectus and carried out door-to-door collection seeking £2.00/week from each wage earner in the community for four years. A total of £41,000 was raised in the first year and £111,000 in total over the four years. The monies collected over a four-year period from community members was significant as it not only gave the financial basis for the administration and matching funds for projects but also demonstrated the reasonably broad support for the initiative and commitment to ownership (Kelly, 2003).

The Strategic Enterprise Plan was the document that set out the way in which IRD would carry out its activities and meets its objectives. The development programme implemented by IRD to meet its original aims and objectives is divided into four key programme areas. They are Tourism Development, Theme Town Programme, Enterprise Programme and Social Development. It is fair to say that the resources of the area were few when starting off with the plan. In fact the area had more disadvantages than advantages and the programmes for development sought to convert adversity to advantage and many of what are now the resources of an area were initially thought to be problems that could not be overcome. This serves to reinforce that to achieve success the company knew that it must involve its greatest resource, its people and their community spirit. A voluntary working group system was introduced into the company structure with three members per group plus a leader. The groups are sectoral and IRD assists with advice and sourcing of grants. In his book, *The Kiltimagh Renewal*, John Higgins cites 26 voluntary working group leaders that were attending meetings and reporting on their projects. Most of these were not members of the Board of IRD Kiltimagh Ltd, which was real proof that the Kiltimagh system was community driven and a real bottom-up development (Higgins, 1996). Former residents of Kiltimagh were contacted and groups of voluntary workers travelled to England and America to tell those who were forced to emigrate that there maybe an opportunity to come back to live and work in the area. The unique human response to place and the associations they carry in terms of memories and fantasies are the root of attachment. Indeed they are directly related to the process of self-identity (Childress, 1996: 341). In other words, concrete everyday practices give rise to a cultural mediation or 'structure of feeling' (Williams, 1997). As a result, one place as opposed to another becomes the object of identity for the subject (Agnes, 1992: 263). By 1989 the small community of Kiltimagh and its wider community had taken its first steps to come to terms with its economic development needs. To be a successful development group, community empowerment was needed. This must command under-standing, acceptance and support in the society at large. The work of Barr *et al.* (1996) addresses this point and they suggest that a theory of change approach should be adopted, concentrating on the core issues of community development, community empowerment and quality of life. These dimensions, as outlined in Table 9.2, reflect closely on the Kiltimagh community.

Table 9.2 Purposes and core dimensions of community development (Barr *et al.*, 1996)

Community empowerment	Core dimensions
Personal empowerment	A learning community
Positive action	A fair and just community
Development of community organisations	An active and organised community
Participation and involvement	An influential community
Improvement in quality of life	*Core dimensions*
Local economic development	A shared wealth
Social development and services	A caring community
Environmental development	A green community
Crime prevention and public safety	A safe community
Positive perceptions and satisfactions	A good place to live
Sustainability and cohesion	A lasting community

Source: Barr *et al.* (1996: 10)

Empowering the community to pursue the key programme areas of the Strategic Enterprise Plan allowed them to improve their quality of life. These key programmes can be divided into core dimensions depending on the nature of the community organisation and its activities. The core dimensions are the measures of change. 'Community development is about change in people, in communities, in services and in policies. Evidence of change should be sought in each of them' (Barr *et al.*, 1996: 15).

Strategic Enterprise Plan

This plan was divided into five programmes for development.

Tourism Development

Tourism projects are generally initiated by IRD. Although there are no natural tourism resources in the area, IRD decided to provide tourism infrastructure, which would benefit both local people and tourists, and also to enhance and use some of the tourism resources in the surrounding areas. A product development and marketing manager was employed by IRD and actively assists with the two-week long St. Patrick's Festival, family reunions, school reunions, school tours and visiting groups from Ireland and abroad who wish to learn about the 'Kiltimagh Story'. However tourism has not developed like other sectors. There are many reasons for this, in particular major competition from well established nearby regional tourist destinations, a poor natural resource base and IRD's belief in developing facilities for the locals first. By prioritising for the locals, IRD recognised that Kiltimagh had to be a 'place to live' for them.

Arts, Culture and Heritage Programme

IRD Kiltimagh Ltd realised the need to involve other sectors of the community that were perhaps not business orientated. Under the Arts, Culture and Heritage Programme an old school was refurbished and a theatre, seating 200 people, put in place, hosting local, national and international productions. A full-time Arts Officer was appointed in 1998 to coordinate the Arts, Culture and Heritage programme.

Theme Town Programme

Upgrading a town's appearance is crucial for a number of reasons, but the more important ones include a sense of pride of place for local people, attracting investment to the area and of course enticing tourists. IRD gave the town a massive facelift, putting cables underground, bringing traditional-style lighting (supported directly by friends of Kiltimagh in London and America) and restoring the market square. Architects were employed to develop a colour scheme and local people were encouraged to paint their buildings. The aim was to recreate the style of a 19th century market town.

Kiltimagh has two unique assets that distinguish it from other towns: aesthetics and community. One outsider's synopsis of the town: 'Kiltimagh gives the appearance of being a very prosperous town and gives a very good impression. It has a reputation of a town that pulls together. People on the outside look on Kiltimagh as a community as opposed to just IRD Kiltimagh, it is very visible that there is a plan in place'.

Enterprise Programme

In 1992 three derelict houses in the centre of the town were converted into Kiltimagh's first Enterprise Centre. There was an on-going facilitation programme of enterprise development offered to the local community. By 1994, 18 jobs were established at the Enterprise Centre and IRD were also given the responsibility of administering LEADER funding to the East Mayo area (1990–2006). The ongoing work in enterprise development was complimented by a very successful 'Shop Local Campaign'. This Communities Under Threat (CUT) campaign demonstrated the need for local people to support their local retailers and services, encouraging locals to shop locally. The locals in Kiltimagh frowned upon individuals who shopped outside this area. The development of the Enterprise Centres, annual training programmes, growth in services and the LEADER programme led to the creation of 350 direct and indirect jobs. Increased investor confidence brought new businesses and services to the town. Economic activity in the period 1990–94 increased at 15.8% per annum and in the period 1995–1998, increased to 30.2% per annum. This in turn has increased confidence in the wider community.

Social Development

The features of the social programme included the provision of 27 units of social housing, which reduced the number of derelict sites in the town and increased the number of people living in the area. The scheme was funded by a system of 90% nonrepayable loans from the national government. This was not at the expense of the rural hinterland, as most of these people were either returnees, were coming to Kiltimagh to find work in the area or were people moving into the area and working in other towns. The young population holds the lifeblood of the town and is a reason for confidence in the future of any area. Studies in the late 1990s showed that Kiltimagh National School pupil numbers were increasing at a rate of 6% per annum while other comparable schools in the West region declined at 6% per annum. In addition, 40% of those new pupils were not born in the parish but were children of new families that had come into the area.

Community Participation and Empowerment

IRD Kiltimagh recorded considerable success in 'levering' into the development process a good deal of voluntary input, and agency support in time, expertise and funding. O'Brien and Hassinger (1992) pointed out that the 'types of leadership differ from one rural community to another and that efforts of local leaders can make a difference in the response of local communities in meeting problems.' The board leaders placed great emphasis on partnership formation and growth. This strong sense of partnership allowed the voices of the local community to be heard and to foster a sense of shared objectives towards development. This strong sense of partnership is viewed as reflecting the rise of what is called 'the new localism' whereby local actors become involved in designing and implementing solutions to local problems (Goodwin, 1998; Moseley, 1999) Ireland has one of the strongest records in Europe of using partnership to address the challenges of rural development. The partnership approach between the community, state agencies and private sector has worked very effectively for Kiltimagh.

This IRD Kiltimagh structure was ahead of its time in catering for local development. This is attributed to having a formal structure – IRD Kiltimagh Board with a Professional Manager employed to drive the strategic plan. This was backed up by informal working relationships between the community and members represented on the board. Successful and sustainable development is better achieved where it starts from a local physical, social and cultural resource base and involves inclusive participation in planning and implementing development (Lynch, 2002).

There is no doubt that community empowerment through voluntary input is the key criteria throughout the latter stages of the community's lifecycle, as outlined in Figure 9.2. The formulation of working groups was very important, as it gave the community a sense of being involved in the development process of their area and of course provided some very successful smallscale projects. It must be noted that at this time there was the huge crisis of emigration in Kiltimagh and only for the strong 'sense of place' and 'voluntary input' from those left behind could the community reach that 'pride of place' stage that they are at now. IRD is one of the best examples in Ireland of a local development organisation's ability to encourage participation. Encouraging participation reduces begrudgery (i.e. where people try to prevent the positive side of things) and denies a 'them and us' situation. John Higgins (1995: 7) wrote that 'no other single factor impedes the bottom up development and expression of communities that the national pastime of begrudgery.' One retired elderly couple that moved to Kiltimagh four years ago believe that encouraging participation is the key to sustainable community development and the key to capitalising on the great work that has been initiated by IRD to date (Interview with Community Member,

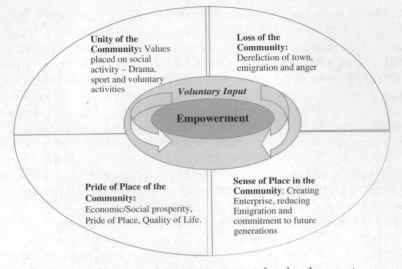

Figure 9.2 Stages of community empowerment for development
Source: McGettigan and Burns (2004)

22.6.01). This great work is reflected in the organisation winning every major award for enterprise development. A list of the national awards is outlined in Table 9.3.

This has reinforced the 'pride of place' felt amongst the local community. Kiltimagh is frequently held up as a model of best practice. IRD have made good use of the media in publicising the successes of Kiltimagh, which heightens the pride of place felt by residents as they receive national coverage. Kiltimagh can be credited with capitalising on the tangible factors of leadership, partnerships and funding to achieve the development process, but the intangible factors such as community spirit, sense of place and pride of place have made it successful. The action plan for the last 10 years has focused on the following sustainable developments: Built Environment Renewal (BER). Local Economic Innovation (LEI) and Social and Cultural Stimulation (SCS), which have achieved great success. Throughout all stages of the development process the community's spirit, which was generated from their values and sense of place, empowered them to become the driving force in Kiltimagh.

This can only happen when the community is part of the development process. Hall and Jenkins (1995) state that 'values are the overarching criteria people use to make decisions'. The decision-making process for

Table 9.3 IRD Kiltimagh Ltd. National Awards

Year	Award	Prize
1991	National Award Winners of ESB Community Enterprise Awards	£60,000
1994	National Award Winners in the Bank of Ireland/Farmers Journal Community Enterprise Awards	£12,000
1994	Runners up in the Irish Planning Institute National Award for Urban In-fill and Re-development	
1995	National Finalists in FAS Community Initiative Awards	
1996	Winners of AIB Better Ireland Awards	£25,000
1999	Regional Winners of AIB Better Ireland Awards	£16,000

Source: Internal document, IRD

this community varied between making personal financial contributions to save the town or deciding to 'emigrate', all of which sought a better 'quality of life'. Max-Neef (1992) defines 'quality of life as the way we experience our lives', which is related to the degree and the way in which fundamental human needs are satisfied. The needs of the society in Kiltimagh have changed because the community has overcome crisis point and a more modern world dictates that time is necessary for self-fulfilment as a priority. Thus the level of voluntary work declines and community empowerment fades, resulting in a 'gap' between leaders and followers. The future for the community in Kiltimagh lies in regenerating empowerment among its members through an integrated tourism development strategy.

At the outset the community along with IRD decided to pursue development for local needs and priorities before considering the development of tourist needs. Tourism should be managed as a local resource where local needs and priorities take precedence over the goals of the tourism industry (Murphy, 1995 in Burns, 1999). Unlike other economies, Kiltimagh, despite doing badly, never lost sight of the 'quality of life' concept throughout the last decade. It is in adopting this holistic approach that the community is now in a 'stage of readiness' and Kiltimagh, as a place empowering its community, is ready to pursue a form of tourism based on targeting the wider Kiltimagh community as 'emigrant tourists'. In using this argument we need to understand what constitutes 'community'. The term 'community' has been used (and misused) in such a wide range of contexts that it is almost impossible to proffer a workable definition. The term is best approached contextually. It is frequently used to describe both a geographical area and communities of interest. But the word also has other connotations. For example a number of rather intangible factors that we often think of as 'community spirit' are important in creating positive feelings about neighbourhoods and neighbourhood organisations, in turn feeding into a 'sense of place' and 'place attachment'. Hummon (1992) suggests that we approach the issue of community through exploration of people's 'sense of place' and self-identity.

State of Readiness for Tourism Development

The 'state of readiness' may be defined as a stage reached by a community where the development process has satisfied community needs as a 'place to live' and now can offer it as a 'place to visit' to the wider community of tourists (Figure 9.3).

The relationship between the place to live and the place to visit is *place empowerment* for tourism development based upon community values, which are the starting point for formulating and developing a form of tourism for this place. It is focusing on targeting the emigrants from the wider community to return as tourists and reverse the push of emigration with the pull of Kiltimagh. The networking between the hosts (friends, relatives and other local people) and the tourist has social and economic benefits. This place empowerment will encourage participation by the community to further community tourism empowerment. 'Kiltimagh Community Tourism Empowerment' is based on

Figure 9.3 Place empowerment
Source: McGettigan and Burns (2004)

attracting the visiting friends and family (VFR) market, which will contribute to the 'quality of life' for the tourist and host and satisfy the lack of tourism development. The 'quality of life' of the community is taken as the starting point and tourism as one of the possible instruments to improve it (Postma, 2002). In this instance the community's sense of place drove the hunger for economic and environmental development through voluntary effort, and now will be the backbone of emigrant tourism development.

Community Tourism Empowerment (CTE)

Voluntary input is now diminishing and to reverse this decline the aim of the Community Tourism Empowerment (CTE, Figure 9.3) concept is to tap into the community's 'sense of place' and 'pride of place' and regenerate the voluntary community effort, empowering the community to undertake an integrated tourism development strategy for emigrant tourism (Figure 9.4). By involving them in the process for developing CTE, the community will realise the social and economic benefits for the host and tourist.

Through the CTE concept (Figure 9.4) these emigrants will be attracted back to Kiltimagh to become embedded in the local area using the tourism system where the public, private and voluntary sector work together for tourism development. In exploring the CTE. concept the relevance of place attachment and its importance to quality of life for both the host and the guest is vital. Kiltimagh has now established itself as a place empowering a community of residents and emigrants to

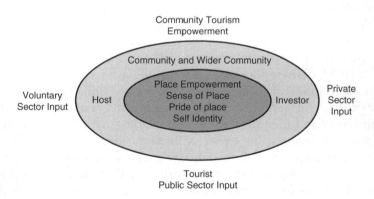

Figure 9.4 Community tourism empowerment

Source: McGettigan and Burns (2004)

participate in tourism in an integrated way where the focus of development is on networking, sustainability, partnerships and owner-ship of the resources. The local community have been driven by their values and spirit to achieve success, where 'civic togetherness, participation and commitment to the area are evident'. A traditional part of the seasonal rhythm of many Irish villages is the return of the emigrants for holidays, and this continues to be an important and integral part of local place identities. This type of visitor has different expectations to the 'tourist' and tends to blend in with local lifestyles and habits, staying in relatives' homes, and socialising with family and friends in local bars. It can be argued that this segment of tourist flow of people contributes to a global sense of place, a fluid interchange between the local and its global outputs, which weakens the boundaries between hosts and guests. CTE is taking Relph's suggestion that 'an authentic sense of place is above all that of being inside and belonging to your place both as an individual and as a member of the community, and know this without reflecting upon it'.

The CTE concept focuses on creating a sense of belonging due to high levels of social capital, which represents a sense of place and cohesion among the community (Richards, 2003). In this era of globalisation it has often been commented upon that we need notion of 'place' as stable, secure and unique. According to Relph (1976: 6), if places are 'sources of security and identity for individuals and groups of people, then it is important that the means of experiencing creating and maintaining significant places are not lost'. Emigrants' memories of Kiltimagh, the place they came from, are vivid, and despite living in new locations many are rooted in the past and to their birthplace.

As the forces of globalisation bear down on places and locales, this kind of approach seems useful as a way of understanding the mechanisms underlying place attachment and the creation of symbolic locales. Agnew (1992) defines place as 'a discreet if elastic area in which settings for the constitution of social relations are located and with which people can identify'. This definition clearly links the idea of place with both self-identification and identification with a community. The vast number of emigrants represents the wider Kiltimagh community and the CTE concept is focussing and understanding peoples' sense of place and place identity contributing to the quality of life of all participants. Kiltimagh satisfies the basis for a 'sense of place' or 'place attachment' through the CTE concept, which will deliver further community empowerment in the Kiltimagh area.

Conclusion

The analysis of this community has presented us with how the holistic and participatory approach to development harnessed the intangible factors of the community's 'sense and pride of place', backed up by tangible factors, for development. The outcomes of this process identified gaps in tourism development which only now can be addressed as the community is in a 'stage of readiness' to offer the 'place they live in' as a 'place to visit'. The concept of converting place empowerment into the CTE is the key criterion for a sustainable approach to 'emigrant tourism' where the host, tourist and investor are active participants and beneficiaries. This embeds the emigrant community as stakeholders in the development process and regenerates the voluntary input in partnership and networking with the public and private sector. In terms of CTE, emigrant tourism is likely to be the most sustainable approach for future tourism development in the region.

References

Agnew, J. (1993) Representing space, scale and culture in social science. In J. Duckan and D. Ley (eds) *Place, Culture and Representation* (pp. 220–224). London: Routledge.

Burns, P. (1999) *An Introduction to Tourism and Anthropology*. London: Routledge.

Childress, H., Atlman, I. and Low, S. (2004) Place attachment. *Journal of Architectural and Planning Research* 13 (4), 334–339.

Christensen, N.A. (1995) Sustainable community based tourism and host quality of life. In S. McCool and A.E. Watson (eds) *Linking Tourism, the Environment, and Sustainability*. Ogden, UT: USDA Forest Service.

Corcoran, M.P. (2002) Place attachment and community sentiment in marginalised neighbourhoods: A European case study. *Canadian Journal of Urban Research* 11 (1), 47–68.

Dicken, P. (1998) *The Global Shift: Transforming the World Economy*. London: PCP.

Goodwin, M. (1998) The governance of rural areas: Some emerging research issues and agendas. *Journal of Rural Studies* 14 (1), 5–12.

Gray, B. (1989) *Collaborating: Finding Common Ground for Multiparty Problems*. San Francisco: Jossy-Bass.

Hall, C.M. and Jenkins, J.M. (1995) *Tourism and Public Policy*. London: Routledge.

Higgins, J. (1996) *The Kiltimagh Renewal: Best Practice in Community Enterprise*. Dublin: Oak Tree Press.

Hummon, D. (1992) Community attachment local sentiment and sense of place. In N.I. Atlman and S. Low (eds) *Place Attachment* (pp. 253–278). New York: Plenum Press.

Kelly, J. (2003) Strategic Enterprise Plan Discussion for Kiltimagh IRD. Interview, February, 2003.

Max-Neef, M. (1992) Development and human need. In P. Ekins and M. Max-Neef (eds) *Real Life Economics: Understanding Wealth Creation* (pp. 52–60). London: Routledge.

McGettigan, F. and Burns, K. (2004) Community Tourism Research in Kiltimagh 2003/04. In *Quality of Life – Competing Value Perspectives in Leisure and Tourism*, ATLAS Conference Leeuwarden, The Netherlands, 19–21 June.

Moseley, M.J. (1999) The Republic of Ireland: The new localism as a response to rural decline. In E. Westholm, M.J. Moseley and N. Stenlas (eds) *Local Partnership and Rural Development: A Literature Review of Practice and Theory* (pp. 25–43). Falun and Cheltenham: Dalarna Research Institute, Sweden in Association with the Countryside and Community Research Unit, Cheltenham and Gloucester College of Higher Education.

Moseley, M.J., Cherrett, T. and Cawley, M. (2001) Local partnerships for rural development: Ireland's experience in context *Irish Geography* 34 (2), 176–193.

Moser, C.O.N. (1989) Community participation in urban projects in the third world. *Progress in Planning* 32 (2), 81.

Nolan, B., Whelan, C. and Williams, J. (1998) *Where are Poor Households? The Spatial Distribution of Poverty and Deprivation in Ireland.* Dublin: Oak Tree Press.

O'Brien, D.J. and Hassinger, E.W. (1992) Community attachment among leaders in five rural communities. *Rural Sociology* 57, 521–534.

Porter, M.E. (1987) From competitive advantage to corporate strategy. *Harvard Business Review* May–June, 43–59.

Postma, A. (2002) An approach for integrated development of quality tourism, in tourism destination planning. In N. Andrews, S. Flanagan and J. Ruddy (eds) *Tourism Destination Planning* (pp. 205–217). Dublin: DIT.

Postma, A. and Jenkins, A.K. (1997) Improving the tourist's experience: Quality management applied to tourist destinations. In P. Murphy (ed.) *Quality Management in Urban Tourism*. New York: Wiley.

Relph, E. (1976) *Place and Placeness.* London: Pion.

Richards, G. (2003) Social capital: A measure of quality of life and determinant of quality of experience? Quality of life – competing value perspectives in leisure and tourism. ATLAS Conference, Leeuwarden, The Netherlands, 19–21 June.

Richards, G. and Hall, D. (2000) The community: A sustainable concept in tourism development? In G. Richards and D. Hall (eds) *Tourism and Sustainable Community Development* (pp. 1–15). London: Routledge.

Riley, R. (1992) Attachment to the ordinary landscape. In S.N. Low and I. Altman (eds) *Place Attachment.* New York: Plenum Press.

Sabel, C. (1996) *Ireland – Local Partnership and Social Innovation.* Paris: OECD.

Websites used

www.teagasc.ie/

Chapter 10

Raising the Status of Lappish Communities through Tourism Development

SATU MIETTINEN

Introduction

Inari is a municipality located in the northernmost area of Finland. It is a place where different cultures overlap and mix through the history and geography of the area. Inari has national borders with Russia and Norway. There is a lot of traffic between all three countries. The Sami people from Finland, Russia, Norway and Sweden have succeeded in maintaining their cultural heritage and traditions throughout the Barents Sea region. In this region, both the Sami and Finnish people bring together their cultural heritage and way of life. The Inari community earns its livelihood from forestry, tourism and reindeer husbandry. Tourism is becoming an increasingly important means of livelihood for the local communities.

This chapter focuses on the development of cultural tourism and community empowerment in the local communities of Inari. There are several active communities, like Lemmenjoki located within a National Park area, as well as Koppelo and Nellim, which are located next to the Russian border. All the communities have been activated through community participation in various cultural tourism development projects. The focus of this chapter is on those projects where elements from cultural heritage or material culture are used to create new tourism services. These services are aimed towards generating income for the members of the local communities. Many of the cultural tourism development projects deal with local material culture, such as locally produced arts and crafts. Material culture is here defined as local arts and crafts, which are either functional or decorative. Arts and crafts production is an important means of income generation, as there are not many alternative employment opportunities within the region. Tourists are the major market segment for local arts and crafts production, as

159

almost 90% of the arts and crafts are sold to tourists visiting the area. The aim of this research is to investigate different development strategies in community participation and examine the factors that have made the case study successful through community participation.

Background to the Study

The researcher has been actively involved in cultural tourism, especially arts and crafts tourism development in Lapland, since 1997. Arts and crafts tourism is defined by Richards as tourism development whereby the buying or collecting of arts and crafts, or learning about traditional arts and crafts, is a part of the local tourism experience (Richards, 1999). The researcher worked as a 'EUROTEX' project coordinator from 1997 to 1999. The EUROTEX project was a cultural tourism development project funded by the Regional Development Fund of the European Union. The ATLAS organisation was also involved in the project. One of the activities during this period was to assess the tourism-related skills development needs of local microscale entrepreneurs. The researcher was also very involved in cultural tourism and product design development in the local communities. The fieldwork experience and research material collected during this project provided the researcher with a good insight into community participation and its development since 1997.

From 2002 to 2003, the researcher was again engaged in a tourism development project called 'There is more than snow' in the Inari region. During this project, she had an opportunity to compile data on tourism development that had taken place since the EUROTEX project. Another skills development needs assessment was made during this period among the same entrepreneurs that took part in the EUROTEX project. Analysis of the data provided good background information about good practices implicated during the EUROTEX project. A number of the projects dealing with community-based tourism development focus on product design and marketing. The services and products that local communities offer are aimed at the tourism market. Different projects try to develop specialised tourism events based on local arts and crafts traditions, eco-food products and other forms of local culture. The results of these two assessments provided the researcher with a better understanding of success factors and the importance of community participation.

Furthermore, this project provided the researcher with an opportunity to spend time in the local communities, take part in the tourism development workshops and interview project participants, project leaders and tourism business people who were initiating different projects and development actions. The project also enabled her to actively take part in them.

The main methods of this research were interviews and participant observation. A major part of the interviews were either open and rather long thematic interviews or group discussions in the local communities. Interviews took place in the participants' homes, at their workshops or at their offices. Because of the long driving distances between participants' homes, the researcher also stayed overnight at some of their homes and took part in their daily lives. This provided her with a good opportunity for participant observation and for long discussions about tourism and its effects on their lives.

The Inari region is sparsely populated. There are 7500 inhabitants in a land area of 17,400 km^2; the local communities are small. The population of some villages comprises approximately 30–40 inhabitants, while the largest villages comprise several hundred inhabitants. Most of the villages have village associations. The role of the village associations, in many cases, is to take care of the village development. These village associations are formed around different themes: folk dancing, folk tradition, sports and so on.

The term 'local community' can be defined in various ways, but in the end it is always about groups of people involved in a certain kind of action. It can refer to an entire village, a village association, a cooperative or other group of people who have shared interests. On many occasions, a real dilemma arises when the interests of the local community and regional or national administration collide. Then, an official definition of local community is needed. In the Lapland region, local communities can include representatives from various interest groups and different ethnicities. The small villages of Northern Lapland suffer from an absence of communal and administrative services. For example, many of these small villages lack elementary education for children, as the village schools have been closed down.

Living in a small village in Northern Lapland is a tough job, as there are not many free utilities and services provided by the local administration. The people take care of their water and heating services themselves and construct the infrastructure for these services. This is rather costly, as the regional maintenance does not reach out to villages located far away from the urban centres. Those living away from urban centres certainly feel discriminated against. Eventually, smaller villages disappear when they do not have many of the basic services that can be obtained in urban centres. Long distances also influence quality of life and employment opportunities: having to drive hundreds of kilometres daily in order to reach the closest urban centre is not easy.

Tourism Development and Community Involvement

The EUROTEX project initiated arts and crafts tourism in Lapland. The project idea was to develop arts and crafts tourism routes and services in the region. This work was conducted in cooperation with a local tourism development agency and tour operator, Lapland Tourism Oy. The project worked directly with small communities of craftsmen and small- and medium-size tourism entrepreneurs. One of the communities, called 'Inarista käsin' (*Handmade from Inari*), was located in an Inari village. Other arts and crafts producers in Inari were also involved in the project. Most of the participants in the project had their own companies or cooperatives.

Inari is a great example of an arts and crafts tourism product. The village has several workshops where arts and crafts are produced, and tourists are given the opportunity to see how objects are made by hand. There are both Finnish and Sami producers in the village. Inari has a beautiful Sami museum called SIIDA, a Sami arts and crafts school and Sami Duodji, a place where handmade Sami arts and crafts are sold. Sami Duodji has initiated a brand for authentic Sami arts and crafts. These objects are produced by the Sami people according to the Sami tradition. In the summer season, from June to August, the village is packed with tourists. The village has a couple of hotels, several campsites and specialised tourism events. A typical specialised tourism event is a boat trip on Lake Inari. Inari village is a popular stop on the way to North Cape or on the way to salmon fishing further north.

The EUROTEX project provided seminars on marketing for arts and crafts producers; in order to help with product development, a 'round-trip' tour was designed and successfully marketed to Dutch special interest tourists. The project was also involved in export. 'Round-trip' tours and arts and crafts products were marketed at the Kitakyushu Fair on Kyushu Island in Japan. The Lapland region is very popular among Japanese tourists. The goal of the export project was twofold: to find additional distribution channels outside the tourist season and to attract more special interest tourists to take part in 'round-trip' tours.

A lot of development work was conducted either through one-on-one meetings or as group discussions at the producers' homes or workshops. The project was initiated with a skills development analysis and an assessment of the general development needs. These development needs were defined together with the participants of the project. This gave the participants a commitment towards the common goals. The project had certain goals that were defined in the project plan, which were, of course, achieved. However, more important goals for practical work were set by the representatives of the local communities: arts and crafts producers and tourism entrepreneurs involved in the project.

Representatives of the local communities were committed to the practical work of the project: planning and designing new specialised tourism events, planning marketing materials and designing the 'round-trip' tour. This kind of work was very productive as they could benefit from it in the long term. It was deemed important to discover concrete benefits for the project participants and communicate these benefits in a way that the participants could understand.

There were general patterns in the participation of the local communities. Usually, there were one or two key persons who were actively involved in the development work. Local communities are sometimes rather closed communities where resistance to change can be quite strong. It can be hard for a newcomer or a visitor to fit into the small community, and it takes time before the community accepts one as a full member. It is always good to find key persons within the local community that share the same interests. Only after one has proven oneself to be trustworthy would it be possible to begin the actual project work. Trustworthiness was obtained through creating down-to-earth goals that one could keep to, not raising false hopes about expected results, and in keeping a very low and committed profile among community members. In many development areas, there are numerous projects going on where participants are promised more than is realistically possible to achieve during the project. This causes a lot of disappointment and complicates development work.

In addition to this proven trustworthiness, it was important to obtain very concrete results that benefited the local community. These concrete results could be related to promotion. For example, a good article about development projects, or an important topic for the local community in the regional newspaper was very useful. Furthermore, help in product design work or in promotion planning was usually warmly welcomed by the local community. The initial results did not need to be overwhelming; something that would simply show that the project is about practical actions for the local community would be adequate. For long-term commitment, however, local investment is usually needed, or good results have to be seen in product sales and promotion.

Improved Skills and Networking

During the EUROTEX project, an assessment of the skills development needs of local craftsmen was conducted in 1997. This assessment was conducted through a series of interviews and an assessment form that was filled in together with a craftsman. The results showed that craftsmen were suffering from a lack of business and marketing skills, and many of them were lacking professional training. The majority of producers were involved in arts and crafts production as a way to earn additional income. Tourism-related skills like language skills needed improvement. The majority of the producers had learnt their trade from their parents or had started it as a hobby.

A follow-up survey was done during spring 2003 by the 'There is more than snow' project of the Inari municipality. The aim of this survey was to discover how arts and crafts people were benefiting from tourism in Lapland. Specifically, the survey focused on discovering their major problems, how they were using marketing and networking skills and how the products aimed at the tourism market were designed. Another part of the survey was aimed at tour operators and companies selling specialised tourism events, mainly snow mobile tourism marketed locally as snowmobile safaris. Snowmobile safaris, where groups of tourists learn to drive snowmobiles, are very popular in the Lapland region. A further aim of the follow-up survey was to discover how arts and crafts people and tour operators could cooperate, and if there was a need for a certain kind of product development.

The networking stage had improved since the EUROTEX project. Most of the arts and crafts people had received help from regional business development centres. The majority of the arts and crafts people in this group had both training in business skills and in arts and crafts.

How Craftsmen Benefit from Tourism

A survey done during spring 2003 by the 'There is more than snow' project of the Inari municipality provided information about the customer segments of the arts and crafts producers. Tourists are the most important customer group, mostly comprising Europeans (central and southern), visiting as independent travellers. Finnish tourists, by comparison, mostly travel in groups. Furthermore, Finnish companies and individual travellers also form an important customer group.

Concerning marketing strategies, it appeared that those employed within the arts and crafts sector believed that they themselves could sell their own products best. This marketing strategy included participation at various fairs, the installation of roadside signs and the printing of brochures. However, in subsequent personal interviews with arts and crafts producers, many actually reported that they would prefer someone else to market their products for them. Since then, the degree of networking within the EUROTEX project has improved. At present, a larger percentage of arts and crafts producers appear to be participating in different projects and have learnt to market their products collectively. However, many arts and crafts producers still believe that they have to manage all the business areas from production to the marketing of their products. When arts and crafts producers learn to cooperate and join different networks, they discover that they can divide the work load and concentrate more on their strengths, i.e. certain members of the network can work with marketing, and others can focus on production.

Most of the arts and crafts producers believed that the current trend was to provide tourists with an opportunity to participate in arts and crafts production or in other cultural activities. Most of the arts and crafts producers designed their own products for a wide customer group, from children to elderly people, and tourist needs were not automatically taken into consideration. Arts and crafts producers weren't using professional help in product design. Their development needs were partly the same as during the EUROTEX project. At present, products are still designed to satisfy everybody's needs in very general terms. A positive development, however, is that all the entrepreneurs have a strategy for receiving information about their products from their customers.

Five out of 14 of the respondents were receiving special interest tourist groups. All five respondents provided different responses to the question concerning how often tourists visit them, i.e. every day, the summer season only or a couple of times per year. Group sizes varied from 3–6 individuals to 23 individuals. A more developed business could receive larger groups. Most of the arts and crafts producers had such small workshops that they could only receive a few individuals at a time. Different specialised tourism events, such as felting wool or learning about traditional Sami crafts, lasted from three to seven hours. The most important qualities that entrepreneurs mentioned when designing their services were: locality, authenticity, originality, high degree of craftsmanship and taking care of customer needs. Arts and crafts producers running the programmes stressed that the knowledge of local cultural heritage is essential. The marketing of these products goes by word of mouth, other entrepreneurs and professional marketing people. There are still development needs in both product design and in marketing.

Since the EUROTEX project, the profile of Lappish arts and crafts producers has developed in a more professional manner. As there are numerous development projects in the Inari area, it is hard to specifically state what the real effects of a single project are. Yet, it can be mentioned that part of the development actions that were initiated during the EUROTEX project were very fruitful. Participatory methods in the project work were important and the developments based on common development goals were the most successful.

Creating a Tourism Product Based on Local Sami Tradition in Nellim Village

Nellim village is located next to the Russian border of the Inari municipality. The village is also located close to Lake Inari. This village has a very special history, as it is a place where different Finnish and Sami cultures meet. Nellim is called a village of three cultures. The Inari Sami are the original inhabitants of Nellim village. Later, Finnish families and, after the Second World War, Skolt Sami from Petsamo moved into the area. Nellim village is a place where the Eastern and Western Sami cultures meet. There are approximately 260 inhabitants in Nellim village. Reindeer herding, fishing and forestry are the main sources of livelihood. Furthermore, Nellim village is a destination for day visitors from the Saariselkä and Ivalo ski-resort areas. One of the most important sights in the village is the Nellim Orthodox Church, dedicated to the Holy Trinity and Trifon of Petsamo. Trifon of Petsamo was an Orthodox priest who baptised Skolt Sami people in the 16th century. He established a convent in Petsamo in 1556. The Nellim Orthodox Church is dedicated to the memory of Father Trifon. The village also has a village museum, which represents the archaeological findings of the local area and Inari, as well as the Skolt Sami traditions. This museum was initiated by local villagers who were interested in their own Sami traditions and material culture.

Nellim village has an incredibly vibrant and lively association known as 'Nellimin Pyry'. The association, which focuses on folk dancing and traditions, was established in 1953. 'Nellimin Pyry' is currently formed around two women: one Sami and one Finnish. These two women have worked as tourism incubators and village activists for several decades. They have created a couple of unique tourism products and initiated a village museum that both supports the local heritage and provides a unique tourist attraction.

The idea for the village museum was initiated on a local heritage course, and came about as a result of the village being a meeting point for many cultures and Sami traditions. Course participants were given an assignment to collect old Sami arts and crafts from their homes and look for information and histories related to the objects they found. The course turned out to be very successful and the participants discovered that they had quite a valuable collection of local heritage in front of them. A group of participants designed a project that was funded through regional development funds. The aim of the project was to establish a village museum where the arts and crafts related to local heritage could be presented. Later, the village museum was established in Nellim School with the help of museum professionals from the Finnish National Museum. The school has closed down since the establishment of the museum, but the museum itself is still functioning as a regional tourist attraction.

The museum project is a typical example of community participation related to tourism, as the villagers wanted to preserve their local culture and heritage. The whole process of collecting the arts and crafts, combined with the stories related to their histories, created a feeling of togetherness and appreciation of the local traditions. At the same time, the museum functions as a gateway to the local culture for visiting tourists. The villagers were resourceful enough to initiate a project to fund the professional help and exhibition of the exhibits. The museum is a popular visiting place in the summer season and it presents a unique part of the village history.

Tourism Products from Nellim Village

Nellim village offers two very unique tourism products. These products are mainly operated and run by the two village activists that are also active in the village association. The main product is a Nellim village tour. The guided tour includes the services of the local registered guides, a visit to the local Orthodox Church, a visit to the Russian border, a visit to the village museum and a dinner either at a local tea room or at an entrepreneur's home. The main goal of the tourism product is to generate income for the villagers and a secondary goal is to keep the village active. The main season for these tours is August and September. There are about 1000 visitors during the season and around the same amount outside the season. The majority of visitors are elderly retired people. Although the number of visitors is not particularly high, for the village it means an important additional source of income.

The tour is an interesting experience as the local village activists are working as guides, and one of the women has her own food service enterprise specialising in food that is either produced or collected from the village area. She is a professional cook and has written several books about the Skolt Sami food tradition. The tours usually end by having dinner at her home. She always explains the history of traditional Sami Skolt dishes to the visitors and the origin of the different fish, vegetables, meat, berries and herbs used in the dishes. People living in the small villages around Lake Inari and other parts of the region are usually very self-sufficient. They collect berries, mushrooms and fish and then freeze or preserve these ingredients for the winter. When the dinner is organised at an entrepreneur's home, she serves the food in the garden. It is a very special experience for the tourists to see how local villagers live their daily lives.

Nellim Orthodox Church is one of the tour attractions. It is one of three Orthodox churches in the area and, besides being a place of worship, is a symbol of community participation and togetherness of the village. A major part of the church was constructed with the help of the villagers. It is also a pilgrim destination. There is an annual pilgrimage in August from Nellim to Lake Sevetti, following in the footsteps of Father Trifon of Petsamo. The villagers have also initiated a programme of services related to the Orthodox traditions of the village. There is a dinner celebration before fasting, which is also aimed at tourists visiting the area. The dinner is organised by local villagers. They serve the food by playing roles related to the village history and traditions. The Orthodox church is mentioned on the internet pages of the regional Sami museum. Sources mention that couples from abroad have been coming to hold their wedding ceremony at Nellim Orthodox Church.

A visit to the Russian border is also included in the tour. The proximity of the Russian border makes Nellim village very exotic for many visiting tourists. A visit to the Russian border during the Nellim visit was also a part of the sightseeing programme for the participants of the European Union Summit in Saariselkä. Many of the summit participants found this extremely interesting and even called their families from the Russian side of the border to let them know how extraordinary it was.

Also villagers themselves used to organise small trips to the Russian coast of the Barents Sea and to the Petsamo area. There are still some Skolt Sami people living in this region. There are also several projects attempting to develop a tourist route from Inari to the coastal area of the Barents Sea. Nellim village is also populated by Finnish frontier guards patrolling the Finnish–Russian border. They visit the village quite regularly and participate in village meetings occasionally. There are also some interesting sights in the Nellim area relating to Lapland's war history that are occasionally visited by tourists.

The Importance of Tourism for Nellim Village

The number of tourists visiting Nellim village is relatively small. Yet, tourism is an important activator of the local village and it also brings much-needed additional income to the villagers. Sources were very specific about the goals of tourism development in the interviews. One definite goal for tourism development was to activate the community and especially 'Nellimin Pyry', the village folk dancing and heritage association. Even though they were also concerned about the numbers of tourists coming to the village, they said that they would be happy to receive more tourists outside the season.

The sources had been working with tourism for several decades and had a professional attitude towards the quality of tourism services provided. Both of the sources were involved in the tourism business in the nearby ski-resort area. They felt threatened by the larger tourism industry of the nearby resorts. They mentioned that some of the nearby hotels have started to run their own Nellim village tours in imitation of the villagers' concept.

Nellim village is a good example of community participation and tourism, as tourism products have been planned and realised by the local community. They have even become symbols of togetherness and local traditions of the village. At present, the amount of tourism is still manageable and beneficial to the local community. However, one of the largest threats for the local communities is the ageing of the population. As local services have been reduced, remote villages are no longer seen as being attractive places to inhabit by the younger population. One major reason is the fact that there are not many educational opportunities. The tourism industry is the main option for employment in addition to the traditional trades: reindeer herding, fishing and forestry.

Women and Empowerment in the Local Communities of Inari

Tourism has provided Sami and Finnish women with a possibility for both income generation and empowerment. A group of local arts and crafts women at Inari established a cooperative called *Handmade from Inari* (Inarista käsin). Cooperation between arts and crafts women started with exhibitions that they organised together in the hotels of a nearby ski-resort. Soon they noticed that they benefited from cooperation, as they could share the workload and costs. All the women had their own businesses and a cooperative was established in order to market their products. There were five women who established the cooperative and all of them worked in turns in a shop that the cooperative rented. The shop was located in the centre of Inari village and its high season was the summer season. Tourists from the ski-resort area also visited the shop occasionally during the winter season. The women also sold their arts and crafts products at different fairs and even took part in export projects. One or two of the women would sell the products at different fairs. This way they could save money in travel and hotel costs.

The various cooperatives and women's networks provide female artists with the support and encouragement they need in order to continue their work. Many female artists feel that they are not strongly supported by the local communities. It is always challenging to expose oneself to the critique and opinions of the local community if an artist is not producing traditional arts and crafts items, or is somehow breaking the boundaries of standard behaviour. However, in many cases, tourists are more open to the opinions of these women. For visiting tourists, it may be enough that a product is produced by a local person to make it authentic. Tourists may also have a broader concept of what is traditional, or they simply buy products based on aesthetic values. The tourists are sustaining a number of female artists and form an acceptable audience for their products.

One of the women spoke about her experiences from the beginning of the cooperative. She said that it was really difficult for her to break free from a closed Sami society and present her arts and crafts products in exhibitions. She was known as being a Finnish woman who had married a Sami man. She had stayed at home with the children but she had also wanted to have a job where she could take care of the children at the same time. Handicraft production was a craft that made both of these things possible. She knew that her products were of high quality, yet she felt a little bit intimidated by the Sami community, which was giving her negative comments about her traditional Sami arts and crafts products. She was breaking boundaries by producing traditional items as a Finn and not as a Sami. She was empowered by the success of the exhibitions and by the fact that she was able to sell her products to the tourists.

In 1993 she learnt how to felt lambs' wool and this was a real start for her business. She had a good artisan education in various arts and crafts skills and could learn more about felting. Gradually, she became a master in the art of felting. Today, she uses the nature and life in the Sami region as the source for her designs. One can find all the colours of different seasons and symbols of the Sami way of life in her work. The success of her products empowered her and she broadened her knowledge in felting by visiting various Turkish felt makers to learn more about this ancient craft.

As her own business developed and she started to have her own private exhibitions, she realised that she had come to an end with the cooperative. She had developed her own marketing and business concept that now worked independently. The EUROTEX project had helped in the development of special interest products: part of her product range had been developed during the project. One of the success stories of this development is her felting company. She succeeded in developing a good special interest product concept within ten years.

Her business is located in Lemmenjoki, which is approximately 40 km from the centre of Inari. Her husband runs a riverboat company and they have been involved in local tourism for 20 years. He sells boat trips to tourists. During the EUROTEX project, a cultural 'round-trip' tour was developed. Her felting company was included in the tour. She had planned a specialised tourism event for visitors. She would teach the visitor group some of the basic techniques in felting and inform them about her work and art. As a result of providing these events, she developed her idea of a Felt Art Studio where tourists could visit her, try out the technique and buy her products. She constructed a studio for the groups and it has turned out to be a success. She has developed a creative tourism product where visitors can try out something new and learn new things about the local culture and way of life.

Later, she developed a product with her husband where half of the group goes in a boat to wash gold and the other half stays with her and learns to felt wool. There is a tradition of gold expeditions in the Lapland region. At noon, both of the groups have a traditional meal made of reindeer. After this, the groups swap. She said that her goal is to focus on designing interior textiles and sell them to these special interest groups from her home. She also offers tourists a presentation of her felting technique and informs them about her artwork. At present, her business is fully thriving from tourism. She is selling only through her studio and through exhibitions. The future looks good for her. She is actively involved in different projects and marketing efforts to improve her business.

Sami Artist's Studio by Lake Inari

One member of the cooperative was a Sami artist whose special skill was porcelain painting. It was very interesting to learn about her experiences as a member of the cooperative. She was also an original member of the *Handmade from Inari* cooperative. She lives in a small village by Lake Inari, which is the same village where her family comes from. She used to live in the South of Finland for some years, but later returned to the village. The village is very close to the Norwegian border.

This particular Sami artist has her own studio with a beautiful view over the lake. Her experiences from the *Handmade from Inari* were rather good. The cooperative had offered her a place where she could sell her products and works of art. As an artist, she had already won several nominations in visual arts. She is a Sami artist who looks at her identity from different perspectives using modern art techniques and materials. Whilst being interviewed, she said that the local communities were wondering about her works of art, as she wasn't producing traditional Sami objects. However, it is easy to recognise the influence of the local natural environment in her work. Moreover, tourists are very fond of her products as they have very unique motifs related to Lappish nature, and her materials and techniques can fit easily into the average home. She was encouraged by the tourists who were buying her works of art and porcelain, and this success has helped her to form her identity as a contemporary Sami artist producing modern art and design products.

During the interviews she said that the cooperative served well as a sales outlet for her products. However, the problem with the cooperative was that they were taking turns in the shop when it came to selling the products. According to the interviewee: 'It takes a lot of effort to drive a couple of hundred kilometres and spend a day in a shop. It is also time away from your production.' After the cooperative stopped working she began to concentrate more on exhibitions and selling her artwork through them. She also began to work part-time as a local art teacher, which was more profitable for her. This job meant that she could now spend more time concentrating on her production and artwork. Occasionally, tourists would visit her studio from the holiday village nearby.

Tourism and Women's Empowerment

The history of the cooperative, *Handmade from Inari*, was very interesting, as it was a very powerful connector between the five women who took part in it. The cooperative worked as a marketing tool for the women and as a showroom where they could present their products for the tourists. It was also a social arena where the women could share the pressure coming from the local communities. Many of them explained how important it was to have colleagues with whom one could talk about the problems that a new entrepreneur has to face. They said that they met at the shop in order to discuss the cooperative and make decisions concerning it. However, they also phoned each other and were empowered by the support that they could provide.

It was also interesting to notice that the tourists had played an important role in the identity construction of two of the women. Both of them had broken free from the roles that the community had given them. Income from the sales of their artwork had provided them with an opportunity to develop their ideas and look for the business and working concepts that they felt good about. In some respect, the feeling of acceptance that they received through the success of their products was also an important factor in their identity construction. They received the acceptance from the tourists that they didn't receive from the local community. This empowered the women to continue their work.

The well known Sami researcher, Veli-Pekka Lehtola, writes about the Sami identity as a transforming resource that enables the changing and renewing of cultural identity. The Sami identity adapts to contemporary living. These two craftswomen are an example of women who have new cultural identities as Sami artists and modern business women (Lehtola, 1997).

Handmade from Inari was a small community of five women. It was a good example of a small active community that had its pros and cons. The women were active members of the community and together they could have more resources for marketing than everyone working separately. All the women had their own histories related to the cooperative, and it eventually provided something to all of these women. In the end, the cooperative should have been processed again according to the needs of the women. Many of them had been empowered and their needs and demands had changed. Although the cooperative stopped working in 2003, all of the women are now running their own successful businesses.

Conclusion

All three of these case studies illustrate different aspects of community-based tourism and rural tourism. Empowerment through tourism occurs when tourism is implemented through a participatory process, where locally based key resource persons are able to influence tourism development. Alenka Verbole, writing about rural tourism development in Slovenia, notes that the rural tourism process involves many social actors who continually reshape and transform policies through interaction and negotiation (Verbole, 2000). In many Lappish villages, key persons are involved in tourism planning and product design, yet local communities may see development strategies in a different way than the elite. Sustainable tourism development has good opportunities of success when the level of community participation is high.

In all of these case studies, tourism development has had some positive effect on local communities through income generation that sustains traditional or contemporary arts and crafts trades. Dallen discusses community-based tourism as a more sustainable form of tourism than mass tourism. Community tourism is grassroots empowerment where needs, traditions, culture and local identities are taken into consideration when developing tourism products and infrastructure (Timothy, 2002). Yet, there are serious concerns about the effects of tourism in the local community. Koppelo villagers were concerned about the number of tourists that villagers and the village environment could sustain. Small villages in many locations are also suffering from the effects of tourism concentration in ski-resort areas. The population in the villages is ageing and fewer services are available as they are transferred to the ski-resort areas.

The most surprising result of this research is definitely the empowerment of women in the local communities. Women were very active in creative industries such as visual arts, arts and crafts production, and theatre. Tourists were providing these women with an audience that the local communities couldn't provide. This benefited their identity construction and feeling of independence through income generation and self-esteem.

References

Richards, G. (1999) Culture, crafts and tourism: A vital partnership. In Richards, G. (ed.) *Developing and Marketing Crafts Tourism* (pp. 11–35). Tilburg: ATLAS.

Timothy, D. (2002) Tourism and community development. In R. Sharpley and D.J. Telfer (eds) *Tourism and Development: Concepts and Issues* (pp. 149–164). Clevedon: Channel View Publications.

Veli-Pekka, L. (1997) *Saamelaiset: Historia, yhteiskunta ja taide Kustannus-Puntsi* (pp. 86–87). Jyväskylä: Gummerus kirjapaino.

Verbole, A. (2000) Actors, discourses and interfaces of rural tourism development at community level in Slovenia: Social and political dimensions of the rural tourism development process. *Journal of Sustainable Development* 8 (6), 479–490.

Part 3
Authenticity and Commodification

Chapter 11

Cultural Tourism: Aspects of Authenticity and Commodification

NICOLA MACLEOD

Introduction

Discussions of authenticity and commodification pervade the literature of tourism studies and have been considered to be central to explorations of the sociocultural impacts of tourism since Dean MacCannell published his influential text *The Tourist* in 1976. The increasing influence of the tourism industry, the greater ease of travel and ever-widening arena of visited places have increased the urgency of debates on the impacts of tourism on the authenticity of cultures. These debates cluster around the ways in which tourism has impacted on the authenticity of the tourists' experience of places and culture, on the culture of the hosts themselves, on the nature of the host–guest relationship and on the production of cultural objects and events consumed (but not necessarily exclusively) by tourists.

This chapter explores the issues of authenticity and commodification within global cultural tourism through three case studies that reflect a variety of perspectives and concerns within these debates. The agents of change, including tourism, that have impacted on the concepts of the genuine within cultures are explored and the main theoretical approaches to the question of authenticity are outlined. The case studies hail from Brazil, Holland and Bali and, in exploring ethnic handcrafts, national souvenirs and dance performances, illustrate a number of important perspectives on this most pervasive of tourism issues.

Tourism as an economic activity has been blamed for the commodification of cultures. Objects and performances that were once created for local consumption become geared towards the tourism market and consequently are said to be exploited, debased and trivialised (Cohen, 1988). Such commodification can therefore be seen to destroy the authenticity of local cultural products and relationships and lead to the 'staged' or faked experiences created specifically for external consumers

(MacCannell, 1976). Such loss of authenticity is damaging to the host community and to the experience of the visitor. However, ideas surrounding authenticity and commodification in relation to tourism are more complex and contradictory than the above suggests. From the perspective of the tourist, the consumption of genuine products and experiences may be seen as being either the central raison d'être of tourism or as irrelevant to the enjoyment of a holiday. Consider a tailor-made holiday that takes a discerning traveller 'off the beaten track' to uncover the unadulterated culture of a remote community. Such a traveller will experience real events and rituals, buy authentic craft items, get to know the local people and will enjoy an experience based on hospitality and friendship. This experience is of course worlds apart from a theme-park-based vacation spent consuming simulacra in a completely artificial, purpose-built environment. Here the holidaymaker will consume events and products created specifically for the tourist market, will experience encounters and transactions that are purely financial and will spend virtually no time within the host community. Both of these holidays are popular products of the global tourism industry and to their consumers, we imagine that both experiences are equally 'real'. Are we to assume therefore that authenticity is simply a matter of taste and that real holidays are a form of niche tourism available for those with sufficient cultural capital to appreciate them? Obviously not. If we examine these two products more closely we may of course decide that the adventurous traveller is actually being presented with an inauthentic staged version of local tradition whilst the hedonistic theme-park reveller is honestly consuming a product that genuinely reflects the contemporary global culture of the host community.

The very act of being a tourist is to consume inauthentic and com-modified products and events and to consider contemporary tourism as being deleterious to the concept of authenticity is perhaps to romanticise the notion of tourism itself and to hark back to a 'golden age of travel'. Kevin Meethan suggests that:

> ...the processes of commodification, rather than being a side issue, are in fact central to the whole basis of tourism and, what is more, that tourism is one aspect of the global processes of commodification rather than a separate self-contained system. (Meethan, 2002: 5)

Despite the contradictions inherent in the admittedly reductionist examples above, traditionally the central concerns regarding authenticity and commodification within tourism rest on either the changes that tourism has brought to host destinations or to its impacts on the cultures of the tourists themselves. Thus, discussions revolve around the tourist, the nature of their relationships with hosts and the cultural products so central to the tourism industry.

The much-quoted work of Dean MacCannell, *The Tourist* (1976), first brought critical attention to the role and experience of the tourist within the ever-expanding 'tourist settings'. His concept of 'staged authenticity' suggested that in the modern world, real events and culture are increasingly hidden from tourists' eyes and instead, a variety of artificial experiences are staged for their consumption. MacCannell depicts the modern tourist as a hopeful creature, ever optimistic of discovering the authentic on their travels. However, their very presence as tourists, and the encroaching influence of the tourism industry renders this impossible. MacCannell's work is often contrasted with that of Daniel Boorstin, whose tourists in *The Image: A Guide to Pseudo Events in America* (1964) are rather less idealistic figures. Boorstin's tourists are actively in search of the pseudo-event – a contrived and artificial experience – and consequently are to blame for the lack of authenticity evident in the modern tourists' world. MacCannell believes that Boorstin's views reflect the elitist traveller–tourist dichotomy, a commonplace and simplistic approach that valorises the efforts of the energetic and independent traveller over the more passive and hedonistic motivations of the modern tourist (MacCannell, 1976: 104).

Concern has also frequently been voiced over the impacts of tourism on the host communities, in particular on the nature of the host–guest relationship and the cultural products of those communities. The increasingly commercial relationship between hosts and guests has been seen to adulterate both parties by reducing the apparently authentic tradition of hospitality to a mere commercial transaction. The cultural products of a destination are particularly important players within the tourism industry, as the case studies in this chapter exemplify. Cultural events, products and other markers are commonly used in place promotion and serve as tourist entertainment (as in the case of Balinese dance) and souvenirs (in the instance of delftware and Pataxó ethnic arts). Much has been written about the role that tourism has played in the adaptation of cultural forms, for example 'tourist art' (Graburn, 1976), the increasing 'heritagisation' of destinations (Hewison, 1987; Walsh, 1992) and the commodification and adaptation of rituals, dances and festivals for tourist consumption (Greenwood, 1989).

Tourism, Globalisation and Authenticity

Tourism has been a major agent of change both in host destinations and within the culture of the tourist-generating countries, which, until recently, have been the industrialised nations of the West. Tourism is clearly part of the process of globalisation that has transformed our identification with local cultures and replaced this with a global awareness. The ever-expanding communications network, intensified international travel flows and the increasing dominance of global brands supplying worldwide markets have contributed to the globalisation of tourism, cultures and economies. The notion of the 'global village' denotes a sense of community and shared cultural references albeit on an increasingly virtual, mediated plane. Global villagers are therefore becoming increasingly curious about, and capable of visiting, their worldwide neighbours, as forecasts of international tourist arrivals suggest. The World Tourism Organisation predicts that by 2020, 1.56 billion international trips will be made and that the new tourism-generating regions of India, Eastern Europe and China will contribute to this number on an increasingly significant scale, augmenting the multicultural nature of international tourist culture (WTO, 2001).

As long-haul travel becomes easier and cheaper and a maturing tourism market seeks differentiation through novelty, more and more regions of the world are entering the tourism industry and the tourists' points of cultural reference become increasingly global (Urry, 2002). Tourist sites and events are marketed on a global scale and have international significance and appeal, for example the growing list of UNESCO World Heritage Sites and international spectacles such as the Olympic Games. The mature tourist market is also keen to seek out more specialised, niche tourist experiences and thus the travel industry offers more special interest holidays to remote locations and unique, colourful cultures.

The globalising processes described above have led to the emergence of the postmodern condition (Harvey, 1989), which is characterised by a recent intensification of the changes set in motion within the modern period. Kevin Walsh (1992: 53) suggests that:

> [Post]-modernity is a condition – one which is not an experience of radical rupture, nor so different from modernity that the two share no characteristics at all, but rather one that is an intensification of those experiences and processes which emerged during the eighteenth and nineteenth centuries especially.

The experiences and processes indicated by Walsh include multi-national capitalism, transportation and mass communications, all of which have intensified over the last two centuries to create the phenomenon of time–space compression (Harvey, 1990) – the shrinking of distance and time so that events, financial transactions and communication can happen instantaneously. New technologies have promoted the culture of the mass-produced replica and the simulated experience to the extent that the postmodern tourist may actually prefer the reliability of the artificial hyper-real attraction as Umberto Eco describes in his *Travels in Hyper-reality* (1986). Urry notes that the character that he calls the 'post tourist' actually enjoys the playfulness of the simulated experience, aware of, yet revelling in, the artifice. Critics of contemporary culture have noted that postmodernism and tourism have created placelessness – spaces devoid of any local meaning or indigenous culture (Relph, 1976). Within these soul-less places, culturally impoverished individuals consume mediated experiences far removed from the authentic lives of their ancestors, who were in touch with their locale, the land, ancient traditions and their community. In this worldview, contemporary culture is characterised and greatly impoverished by its lack of authenticity. Conversely, postmodern theorists and post-tourists are unconcerned with issues of authenticity, which are now anachronistic. In this vision of the world, all places are simultaneously real and inauthentic and the traditional boundaries that existed between the real and the fake have dissolved.

The issues of authenticity and the commodification of cultures and places have continued to feature in the literature of tourism studies and in order to understand their enduring resonance it is necessary to explore the evolution of a theoretical perspective on tourism's relationship with these related discourses.

Theoretical Perspectives on Tourism and Authenticity

A number of commentators have deconstructed the concept of authenticity in an attempt to address the complexity of the ideas inherent in this issue. Selwyn (1996) accepts that authenticity may lie as much within the experience of the consumer as in the genuine object or event itself, as his categories of 'cool authenticity' (genuine and real) and 'hot authenticity' (admittedly fake but enjoyable) exemplify. Both Wang (1999) and Jamal and Hill (2002) differentiate between 'objective authenticity' – an externally verified truth; 'constructive authenticity' – an emergent form of authenticity; and 'existential authenticity' – an approach to the genuine that takes into account the individual's own experience. These three categories are a useful means by which to explore the discourse of authenticity and consequently they will be adopted here.

Objective authenticity

One approach to the question of tourism's impact on authenticity is based on the assumption that real and genuine touristic experience and products exist, can be verified as such, but are perhaps less easy to find in contemporary society. Importance is placed on objects made from what we consider to be authentic materials and by indigenous craftspeople or on events and rituals that we perceive as being traditional emanations of genuine cultures. As Wang (1999: 352) suggests:

> [o]bjective authenticity refers to the authority of originals. Correspondingly, authentic experiences in tourism are equated to an epistemological experience (i.e. cognition) of the authenticity of originals.

Therefore this approach to authenticity concentrates on original objects that provide genuine touristic experiences for those who recognise the authenticating signs. Schouten's case study of delftware souvenirs explores the importance that some tourists place on obtaining authenticated objects. Every piece of delftware comes with a certificate of authenticity and for overseas visitors these pieces have become synonymous with Dutch national identity. Cohen cites the work of Trilling (1972), who traces the provenance of the word 'authenticity' to the world of museums where experts authenticate objects using a range of strict criteria (Cohen, 1988: 374). Objects displayed in museums, and importantly, the information provided on these objects, are generally perceived by the visitor to be genuine and meticulously researched. The mode of display, the highly visible security and the temple-like architecture and atmosphere of the traditional museum all contribute to the aura of the genuine object and convince us that if reality exists at all, then it is to be found within these revered institutions. Of course the objectivity and authority of the museum and museum curator are now no longer taken at face value and museums are seen as products of the societies that support them: a selective treasure house reflecting past and contemporary power relations (Bennett, 1995; Macdonald & Fyfe, 1996). However, the idea that objective facts can be known about objects or historical events is still central to scientists, anthropologists and archaeologists who hold the view that 'an authentic historic event or site is one that has been scientifically and objectively situated in the original time period, setting materials etc. of that era' (Jamal & Hill, 2002: 84).

This approach to authenticity places emphasis on both the integrity of the materials and the context within which an object is made. Thus Cohen (1988) refers to a recent trend in curators of primitive and ethnic art to apply increasingly stringent criteria to the art in their museums: objects may have been made from traditional materials by a native craftsman but if they were produced primarily for the acquisition of outsiders then they were to be considered fakes (Cohen, 1988: 375). This approach is no longer valid as commerce and the intervention and power of the international art market are now considered to be a part of the authentic history of ethnic and primitive art.

MacCannell noted that the authentic is a characteristic of premodern or primitive societies and that modern tourists are on a pilgrimage to seek that lost innocence. Our contemporary lives have alienated us from the genuine experiences and relationships of our ancestors and from their close association with place. Instead of simply living our own lives, we are increasingly consuming experiences and products that are based on other lives and times and created by the tourism industry. Thus:

> [t]he modernisation of work relations, history and nature detaches these from their traditional roots and transforms them into cultural productions and experiences...Modern Man is losing his attachments to the work bench, the neighborhood, the town, the family, which he once called 'his own' but, at the same time, he is developing an interest in the 'real life' of others'. MacCannell, 1976: 91

The tourist then becomes a modern-day pilgrim in search of the authenticity and meaning that is absent in their own lives. As Jamal and Hill (2002) suggest, the very existence of tourism suggests a society who wishes to escape their own reality. Consequently, 'tourism and the tourist metaphorically represent the inadequacies of the modern world' (Jamal & Hill, 2002: 78). Indeed authenticity is essentially a modern concern (Cohen, 1988: 373) and one which particularly exercises the industrialised West. The Romantic Movement of the 18th century mourned the triumph of science and the loss of innocence effected by the industrial revolution and saw nature as being the centre of genuine emotions. The most celebrated Romantic poet, William Wordsworth, was an early tourist-pilgrim in the MacCannell mode, finding authenticity in the plaintive Gaelic song of a Highland girl encountered on his travels and described in his poem 'The Solitary Reaper' published in 1805. By seeing her as an authentic remnant of a primitive race, he at once exalts and objectifies her, turning her into yet another visitor attraction on his Scottish Highland tour (Aitchison *et al.*, 2002).

Thus the premodern is seen as a source of genuine, unadulterated culture. MacCannell (1976) suggests that 'primitive' people have no concept of authenticity and, as they remain unvisited, have not yet developed a system of 'front and backstage' to protect their privacy. Once visitors begin to arrive, communities set up staged events to satisfy their guests' desires for authentic, colourful cultural emanations. Meanwhile, backstage, real life continues unadulterated. Backstage regions become holy grails for adventurous independent travellers, but, MacCannell (1976: 106) suggests, they will never gain entry or stop being tourists: '...once tourists have entered touristic space there is no way out for them so long as they press their search for authenticity'. The truth is out there, but inaccessible to outsiders.

Constructive authenticity

Whilst the objective approach to authenticity assumes that real tourist experiences exist if only we could track them down, the constructive paradigm posits that reality is in fact a constructed phenomenon. This reality is created in our own minds, which are influenced by our personal worldview and external social, cultural and political factors. Thus notions of what is authentic are not static but emerge over time and are relative and negotiated. According to Wang (1999: 355):

> ...authenticity is thus a *projection* of tourists' own beliefs, expecta-
> tions, preferences, stereotyped images and consciousness onto toured
> objects, particularly toured Others.

However, these notions of authenticity are not simply an individual's perspective but are created and shared within communities. In their work entitled *The Invention of Tradition* (1983), Hobsbawm and Ranger explore how seemingly ancient traditions are created for contemporary purposes (including tourism) and very quickly become accepted as part of a community's or nation's history. The British Coronation ceremony, the Romantic iconography of Wales and the Scottish Highlands and the paraphernalia of nationhood (for example flags and national anthems) have all involved rituals and myths that have been deliberately, and relatively recently, created to induce patriotism, loyalty or even subser-vience and yet are considered to be authentic from both the community and the visitor perspective (Hobsbawm & Ranger, 1983).

Much of the concern about the adverse impacts of tourism on communities revolves around the commodification that inevitably occurs when societies are exposed to tourists, become economically dependent on tourism and eventually produce artefacts specifically for the tourism market. Graburn defines such production as 'tourist art' (Graburn, 1976) and this term reflects the fact that the cultural artefacts are produced not for an internal but an external audience. Grunewald's case study of the handcrafts production of the Pataxó people of Southern Brazil illustrates these concerns but demonstrates that an emerging sense of identity and new traditions are the benefits to be gained from the Pataxós entering into the tourism industry. It is apparent that three different types of products are made and recognised by both producer and consumer. Firstly, there are items reflecting indigenous traditions, secondly there are transitional objects that are made by native people but are inspired by external influences and thirdly there are nonindigenous pieces that represent global tourism influences. As Frans Schouten states in his case study of delftware, 'one can argue that there has evolved a kind of universal stock for souvenir retail on the tourism market... it is interesting in this respect that the "otherness" is emphasised with objects that are iconic for a feeling, not for the place itself'. The Pataxó people have developed their souvenir industry out of necessity but have used it to diversify their cultural production and gain a new sense of identity.

The tourism industry and its associated media are involved in the business of constructing authenticity as part of the product presented to visitors. Such articulations of reality become accepted by tourists as part of the package of holiday experiences and the power of the industry, the media and other stakeholders in creating attractive versions of reality is considerable. As Jamal and Hill (2002: 87) suggest, '...authenticity is not a quality of objects themselves, but one that is ascribed to them, often by those with the authority to do so'.

The stereotyping of cultures that the tourism industry has created become more real to visitors (and sometimes even to the local community) than the actual everyday life of societies themselves. Two examples from Scotland illustrate this point. In 1953, the Hollywood film producer Arthur Freed visited Scotland on a location hunt for a suitable village in which to set his film *Brigadoon* (1954), a whimsical tale about a Highland village that only wakes up for one day every hundred years. He was shown a number of genuine Highland communities but returned disappointed to Hollywood to film *Brigadoon* in a studio, claiming that 'I went to Scotland but I could find nothing that looked like Scotland'

(Hardy, 1990: 1). His film, replete with tartan, misty hills and bagpipes, reaffirmed the external image of Scotland that the Scottish tourism industry has used to its advantage in creating a highly recognisable 'brand' (McCrone *et al.*, 1995).

But residents also consume and renegotiate touristic images to create a new form of authenticity for themselves. A Scottish tourism boom followed the highly successful film *Braveheart* (1995), which exploited notions of patriotism and courage embodied in the character of hero William Wallace. Such images of Scottish valour represented at associated historic sites in Stirlingshire were consumed not just by overseas visitors but by young Scots, rediscovering their heritage through this highly glamorised touristic image of people and place. Ironically:

> ...in contrast to recognized profiles of tourists and visitors to heritage sites, many of Scotland's new visitors were young Scottish men with a reasserted interest in Scottish nationalism motivated by *Braveheart* and the exploits of an Australian actor (Mel Gibson) filmed largely in Ireland. (Aitchison *et al.*, 2002: 130)

Much about the film is inauthentic in objective terms but we must assume that the sense of identity that was produced is genuine.

The tourists themselves are also involved in what Cohen (1988) describes as the creation of emergent authenticity. Cohen's classification of tourists in relation to their attitude to authenticity produces a range of expectations from the existential tourist (one who spiritually abandons modernity and embraces the Other), the experimental tourist (one who experiments with a range of Others), the experiential (a tourist who wishes vicariously to participate in the lives of other societies), the recreational tourist (one who is seeking enjoyable relaxation and has a playful attitude to authenticity) and finally the diversionary tourist who is simply seeking amusement and has no concern for authenticity within their experiences. The recreational tourist seems similar to Urry's later post-tourist (Urry, 2002), who enjoys the artifice of staged authenticity whilst being aware that this is a game to be played. Their collusion in this game produces new forms of authenticity as Cohen (1988: 379) suggests:

> ...such tourists may playfully consent to buy fake products or experiences as if they were genuine, merely because their resemblance to the genuine thing gives these tourists an inkling of authenticity.

As part of tourism's dynamics, tourists may also be the instigators of creative innovation within host communities, as Grunewald explains in his case study of Pataxó tourism art. Here visitors have made suggestions to the Pataxó people for new objects to be sold as souvenirs. Non-indigenous earrings, hairpins and hats are now produced for the tourist market and represent the emergence of creative cultural adaptations through tourism.

Existential authenticity

We have questioned the notion of objective authenticity and explored the idea of an emergent, constructivist authenticity where meaning evolves over time. Authors have also argued for a more existential approach to the question of authenticity (Hughes, 1995; Wang, 1999) where the individual creates a sense of truth within themselves. The demands of everyday life have led to concerns that we are losing sight of our true selves – the simpler, more playful, natural selves that are repressed by work and responsibilities. The rituals of tourism include relaxation, freedom from constraint and a simpler, more pared-down routine based on sensual enjoyment. Therefore tourism itself can be seen not as a corrupting and commodifying influence but as a way of being that is genuine and natural. Wang suggests that 'as a contrast to the everyday roles, the tourist is linked to the ideal of authenticity' (Wang, 1999: 360).

Tourists involved in active participation rather than observation are more likely to experience a sense of existential authenticity. Ooi (2002) notes that there is more chance of this happening if cultural mediators absent themselves and allow the tourists to feel they are both part of the local community and experiencing culture bodily. Events such as the Balinese dance performances described in Barker's case study may become more meaningful if spectators were to take part in the touristic version of the dance. Having a sense of performing within a culture and creatively adjusting the body to the shape of the dance and the music will, Daniel (1996: 789) suggests, create an existential authenticity based on 'sensations of well-being, pleasure, joy, or fun, and at times, frustration as well'.

There may be few opportunities and places within our daily lives to experience such existential authenticity and so those environments that do offer such liberation have become increasingly prized. It has been argued that the alienation of people from the land as a consequence of the industrial revolution resulted in a fetishisation of Nature as a place of true repose and spiritual refreshment (Bunce, 1994; Coates, 1998). Tourism activities that involve a close association with the countryside such as camping or hiking are therefore popular because they allow individuals to test themselves and rediscover their essential selves. These tourists are seeking authenticity within themselves rather than in toured places or objects (Wang, 1999).

Wang suggests that existential authenticity can also be experienced within close family relationships that become more genuine and binding in tourism's ludic environments. Other relationships can be equally genuine however – the experience of being with a like-minded group or 'touristic communitas' is akin to a pilgrimage or rite of passage with the places and events being of secondary importance:

> Tourists are not merely searching for authenticity of the *Other*. They also search for an authenticity of, and between, *themselves*. The toured objects or tourism can be just a means or medium by which tourists are called together, and then an authentic inter-personal relationship between them is experienced subsequently. (Wang, 1999: 364)

The Case Studies

The following three chapters address the issues of authenticity and commodification from the perspective of cultural products based on local identity but produced for an external audience. The first case study explores the importance of souvenirs for reflecting what Schouten calls the 'spirit of place'. He traces the development of an authenticating process for souvenirs, namely delftware in Holland. These expensive, certified products, originally produced in China, have come to represent Dutch identity for overseas visitors and expatriates, whilst Dutch nationals have long ago stopped using these items in their homes. The association with the royal family and important institutions has created products that represent official Dutch culture but not the everyday lived experiences of the local community. Thus their apparent official authenticity make them attractive souvenirs and markers of Dutch culture for visitors. As receptacles of seemingly authoritative national culture, the production of delftware reflects the significance of apparently objective authority for the tourist.

Grunewald's case study explores a very different type of cultural product, the tourist art produced by the Pataxó natives of Southern Brazil. Forced into finding alternative means of supporting themselves when they lost access to hunting, gathering and agricultural activities, the Pataxós began producing handcrafted articles to sell to visitors. These items were based on everyday Pataxó objects but were more highly decorative for the tourist market. Soon, the range of items developed and began to lose their traditional function. Thus, three different categories of souvenirs began to appear – those reflecting indigenous traditions, those that are transitional (made by native peoples but with nonindigenous inspiration) and those that are nonindigenous and recognisable as global tourist souvenirs, for example ashtrays and carvings of saints. The interplay between tourist and producer and the emerging handcraft traditions of the Pataxós reflects the constructed nature of authenticity.

Finally, Barker *et al.*'s case study of the impacts of tourism on Balinese dance performances reflects the concerns that commodification of a spiritual ritual leads to loss of authenticity. Dance is an important aspect of Bali's cultural tourism product as well as having religious, political and social meaning for the Balinese people. Complex dances have been reworked and staged for tourist consumption in an attempt by the host community to protect the 'backstage' performance of authentic religious rituals. However it is suggested that the shortened tourist version is actually performed more frequently than the 'authentic' dance and is 'more relevant and acceptable to present day Balinese'. Thus the integration of touristic culture into contemporary Balinese society seems to highlight the emergent nature of authenticity over time.

References

Aitchison, C., MacLeod, N. and Shaw, S. (2002) *Leisure and Tourism Landscapes: Social and Cultural Geographies*. London: Routledge.

Bennett, T. (1995) *The Birth of the Museum: History, Theory, Politics*. London: Routledge.

Boorstin, D. (1964) *The Image: A Guide to Pseudo Events in America*. New York: Harper and Row.

Bunce, M. (1994) *The Countryside Ideal: Anglo-American Images of Landscape*. London: Routledge.

Coates, P. (1998) *Nature: Western Attitudes since Ancient Times*. Cambridge: Polity.

Cohen, C. (1988) Authenticity and commoditisation in tourism. *Annals of Tourism Research* 15, 371–386.

Daniel, Y.P. (1996) Tourism dance performances: Authenticity and creativity. *Annals of Tourism Research* 23 (1), 780–797.

Eco, U. (1986) *Travels in Hyper-reality*. London: Picador.

Graburn, N.H. (ed.) (1976) *Ethnic and Tourist Arts: Cultural Expressions from the Fourth World*. Berkley: University of California Press.

Greenwood, D.J. (1989) Culture by the pound: An anthropological perspective on tourism as cultural commoditization. In V.L. Smith (ed.) *Hosts and Guests: The Anthropology of Tourism* (2nd edn). Philadelphia: University of Pennsylvania Press.

Hardy, F. (1990) *Scotland in Film*. Edinburgh: University Press.

Harvey, D. (1989) *The Condition of Postmodernity*. Oxford: Blackwell.

Hewison, R. (1987) *The Heritage Industry: Britain in a Climate of Decline*. London: Methuen.

Hobsbawm, E. and Ranger, T. (eds) (1983) *The Invention of Tradition*. Cambridge: Cambridge University Press.

Hughes, G. (1995) Authenticity in tourism. *Annals of Tourism Research* 22 (4), 781–803.

Jamal, T. and Hill, S. (2002) The home and the world: (Post)touristic spaces of (in)authenticity. In G. Dann (ed.) *The Tourist as Metaphor of the Social World* (pp. 77–107). Wallingford, CABI Publishing.

MacCannell, D. (1976) *The Tourist: A New Theory of the Leisure Class*. London and Basingstoke: MacMillan.

McCrone, D., Morris, A. and Kiely, R. (1995) *Scotland the Brand: The Making of Scottish Heritage*. Edinburgh: Edinburgh University Press.

Macdonald, S. and Fyfe, G. (eds) (1996) *Theorizing Museums*. Oxford: Blackwell.

Meethan, K. (2001) *Tourism in Global Society: Place, Culture, Consumption*. Basingstoke: Palgrave.

Ooi, C. (2002) *Cultural Tourism and Tourism Cultures*. Copenhagen: Copenhagen Business School Press.

Relph, E. (1976) *Place and Placelessness*. London: Pion.

Selwyn, T. (1996) *The Tourist Image: Myths and Myth Making in Tourism*. Chichester: John Wiley & Sons.

Urry, J. (2002) *The Tourist Gaze* (2nd edn). London: Sage.

Walsh, K. (1992) *The Representation of the Past: Museums and Heritage in the Postmodern World*. London: Routledge.

Wang, N. (1999) Rethinking authenticity in tourism experience. *Annals of Tourism Research* 26 (2), 349–370.

WTO (2001) *Tourism: 2020 Vision – Global Forecast and Profiles of Market Segments*. Madrid: World Tourism Organisation.

Chapter 12
The Process of Authenticating Souvenirs

FRANS SCHOUTEN

Introduction

Tourism is about selling dreams. The core of the tourism industry is the commodification of escapism, the commercial answer to the longing of mankind for another reality beyond the dull and grey of the everyday life. Tourism is about experiencing beyond the ordinary, to step out of the daily treadmill into a more wonderful, exciting and challenging world. In this respect Mason rightly states that the core of the tourism product is to 'mystify the mundane, to amplify the exotic, minimize the misery, rationalize the disquietude and romanticize the strange' (Mason, 1994). We are really making quite an effort in improving reality. In his book *The Language of Tourism, a Sociolinguistic Perspective* (1996), Graham Dann explores the ways in which images of destinations are created and communicated and how language is used as a means of social control in sustaining the prototypical images of destinations. Ian Littlewood provides us, in *Sultry Climates, Travel and Sex since the Grand Tour* (2001), with a fascinating overview of how in the history of travel such prototypical images of other cultures have evolved, and how deep they are imbedded in the conceptions we have of destinations. These tourism dreams have to be sustained by both the consumer and the producer of the product and the perception of authenticity through souvenirs plays an important role in achieving this objective. Souvenirs as well as experiences are conceived as being authentic when they reflect the perceived core values of the visited destination. These core values are basically prototypical, but not always identical, they differ based on motivation for travel, previous experiences and expectations. Mary Littrell distinguishes tourists looking for souvenirs into *Ethnic, Arts and People*, *History and Parks*, the *Urban Entertainment* and the *Active Outdoor* (Littrell, 1994). Shenhav-Keller provides, in her paper 'The Jewish pilgrim and the purchase of a souvenir in Israel' (1995), a good insight into the way value systems determine the purchase of particular types of souvenirs. She also shows that in the exchange between buyer and seller meanings are attached to the choice of souvenirs.

In this contribution we will concentrate on the way souvenirs are authenticated. We focus on souvenirs as objects from a local arts and crafts tradition that are considered to reflect the 'spirit of the place' visited by the tourist. The tourists categorised by Littrell as the *Ethnic, Arts and People* people. This narrows the subject down considerably, for there is a whole range of souvenirs on the market that do not meet this criterion. We are not concerned here with Littrell's *Urban Entertainment* people or the *Active Outdoor* people. Many souvenir shops in mature destinations in Europe are catering for these groups and sell a wide range of objects that are not representative of the destination. In fact one can argue that there has evolved a kind of universal stock for souvenir retail on the tourism market, which is virtually the same all over Europe. Pictures of girls taking a bath in a pond are for sale everywhere, as well as portraits of children with a teardrop. And no one has been able to give me a reasonable explanation for the occurrence of sets of Japanese samurai swords in many souvenir shops all over Europe. Equally universally for sale are 'dream catchers', based upon a design that originates from Native American tribes. They are available all over the world, from Ireland to Bali. Their popularity remains so far unexplained but one could argue that they have become the very icons of the 'otherness' of a visited place. It is interesting in this respect that the 'otherness' is emphasised with objects that are iconic for a feeling, not for the place itself. The dream catcher as an omnipresent souvenir confirms in a way that tourism is dreamtime. The phenomena of 'universalia' in souvenirs at tourism destinations are an interesting field for further research.

A Conceptual Framework

Authenticity is a modern Western concept, closely related to the impact of modernity. Modernity is characterised by breaking away from tradition and the past into a realm where innovation and personal creativeness are favoured above walking the trodden path. In modernity discontinuity is both the expectation and the norm and as such has uprooted Western society. Westerners conceive their own cultural environment as inauthentic and they increasingly look for it elsewhere. They either seek it in 'unspoilt' exotic destinations, the past (the heritage experience), in nature (looking for paradise) or in the 'simple' life as in rural tourism (Dann, 1996). Despite the emphasis in tourism literature on the 'authentic experience', an authentic experience is not necessarily a good experience. Field research among tourists on an adventure tour in Latin America revealed the contrary: the more authentic the experience the higher the amount of complaints from the tourists. Local transportation falling into disrepair, basic sanitary provisions when local food is ruining your intestines and the confrontation with appalling poverty is, however authentic, not the pursuit they had in mind (Hermes, 1998). Rightly McKercher and Du Cros (2000: 40) remark that 'People want "authenticity" but not necessarily reality'.

As most of the tourists are Westerners, it is not surprising that the literature on authenticity and handicrafts is strongly dominated by Western authors. The emphasis Westerners put on creativity, originality and authenticity is not shared with all other cultures around the world. Some non-Western languages do not even have a word for 'copy'. In the East there is less emphasis on authenticity as it is currently used in modern Western societies. Hence the regular violations of international copyright in Asia and the availability of a rich variety of fake expensive trademarked and designed consumer goods. In the Javanese language the term 'son of' is used to differentiate between a remake and an original and there is not necessarily less value attached to the copy as long as it is within the tradition of good craftsmanship. The importance of craftsmanship and its traditions is also emphasised on the island of Bali. In the vicinity of Ubud there are many workshops catering for sculptures that are for sale all over Bali. Cats with long necks, 'African' masks, Egyptian figurines, 'Swiss' dollhouses and characters from 'Tintin' provide a thriving business. Critics complain that these have nothing to do with Balinese culture and that Bali has sold itself to tourism and lost its identity. The Balinese have a different perception and they are not ashamed of these sculptures. Interviews with producers and sellers of these products reveal that the craft of woodcutting as such is what the Balinese are good at and have done so for many centuries (Maas, 2002). Such an attitude makes clear that the act of sculpting is considered more essential for the cultural identity of the Balinese than the forms that are created in the act.

Not withstanding the emphasis in the literature on authenticity, most Western tourists buying these objects are equally unconcerned with authenticity in the classical sense as a reflection of traditional Balinese culture. They are also quite happy to buy locally produced Madonnas and carvings of Leonardo da Vinci's 'Last Supper' at Hindu temples. Touched by the holiness of the visited places they purchase their own icons of holiness as an affirmation of the experience. In a way it can be seen as a reconfirmation in a material purchase of a meaningful experience. In neglecting traditional Balinese design the tourists follow in the footsteps of the Balinese themselves. As most of the 'traditional' Balinese temples are not that old, there are many carved reliefs on them in which the Gods have exchanged their chariots for what now look like nice vintage cars. Likewise, some tourism experts have commented negatively on the development of a new type of monster at the Balinese New Year Festival. Traditionally effigies in the form of huge monsters are made in every village and neighbourhood to drive out the evil spirits from the island. There is a traditional design for these monsters, but increasingly other images are used as well to frighten the spirits. We noticed enormous Hells Angels on motorbikes and tourists depicted as drunkards with a beer bottle. Some view these as derivations of the original design, but one can also perceive them as proof of the vitality of the underlying belief system that uses new images of what locally is considered to be horror, to frighten off the evil spirits even more effectively.

There may be a valid question here whether the concern for the authenticity of local crafts and traditions is predominantly felt among anthropologists and tourism experts.

Authenticity has many different aspects of which the material authenticity is the most obvious. Material authenticity is expressed in aspects like the traditional materials for the production of the object, the genuine decorations used on the object and of course most preferably signed by the maker as the ultimate authentication. There is also the conceptual, contextual and functional authenticity (Ex & Lengkeek, 1996). These different aspects are not always mutually consistent. The conceptual authenticity refers to the original idea behind the object. The Egyptian stele, which is presented in a museum as Egyptian art, is conceptually however a funerary stone. Contextual authenticity is lost if altarpieces – designed to be looked at from a low position – are displayed in an art gallery on the same visual level as the observer. Functional authenticity is often lost in the act of preservation of the object. The functional steam train in its second lifecycle as a visitor attraction ceases to be an authentic means of transportation and is reduced to a tourist ride.

The tourists themselves are much less concerned with the subtleties of authenticity as described above, as long as there is a functional authenticity. Tourist consumption of the other culture is most of the time very superficial, even among the acknowledged cultural tourists. In his paper 'The ethnographer/tourist in Indonesia', Edward Brunner describes his experiences as a tour guide of a group of highly educated American tourists who were on an explicitly cultural tour in Indonesia, accompanied by academics to introduce them profoundly into the culture visited. While visiting Bali, he as an anthropologist noticed that in a certain temple a ritual would be performed that only takes place once a year. The timing of such an *odalan* festival is unpredictable and it is a performance that the Balinese put up for themselves. He decides to go there with the group for a genuine authentic experience. I quote from his description what happens at the site:

> Shortly after noon, the festival started, and it was spectacular. Elderly Balinese women began dancing in a line around the temple courtyard. ...Priests were sprinkling holy water, ... incense was burning, the gamelan playing, ... it was all happening at once, an ethnographer's paradise. At that point, just as the festival was beginning the tour director announced that we had to go back for lunch and that everyone should go back to the tour bus. I protested... Stay, I said, to see this dazzling ceremony. 'But we have seen it', replied one tourist as the group followed the tour leader back to the air-conditioned bus. (Bruner, 1995: 233)

Change in any society will occur, and certainly tourism is only one of the factors in this process. Modern communication systems most probably have a much bigger impact. These processes of cultural exchange are, however, at the same time as old as culture itself. Any culture in the world is shaped in an endless process of giving and taking. Culture is a phenomenon constantly in development, a living identity. Culture is a dynamic pattern and when it is forced into a static pattern it will cease to be a source of inspiration. When conservation of culture is turning into conservatism, the treatment will be worse than the disease and will eventually kill the 'patient'. Vital cultures are constantly interacting with each other. This interaction might lead to cultural change, which in the case of tourism is seen as a negative impact. However when the host population is in control of the process of change, cultural change does not necessarily have to be negative.

Cohen (1989) proposes that authenticity is 'a social constructed concept and its social connotation is therefore, not given, but negotiable'. To give meaning and to attach values to objects and memories is a personal construction and tourists are in this respect active creators of meaning rather than passive consumers. Nevertheless tourists seek regular authentication of their souvenir purchases. Authentication can be provided by experts, institutions and by assurances given by the vendor. In the contribution of Shenhav-Keller (1995), we see how authorisation is convincingly provided by the shop attendants of the *Maskit* handicraft retail chain. Meaning, significance and authenticity are constituted within the exchange between the customer and the shop assistant. In this exchange the 'negotiable' aspect mentioned by Cohen is obvious.

In most cases authorisation as confirmation of authenticity is provided by experts (Ex & Lengkeek, 1996) but as tourists are not usually exposed to experts they turn to so-called 'official' art shops, museum shops and specialised handicrafts outlets. In fact they look for some kind of institution to authorise the purchase. The most notable institutions in this case being museums. Their shops use the authority of the museum as a scientific institution as an added value in the choice of souvenirs they offer the visitors. You buy an object, obviously a copy, but acknowledged by experts as being representative of the best the museum has to offer. The British Museum marks these copies with a 'BM' stamp to distinguish them from the original but which at the same time 'authenticises' the objects.

A museum can also use its weight to authenticate the items for sale in its shop. The Fiji Museum sells souvenirs to which a label is attached telling the visitor that 'This is a reproduction of an authentic traditional artifact from the museum's extensive collection, made by a traditional craftsperson'. Note that in this case the term 'authentic' is used where 'genuine' would have been more appropriate. But obviously tourists are keener for authentic than for genuine objects.

That authentication is closely related to perceived power structures is clear in the above-mentioned examples. Existing power structures can also be applied to give authenticity to crafts. In the course of a cultural tourism development project for Central Java, the Royal Court of the Sultan of Yogyakarta was advised to use its prestige to promote genuine handicrafts as souvenirs. The idea was similar to the Fiji case: give a certain selection of genuine handicrafts a label stating that the item to be purchased has been selected for sale 'with approval of the Royal Court of Yogyakarta'. Apart from the foreign tourism market there was an additional advantage to this proposal. The sultanate is considered to be a holy institution on the island of Java. As a consequence such labels would mean for the rapidly increasing domestic market not just a genuine object of high quality, but a sacred and reverential object. Anything related to the Royal Court is – in the Javanese tradition – considered to be bestowed with a special power, called 'Pusaka'.

Authorisation is essential for arts and crafts souvenirs. In the following case study we will look into a Western example, for there is an abundance of non-Western cases in the literature. For the material of the following case on delftware I'm indebted to the description of the *De Porseleyne Fles* by Debby van der Zalm in her BA thesis.

Aspects of Authentication of Delftware as a Tourism Product

Delftware, white china with decorations in blue, is for tourists to Holland the ultimate souvenir to take home. And for good reasons, for it is considered to belong, next to wooden clogs, to the core of the Dutch culture. The fact that delftware does not originate from Holland, but is based on ceramic techniques (Majolica) the Dutch adopted during the Spanish domination in the 16th century, is of little significance. When trade with the Far East was opened, the Dutch imported enormous amounts of porcelain from China. As the original chinaware was sold in Europe at astronomical prices, the Dutch were among the first who used the Majolica technique in the 17th century to imitate the original white and blue chinaware. Porcelain was an unknown material, so efforts were made to produce this Eastern product with indigenous clay. Especially in Delft and Rotterdam, the efforts succeeded. Soon this was done on a vast scale. Around 1650 more than 30 potteries existed in Delft alone. In the 18th century the delftware industry was in decline. Production of high-quality china shifted to England, where Cookworthy invented white baking clay, which offered a more superior product than the Delft factories could produce. The French soon followed the British in the china factories of the Sèvres porcelain. This new china did not need a white glaze covering and much more sophisticated decorations were made possible due to the transparent glazing. By the middle of the 19th century only one factory *De Porceleyne Fles*, had survived, although they had in the meantime given up the production of the so-called 'old delft' and had started to mass-produce cheap pressed earthenware.

In 1876 Joost Thooft bought the factory with the intention to revitalise the old traditions of the production of blue delftware and the factory has been operating ever since, working in the same tradition. Craftsmen decorate delftware by hand. All painters of *De Porceleyne Fles* are trained at the factory for one year. It is, however, only after five to seven years that they can call themselves experienced delftware painters. Landscapes and portraits are painted by painters graduated from a Dutch academy of arts, and only these painters can become a master painter in due time.

As evidence of the appreciation of the efforts to re-establish the tradition, *De Porseleyne Fles* was granted the title 'Royal' in 1919.

Since 1879 delftware has been coded with a bottle, the initials of Joost Thooft (JT) and the word 'Delft'. At the left side under this trademark are the initials of the painter and at the right-hand side an indication of the year in which the item was made. In fact there is a triple authentication, for apart from the trademark that each product of the *De Porceleyne Fles* carries there is – as an additional form of authentication – a 'certificate' issued. This certificate guarantees the genuineness of the product as hand painted, according to a centuries-old tradition. On top of that there is the authorisation provided by Royal appointment.

The visitors to *De Porceleyne Fles* are predominantly tourists from abroad, in particular American and Japanese tourists prevail. Most visitors participate in a guided tour; this includes a visit to the factory and a visit to the 'museum' where, in a typical 'backstage' setting, a painting demonstration is given. Annexed to the 'museum' is the showroom, where the items are available for sale. Note that here the term 'museum' is being used in an attempt to give even more credibility to the souvenirs for sale than is already provided for in the certificates that are issued when an item is purchased.

Interestingly enough, *De Porceleyne Fles* does not consider itself as part of the tourist industry, but as a crafts industry. In distancing itself from the tourism market the factory makes an effort to give an extra authentication to the product. The relationship between the product and tourism is however evident in the fact that the high season for the factory coincides with the flowering period of the tulips. It is highly unlikely that this crafts industry would be able to survive without the sales made to tourists. In that sense there is not too much difference between delftware and woodcarving on Bali or the production of traditional textile handicrafts in the Andes.

It is interesting to notice that the shop of *De Porceleyne Fles* contains not only items produced in the factory, but also objects produced elsewhere on a more industrial scale. The distinction is made very clear to the visitors and in doing so another layer of authenticity is added to those already available. These noncertified objects are available as affordable souvenirs for visitors, whereas the cheapest item from the exclusive collection from the factory is about €40. This sales strategy is coherent with the findings of Kim and Littrell (2001) in 'Souvenir buying intentions for self versus others'. The less tourists are aware of specific ethnic qualities or generic qualities of handicrafts in a given cultural environment, the more their purchase intentions shift towards items with a high iconic value that is perceived to be unique for the destination. This can be a T-shirt with imagery of the destination or iconic markers such as ceramic windmills, tulips and wooden clogs, etc. in the case of *De Porceleyne Fles*. The more iconic type of souvenirs are also purchased as souvenirs for friends and relatives.

The products of *De Porceleyne Fles* are – apart from its own shop – retailed through a limited number of other sales outlets. Intentionally these shops are not specifically souvenir shops but more sophisticated shops for home decoration. Again we see here an effort to dissociate the product from the tourism industry. Also through this type of retailing an effort is made to sustain the exclusive image of the delftware, but even in these shops the buyers generally are foreigners or Dutch citizens buying gifts for foreign friends. It is a pattern that is applied in other destinations as well with quality handicrafts. The souvenirs sold in the *Maskit* chain of souvenir shops in Israel as described by Shenhav-Keller (1995) operate on an identical principle of exclusiveness.

When we look at the production of *De Porceleyne Fles* from a technical point of view, it is 'authentic' in the sense that it is still made in the traditional way and decorated by hand, very labour intensive, and it is accordingly expensive. Looking at it from a conceptional perspective it is 'authentic' in the sense that it was originally manufactured predominantly as decorative objects, just as its actual functional use as tourism souvenirs. Delftware however has ceased to be a decorative feature in modern Dutch households and is made exclusively for a foreign market. As souvenirs the attached values and connotations are in the terminology of Cohen 'negotiable' and the factory anticipates those connotations and perceived values in the range of decorations they offer to their customers.

De Porceleyne Fles however does not only produce for tourists or visitors to the factory. Also Dutch embassies, ministries and other government agencies are important customers of the factory, which also produces especially commissioned delftware as gifts to foreign dignitaries. Such emphasis strengthens the iconic nature of the items. The fact that delftware is used by the Dutch as a gift to foreigners mirrors and reinforces the image foreigners have of the Dutch. The reinforcement of prejudice is in any case much easier to achieve than trying to oppose it.

Although in the Netherlands delftware is considered to be outdated as a distinctive ornament, it is interesting to notice that for Dutch people who emigrated to the USA, Canada, Australia or New Zealand delftware still is used as an expression of their 'Dutchness'. An affirmation of their distinctiveness as a group follows the conventions of the perceived 'others'. Such is even more so the case in the earlier Dutch Diaspora in

South Africa and Sri Lanka. For a 'Burghers' household in Sri Lanka the amount of delftware decorative elements is an indication of how deep someone is rooted to the Dutch colonial times in Ceylon. It is a status indicator among white Sri Lankans with Dutch ancestry (Orizio, 2000). The same phenomenon can be seen in reverse among Dutch citizens of Indonesian ancestry in the Netherlands. In their houses traditional handicrafts from Indonesia are used as memorabilia that affirm a different identity.

As mentioned earlier, delftware is also manufactured on an industrial scale apart from the traditional and authenticated production of *De Porceleyne Fles*. As everywhere else this production for the tourist market leads to adaptations of the original design. As we can see in many examples all around the world, usually the items become smaller and consequently easier to transport, preferably in larger quantities. Also other forms of delftware appear on the market that did not exist previously in the 'old' tradition, such as delftware puppets in traditional Dutch costume (otherwise also virtually obsolete), delftware 'wooden shoes' (a contradiction of terms) and miniature traditional Dutch houses as can be seen alongside the canals. These vulgarisations obviously are far beyond the level of the production of *De Porceleyne Fles*.

Conclusion

The tourism industry at a destination depends heavily on the image it has in the eyes of its actual and potential customers. Much effort is bestowed both by public institutions and private companies to sustain these images and the value systems that are attached to them. Souvenirs play an important role in establishing and preserving the image of a destination. Many souvenirs reflect the 'spirit of the place' visited whether or not their design is based upon tradition or just reflects the state of mind of the visitor. In particular, arts and crafts souvenirs, which are considered to be an integral part of the tangible heritage that the destination has to offer, are important icons to sustain the image of the destination. In order to fulfil that role handicrafts for sale – as souvenirs – have to meet certain expectations of the buyers. Generally these expectations are expressed in concepts of 'authenticity', 'genuine', 'original' and 'traditional'. The tourist as a layperson is insecure in the purchase of handicrafts, not so much in what they like, but whether their choice represents the above-mentioned values. The tourist seeks confirmation of authenticity. This 'authorisation' of authenticity is to be provided by persons or institutions that are trustworthy. The 'expert' is the prototype of these trustworthy institutions, but they are relatively scarce at destination level. For a tourist access to experts is far from obvious, even if they are around. Often the role of the 'expert' is incorporated in an institution of some kind. Museums can play, in this respect, a vital role as the 'authorisation' institution. In the process of commodification of handicrafts the industry can disguise its commercial character in the form of a museum to add the authority of the institution to the enterprise. Expertise is perceived as a form of dominance or 'power' over the layperson, so it does not come as a surprise to see the role of the expert taken over by other power structures. These power structures can be related to the fabrication of the handicraft in the form of 'official' shops or certified sales outlets or by a certification of the purchased item, either by outside bodies or by the manufacturer. In some cases these power structures relate only by association, as in the case of 'royal' approval or appointment. Generally speaking the 'seller' is not the person to be associated with the expert. However the more trustworthy the sales outlet can make itself, either with certification or any other official status, or is able to support its claim of expertise with the outward symbols of power, the more the seller is in a position to negotiate a special status towards the buyer. The more successful the seller is in this game, the more effective he will be in helping the tourist to purchase the most valuable physical evidence of his visit.

References

Bruner, E. (1995) The ethnographer/tourist in Indonesia. In M.F. Lanfant, J.B. Allcock and E.M. Bruner (eds) *International Tourism, Identity and Change* (pp. 205–223). London: Sage.

Cohen, E. (1979) A phenomenology of tourist experiences. *Sociology* 13, 79–203.

Cohen, E. (1988) Authenticity and commoditization in tourism. *Annals of Tourism Research* 15, 371–386.

Cohen, E. (1989) Primitive and remote, hilltribe trekking in Thailand. *Annals of Tourism Research* 16, 30–61.

Dann, G. (1994) Tourism and nostalgia: Looking forward to going back. *Vrijetijd en Samenleving* 1 (2), 65–74.

Dann, G. (1996) *The Language of Tourism, a Sociolinguistic Perspective.* Wallingford: CAB International.

Ex, N. and Lengkeek, J. (1996) Op zoek naar het echte? *Vrijtijdstudies* 14 (1), 24–41.

Hermes, G. (1998) In the eye of the beholders, the expectations and experiences of tourists travelling through Equator in search of authenticity. BA Thesis, NHTV Breda, University of Professional Education.

Hitchcock, M. and Teague, K. (2000) *Souvenirs: The Material Culture of Tourism.* Aldershot: Ashgate.

Kim, S. and Littrell, M. (2001) Souvenir buying intentions for self versus others. *Annals of Tourism Research* 28 (3), 638– 657.

Littlewood, I. (2001) *Sultry Climates, Travel and Sex since the Grand Tour.* London: John Murray.

Littrell, M.A., Baizerman, S., Kean, R., Gahring, S., Niemeyer, S., Reilly, R. and Stout, J. (1994) Souvenirs and tourism styles. *Journal of Travel Research* 33 (1), 3– 11.

Maas, M. (2002) Reisbijlage. *Volkskrant*, 19 October, 26.

Mason, G. (1994) The 'Fakelore of Hawaii', manufactured myths. *The Eye* 11 (4), 56– 60.

McKercher, B. & Du Cros, H. (2000) *The Fundamental Truth about Cultural Tourism.* Paper Seminar, Hong Kong.

Orizio, R. (2000) *Lost White Tribes.* New York: Free Press.

Shenhav-Keller, S. (1995) The Jewish pilgrim and the purchase of a souvenir in Israel. In M.F. Lanfant, J.B. Allcock and E.M. Bruner (eds) *International Tourism, Identity and Change* (pp. 143– 158). London: Sage.

van der Zalm, D. (2001) Changes in the production of authentic local handicrafts caused by tourism. BA thesis, NHTV Breda University of Professional Education.

Chapter 13
Pataxó Tourism Art and Cultural Authenticity

RODRIGO DE AZEREDO GRÜNEWALD

Introduction

As of the second half of the 20th century, 'tourism impact' and 'tourism development' have deserved more attention not only on the part of social and economic sciences, but also of enterprising agents themselves, who invest political, economic and even symbolic capital in specific societies. Cultural as well as economic changes have noticeably taken place in those societies. Often such changes have been thought of in terms of large-scale acculturation against tourism impact, that is to say, tourism development would make natives from small hosting societies abandon their traditional lifestyle to engage in local businesses fed by tourism development (Smith, 1989). In other cases, the emphasis was on certain traditions that were turned into tourist attractions, and therefore an integral part of a local tourism development perspective. Tourism economic effects on the arts and crafts industry have deserved special attention, as tourism has served to regenerate traditional industries by extending the market to native products. In some cases such products have been kept unchanged; as a rule, though, they have undergone changes (while others have undergone development) to meet tourists' expectations for exoticism, or small, easy-to-carry pieces. In fact, such artefacts, in the opinion of Graburn (1989), are key to a tourism 'journey', when souvenirs are, in addition to 'memories of experience' (materialised), also tangible evidence of a trip tourists share with their family and friends when they return home.

Tourism art is made up of handcrafted products manufactured for external audiences, not familiar with the cultural and aesthetic values of the society that produces it (Cohen, 1993a: 1). These art pieces are not identical to the original objects manufactured in a given society, but rather, in the opinion of Appadurai (1986), correspond to the traditional objects that have undergone changes as a response to commercial and aesthetic imposition on the part of consumers, often from far-away lands. Therefore, these are commercial products that have gone through a 'heterogenisation' process (Cohen, 1993b) to be turned into tourism art, often driven by market imposition through tastes, preferences and demands from a new audience.

The heterogenisation process involves authenticity issues. Cohen (1988) has suggested that ethnic arts should not be classified based on the authenticity versus falsity dichotomy, but rather, on a continuum between one end and the other, with a number of in-between states that may find grounds in authenticity experienced from the point of view of tourists. Littrell *et al*. (1993), for instance, have reported tourists' listing of attributes that would label souvenirs they buy on their trips to be recognised as 'authentic'.

The traits tourists have in their minds to authenticate a cultural product are then focused. If authenticity is not stagnant, but negotiable, then I suggest we take into consideration the possibility of their gradual variation, not only in the eyes of visitors, but of producers and other social actors that have kept some sort of relationship with the *social life* of those pieces as well (Appadurai, 1986), so as to attest their authenticity.

Additionally, as suggested by Chambers (2000: 111):

> We tend to trivialize tourist objects, and when their touristic nature becomes obvious, we are tempted to regard them as fakes. It is worth keeping in mind that, when a 'host' community becomes dependent upon tourism to one extent or another, the goods that it produces specifically for tourists are as authentic in their own right as are any other objects.

If tourists' interests can contribute to alter native objects, 'The challenge is to figure out what, in specific cases, this means for the owners of such traditions' (Chambers, 2000). Therefore, tourist (ethnic) art should not be judged authentic based on the questioning of whether it has been kept unchanged for a long period of time, but rather on its *social vitality*. As Duggan (1997: 31) has stated: 'An authentic culture is not one that remains unchanged, which seems impossible under any condition, but one that retains the ability to determine the appropriateness of its adaptations.' Based on this view I intend to focus on Pataxó handcrafts: by examining the emergence of their ethnic, tourist arts, and how they are perceived by tourists, as well as by Pataxó natives themselves and the population in that region in general in terms of authenticity.

The Pataxós and the Emergence of Tourism Handicrafts

As recently as the mid-20th century, Pataxó natives now located at the extreme South of the Bahia State sea line in Brazil lived in the village of Barra Velha (and adjacent woods), in the most Southern area of Porto Seguro, more precisely, halfway between Caraíva and Corumbau Rivers, also bordering the Atlantic Ocean to the East and Mount Pascoal to the West. The Pataxós underwent severe privation in the 1950s, and especially in the 1960s, when the Brazilian Institute of Forestry Development (IBDF) created the Mount Pascoal National Park (PNMP), in 1961, and the Pataxós were banned from hunting, gathering and agricultural activities. In the early 1970s, upon noticing the severe survival crisis the Pataxós were facing, a high official from the Indian National Foundation (FUNAI) suggested and taught them how to manufacture handcrafted articles that could be sold to visitors to the region, especially after the opening of Highways BR 101 and BR 367. Although not really realising the commercial implications, the Pataxós started necklace production.

In late 1972, one of the natives living in the Barra Velha area moved to Coroa Vermelha (located between Porto Seguro and Santa Cruz de Cabrália municipalities centre), and settled at the very location where the Brazil Discovery Site would later be located. In the following year, some families also moved from Barra Velha to the same location to start marketing their artefacts. In 1974, highways, the Discovery Sites and First Mass landmarks were inaugurated in Coroa Vermelha in a ceremony in the presence of the President, Ministers and other key government figures. At the time, the area did not have electricity, and the population was exclusively made up of fishermen and small merchants. The opening up of paved highways and the creation of a tourism centre with nationalistic appeal acted as an incentive for regional, specifically tourism-related economic development. Intense real estate speculation followed, as well as the building of hotels, bed and breakfasts and restaurants, associated with local colonial architecture restoration. Entrepreneurs began an increasing flow of migration from other states; the Pataxós also started migrating, with a view to develop commercial relations with the tourists that had started being attracted to the area. In contrast to the hippies that had wandered around with their backpacks before the highways were opened up, investment and entrepreneurial activities gave access to growing, mass domestic tourism focusing on both historical sites as well as recreation on the beautiful local beaches. The latter form of tourism is the one that has prevailed in Coroa Vermelha up to the present time.

The Pataxós have kept pace with that change, and have created an urban, commercial Indian village, with its economic basis exclusively attached to commercial interaction with tourists. If in the second half of the 1970s the natives from Barra Velha (a village that had not been reached by tourists) had to walk up to 40 miles on one day to sell their handcraft in Porto Seguro – whether in the retail market, to city visitors, or in wholesale, to city shops – the Pataxós, in their turn, either sold or exchanged their objects (basically necklaces and loincloths, but also some bows and arrows) exposed on cloths on the ground (or hanging in strings between wood poles) under the First Mass Cross. Handcrafted articles are the main source of income for natives in both Pataxó villages nowadays, and practically the only source in Coroa Vermelha, where natives have given up their former agricultural activities in their home villages to specialise in the production and in the commercialisation of handcrafted art.

Today, handicrafts are not the same as daily, common-use objects from former times. Their wooden objects included, for instance, in addition to the traditional canoes, bows and arrows – always kept for hunting – ('quite simple work', that is, different from the ornamented and carved work for tourists), sticks, baskets to carry manioc from plantation, vine baskets and wicker baskets (used for fishing), palm leaf sleeping mats (very special, soft water palm trees) and wicker bags. There were also large bath troughs. The plates, bowls, spoons, combs, etc. they manufacture today are from later development though, as they ate from coconut shells or calabash gourds. They also manufactured loincloths, and usually ornamented their headdress with feathers from colourful birds – immediately forbidden by the IBDF when the National Park was created. The current handcrafted work is very recent, having developed after tourism started, and usually decorative, or playing the part of souvenirs.

As of the 1980s, handcraft started changing in both villages: either existing pieces were changed, or new objects were added to be an integral part of goods to be marketed, but also to help define Pataxó identity. With mass tourism quickly growing in Coroa Vermelha, many non-native merchants started selling objects that competed against native handcraft. Natives, in their turn, quickly changed their craft. The old, large bowls were changed into profitable handcraft for purchasers' use, and changed into plates or dishes of different formats.

Handcraft variety follows the decorative logic required by the tourism art market. Through the development of its craftsmanship Coroa Vermelha exhibited what Costa and Monteiro (1971) called a *'kitschenisation process'*, that is, the *kitsch* element incorporated by Brazilian native population groups as a result of Western culture (Costa & Monteiro, 1971: 126). In its wide sense, bearing in mind that *kitsch* stands for 'an artistic production associated essentially to sales, and having lost its traditional function' (p. 128), all Pataxó craftsmanship marketed both in Coroa Vermelha and Barra Velha would be *kitsch*.

The handcrafted art sold at Coroa Vermelha is quite varied, and can be classified into three kinds: those representing indigenous traditions – although also considered *kitsch* from their 'functional inauthenticity', the objects are made by natives and bear clear reference to that; the transition objects (handcrafted by natives, but from nonindigenous inspiration); and those that are representative of nonindigenous traditions. The first kind includes: bows and arrows, spears, loincloths, gourd rattles, necklaces, headdresses, traditional troughs, etc. The second kind includes: troughs with welded inscriptions such as 'Souvenir from Porto Seguro', heart-shaped troughs, wood clubs, wood knives, forks and spoons, etc. The last kind includes clearly nonindigenous pieces that are sold by the natives such as ashtrays, manioc meal dishes, slippers, caps, hammocks, bags, natives' statues, gargoyles, saints, rugs and numerous typical tourism items, some of them clearly *kitsch* in the tourism art style, others folkloric, etc. Despite such miscellany at the Coroa Vermelha handcraft town centre, natives can tell exactly which items are associated to their traditions, although often they try to lure tourists by saying, for instance, that the colourful feathers are 'xukakai' feathers (chicken), rather than giving the straightforward information that they paint chicken's feathers.

The competition against 'White men' should also be taken into account in sales. Up to the late 1980s, handcrafted art was sold exclusively by natives. After the introduction of wood troughs and other wood items, 'White men' also started producing (even at plants, such as in Itamaraju) and marketing such items not only in Coroa Vermelha, but in Porto Seguro as well, and usually at a lower price than the natives. Moreover, it was easier for natives to buy troughs in the wholesale market and sell at their tents than to manufacture them themselves. As for quality standards, these are closely associated to price, as tourists are not interested in knowing whether pieces are made of jacarandá wood, macawood or common rue – they want a good bargain, at one price.

In Barra Velha, though, artisanship innovation followed a different direction because of the social interaction with tourism in Caraíva – a neighbouring village where solitary travellers or backpackers are the main visitors. At first, Barra Velha craft was exclusively indigenous (necklaces, loincloths, etc.), but as time passed, many orders started being placed with the natives. Very skilfully, those natives started making other products, and included objects that were not traditionally indigenous. In Barra Velha, though, all handcraft is manufactured by natives, and among them necklaces, plates, spoons and little troughs should be highlighted. Actually, what seems to be a specific trait of the Pataxós is the commercial handcraft practice more than the handcraft itself – although it does contain their style and trademark. Materials used are from nature, in contrast to Coroa Vermelha, where materials are also bought.

It has been mentioned that Barra Vermelha natives used to go on walks to sell their objects in the past, but today, tourists come to the village. Barra Velha handcraft is also sold in Caraíva, either by natives that go there (especially children), or at tents that belong to natives' friends or relatives, usually open in the high summer season. Caraíva is a small fishing village where locals and entrepreneurs who have moved in do not allow mass tourism to have access. They have dedicated their efforts to attracting youngsters – not interested in comfort, but rather a meeting point for fun, lively summer parties – and couples as well as people in general who are looking for a quiet place to rest and relax. Those very visitors were the ones to start making suggestions for objects to the Pataxós at those locations, often placing orders for the wholesale market, and thus instigating changes or innovations in Barra Velha craft, such as earrings. The most common model sold these days was designed by Argentinian women, or blades made of turtle shell and ordered by people who are interested in cocaine sniffing, or hair pins called *jarri*, which originated from the first order for *hachis* (chopsticks) by a Japanese visitor to the Pataxós, or the wicker hat brought by a *hippie* who had learned to make it from natives from another region in Brazil and taught the Pataxós how to do so, as well as many other cultural adaptations. Other pieces are also ordered for the wholesale market, such as wooden combs, which have even been sold to Spain.

The Pataxós see this material culture revival as a regular flow for their commercial, productive activity. In the opinion of one native chief, commercial handcraft production is a result of money dependence to buy medicine, clothes and other 'White men's' items. As their lives have changed from their interaction with tourists, the Pataxós even have fun when asked about their lifestyle in the forest. They say they hunt for 'kaimbá', which, in their recently 'retrieved' language means money. But their chief is concerned about the fact that this 'kaimbá hunt' has been leading natives to abandon their 'original handcraft' (children are actually hardly familiar with it). The chief still intends to 'retrieve' it, though. Therefore, although the Pataxós go on working and focussing their efforts on innovations, order placements and demands, some individuals do show concern about 'not forgetting what is ours'; which means to say, to give visibility to original, utility (functional) handcraft concurrently with profitable, modern development, and especially to exhibit it at a Cultural Centre (a museum) to be founded at the village, and where not only tourists but also Indian children could keep in mind the objects and how they were used by their ancestors. However, efforts to organise the people who are able to produce such 'original' handcrafted pieces have not been successful.

Tourism Art and Ethnic Identity

The primitive art concept is not synonymous with this traditional handcraft, neither for style reasons (Boas, 1955) nor for authenticity reasons (Errington, 1994), as the Pataxós are not a primitive population. In addition, Pataxó arts (or artisanship) cannot be judged as Benjamin (1969) sees authenticity. In *artistic* terms, the Pataxós work would better be divided into ethnic and tourism arts, despite Barbosa's (1995) call for the differentiation between art (associated with the concept of new and experimental) and handcraft (associated with the concept of tradition). What is being done is to associate handcraft with tradition. Moreover, if there is any dichotomy between art and artisanship in terms of individual creativity for the former, and collective tradition for the latter, then we must concur with Canclini (1997) that such a dichotomy is actually an obstacle to the advancement of popular art forms. Let us see how Pataxó handcraft is linked to the Pataxós' identity.

Graburn (1976: 1) brings forth his idea of the Fourth World: 'collective name for all aboriginal or native people whose lands fall within the national boundaries and techno-bureaucratic administrations of the countries of the First, Second, and Third Worlds. As such, they are peoples who are usually in the minority and without the power to direct the course of their collective lives'. The arts of these populations would rarely be produced for their own consumption, following their own taste, without any modification. Therefore, the study of the arts of the Fourth World is different from the study of 'primitive' art, characteristic of most earlier anthropological writings, for it must take into account more than one symbolic and aesthetic system, and the fact that the arts may be produced by one group for consumption by another. The study of Forth World arts is, par excellence, the study of *changing* arts – of emerging ethnicity, modifying identities, and commercial and colonial stimuli and repressive actions. (Graburn, 1976: 2)

So, the creation of external consumption objects points towards a special relationship between craft-producing populations and tourism consumers. Often, those objects compete with imported manufactured items and must be subject to innovation and change through not only the availability of new techniques but also continually changing tastes and ideas at different points in time, while at the same time remaining acceptable for consumers worried about buying visually authentic objects rather than understanding native symbolism (Graburn, 1976).

It so happens that an ethnic group's identity goes on reformulating itself as the group's objects are updated. Ethnic identity is constructed, as are objects and their authenticity. And that emphasises the ethnic element in tourism arts that are dependent not only on defined ethnicity but on direct contact between tourists and producers for success.

It seems Nason (1984) has also gone in the same direction while looking at the interactions that took place in Micronesia between tourism, handcraftsmanship and indigenous perceptions. For him, a focus on craft production allows for the understanding of a given native population's perception of foreigners. The analysis of such inter-related data suggests that changes in craft making are the result of socially and economically generated tourism impact, which is also closely associated with ethnic identity perception.

Commodification and Authenticity

To probe Pataxó tourism art commodification authenticity a little further, one could start by looking at how their objects are seen by visitors and by 'natives', as well as how their identity is emphasised through their crafts.

Firstly, it is well worth noting that following in the footsteps of crafts, other traditions have been adapted by the Pataxós as a result of wide-reaching social interactions generated by tourism flow. If craftwork has opened the way for such social interaction, the process of tradition building to promote Pataxó ethnicity followed. In the early stages of craft practice, those natives did not use Indian names, neither did they speak a Pataxó language. Along with crafts, many tourists wanted to know their names, and were surprised to hear Christian names in Brazilian Portuguese. The natives were then suddenly aware of the relevance of bearing *Indian names*, and started using them, as their marketing strategy, especially in their tents while selling crafts at Coroa Vermelha. Tourists also wanted to know about their language. As they spoke Brazilian Portuguese, they decided to start using words that were allegedly Pataxó, to impress visiting tourists at their points of sale. That led many natives to create words, always used in the Brazilian Portuguese language structure. Finally, tourists also asked about dances and music, which led them to create traditions in that area as well. Actually, their crafts made the Pataxós realise the need to present a unique culture, as visitors demanded. Such cultural construction led to a conscious identity production, to a certain extent politically orchestrated, and with consequent enhancement of ethnic unity feelings with the new traditions that had been created (Grünewald, 2001; 2002).

But 'locals' – generations of families living in the area – have been familiar with the Pataxós for a number of years, and know that such traditions have only recently been produced. While in Coroa Vermelha natives are not legitimated as authentic, in Barra Velha such an argument is taken indifferently. Which is to say, Caraíva locals – usually fishermen from the neighbouring Barra Velha – do not develop their discourse on the issue of native culture authenticity. The 'White locals' in their turn – usually merchants from other regions in the country – refuse to acknowledge cultural legitimacy to Pataxó production, also based on the criterion of recent creation of craft and cultural items. As a whole, tourists see them as 'acculturized', and are aware that their objects are not actually 'traditional'. They do not pose the authenticity issue, though, as they see Pataxó items as lovely *souvenirs* to take home for themselves or as gifts for friends. The tourism experience seems to sponsor some sort of complicity between tourists and the tradition-creating natives, resulting in the explosion of the dichotomy between authenticity and simulacrum, as some tourists are willing to share the tourism experience of tourism culture creation (assuming they are tourists purchasing tourism material). But this is not the general rule, and the discussion on the lack of originality of the *tourism natives* is still an ongoing issue. As for the Pataxós, they differentiate between their old objects for regular use and the new ones for sale, while considering them contextually identical. The problem they face is related to advertising: in that area, entrepreneurs, the media and the government promote Bahian culture, and *baianidade* (Bahian-ness), while totally neglecting Indian cultural production. Advertising and promotion, with foreign incentives, of tours and excursions, festivals, food, dance, music, history and souvenirs are only channelled to *baianidade*, hegemonic in the area. Nevertheless, Pataxó objects are well known in different towns and cities in Brazil and Europe, through wholesale purchases and re-sale activities. Anyone who is familiar with Pataxó craft can clearly identify it anywhere (flea markets, airports, etc.). Their objects, even after commodification, are landmarks of their ethnic identity.

The question of authenticity still worries natives though. Pataxó traditions are authentic, of course, as they were created by them and are an integral part of their culture. The question is that in the view of people in general, what should be shown is not what has been fabricated for the tourism arena, but what is 'natural', existing ancestrally, because that is how common sense still expects to authenticate (or legitimate) traditions. Though the Pataxós see this cultural creation process as legitimate for utility purposes, they are hesitant towards invented traditions. The traditions generated in the tourism arena are either for sales (crafts) or to emphasise, as a marketing strategy, craft sales. If an 'authentic native' is presented – and the more authentic the better (here I think of the natives exhibiting a contrast to tourists'/travellers' daily experiences) – then the tourism appeal is greater in the market.

I do not mean to say that invented traditions for commercial interaction in the tourism arena are content void or meaningless for the Pataxós. They are traditions produced from their own background as natives in that region, as well as the aggregation of cultural elements external to the ethnic group, which begin to acquire updated significance for the construction of the very identity of the group.

Additionally, the Pataxó example shows that cultural commodification does not necessarily destroy the significance of cultural products. When tourism oriented, they can take up new meanings for their producers, 'as they become a diacritical mark of their ethnic or cultural identity, a vehicle of self-representation before an external public' (Cohen, 1988: 383). However, the old meanings may also 'remain salient, on a different level, for an internal public, despite commoditization' (p. 383). Finally, if the product transformation through commodification keeps traits that meet tourists' expectations, then they will be kept as authentic in the eyes of those consumers. That way, before taking up commodification, destructive impact on authenticity and the significance of cultural products, I do believe, as does Cohen (1988), that such impact should be submitted to a detailed empirical analysis. The case of Pataxó crafts illustrates well a process of commodification of objects like the trough – present in their memories as something of domestic use, deep in the forests, from remote times. Therefore, it retains internal significance and cultural continuity in the group, while also acquiring new meanings (and formats) following tourism market expectations and not losing authenticity, because while maintaining a reference to the old Indian lifestyle, it also represents their modern commercial configuration.

At this point it is relevant to realise the emergence of a new cultural context. For Simpson (1993), whatever is successful for tourism consumption also defines the parameters of legitimacy and authenticity for native audiences. Whatever is offered to tourists' eyes as images of the dominating host culture is what local population groups should also look at and consider as the mirror image of who they are. Tourism is then turned into a relevant means through which the sense of shared aesthetics and collective identity emerge, or what Anderson (1989), in the context of nationalism, has referred to as 'imagined community'. In this sense, tourism would be truly culturally creative, and the craft traditions built by the Pataxós and enhanced by tourism are authentic, legitimate, positive and connotative of their inherent cultural creativity.

Acknowledgements

The author thanks Regina Alfarano for the English version.

References

Anderson, B. (1989) *Nação e consciência nacional*. São Paulo: Ática.

Appadurai, A. (1986) Introduction: Commodities and the politics of value. In A. Appadurai (ed.) *The Social Life of Things: Commodities in Cultural Perspective* (pp. 3–63). Cambridge: Cambridge University Press.

Barbosa, W. (1995) La artesanía y el tráfico simbólico entre poblaciones del nordeste brasileño. *Artesanías de América* 46 (47) CIDAP, 131–152.

Benjamin, W. (1969) A obra de arte na época de suas técnicas de reprodução. In J.L.F. Grunewald (ed.) *A idéia do cinema* (pp. 55–95). Rio de Janeiro: Civilização Brasileira.

Boas, F. (1955) *Primitive Art*. New York: Dover.

Canclini, N. (1989) *Culturas Híbridas*. São Paulo: EDUSP.

Chambers, E. (2000) *Native Tours: The Anthropology of Travel and Tourism*. Illinois: Waveland Press.

Cohen, E. (1988) Authenticity and commoditization in tourism. *Annals of Tourism Research* 15 (3), 371–386.

Cohen, E. (1993a) Introduction: Investigating tourist arts. *Annals of Tourism Research* 20 (1), 1–8.

Cohen, E. (1993b) The heterogeneization of a tourist art. *Annals of Tourism Research* 20 (1), 138–163.

Costa, M.H.F. and Monteiro, M.H.D. (1971) O *kitsch* na arte tribal. *Cultura* 1, Brasília, 124–130.

Duggan, B.J. (1997) Tourism, cultural authenticity, and the native crafts cooperative: The eastern Cherokee experience. In E. Chambers (ed.) *Tourism and Culture: An Applied Perspective* (pp. 31–57). New York: SUNY.

Errington, S. (1994) What became authentic primitive art? *Cultural Anthropology* 9 (2), 201–226.

Graburn, N.H.H. (1976) Introduction: The arts of the fourth world. In N.H.H. Graburn (ed.) *Ethnic and Tourist Arts: Cultural Expressions from the Fourth World* (pp. 1–32). Berkeley/London: University of California Press.

Graburn, N.H.H. (1977) Tourism: The sacred journey. In V. Smith (ed.) *Hosts and Guests: The Anthropology of Tourism* (pp. 21–36). Philadelphia: University of Pennsylvania Press.

Grunewald, R. (2001) *Os Índios do Descobrimento: Tradição e Turismo*. Rio de Janeiro: Contra Capa.

Grunewald, R. (2002) Tourism and cultural revival. *Annals of Tourism Research* 29 (4), 1004–1021.

Littrell, M.A., Anderson, L.F. and Brown, P.J. (1993) What makes a craft souvenir authentic? *Annals of Tourism Research* 20 (1), 197–215.

Nason, J.D. (1984) Tourism, handcrafts, and ethnic identity in Micronesia. *Annals of Tourism Research* 11 (3), 421–449.

Simpson, B. (1993) Tourism and tradition: From healing to heritage. *Annals of Tourism Research* 20 (1), 164–181.

Smith, V.L. (1989) Introduction. In V. Smith (ed.) *Hosts and Guests: The Anthropology of Tourism* (pp. 1–17). Philadelphia: University of Pennsylvania Press.

Chapter 14
Authenticity and Commodification of Balinese Dance Performances

TANUJA BARKER, DARMA PUTRA and AGUNG WIRANATHA

Introduction

Dance performances form a major part of the global cultural tourism trade. Dance performances can capture expressions of culture within a visually appealing and culturally distinguishable, yet universally under-standable form. However, the impacts of tourism on dance performances have sparked widespread debate, not excluding Balinese dance perfor-mances. Bali is renowned for its exotic and colourful dances and they are frequently used in tourism promotions abroad. An important aspect of the debate centres on the ability of dance to perpetuate meaning for the Balinese people in the light of commercialisation.

This chapter provides an overview of some of the commercialisation and authenticity tourism issues that have been raised in relation to Balinese dance performances. The barong dance is used to illustrate some of the changes that have taken place. The literature, as well as the authors' research on this topic in May–July 2002, is drawn upon. The predominant fieldwork methodology used for the authors' work was informal interviews with dance troupe performers and managers at the Southern end of the island between Denpasar (the capital city) and Ubud, the major tourist region in Bali. In order to gain an understanding of Balinese dance performances, a brief description is provided below.

Tourism in Bali

Bali is a leading international tourism destination. Populated by approximately 3 million people on a land area of 5633 km^2, Bali is situated in the middle of the Indonesian archipelago and is located just south of the equator. The island is a popular destination in the Asia Pacific region given its close proximity to key cities, for example, the flying time from Singapore is 1.5 hours, whilst it takes only 2.5 hours to fly from Perth (Australia) to Bali.

The small Indonesian island region faces numerous tourism challenges given its fame as a tourist destination, its small size, and Bali's politicoeconomic and religious context. For example, the success and consequent reliance on tourism in Bali has spurred an influx of migrant labour and low-quality tourism products (such as imitation souvenirs) onto the island, whilst the numerous economic and political setbacks in Indonesia have led to periodic declines in tourist numbers. Further, given the popularity of Bali with international tourists and it being a predominantly Hindu island located within a dominantly Muslim Indonesian archipelago, the island is vulnerable to acts of violence, as the 12 October 2002 'Bali bombings' have unfortunately illustrated.

While the Bali bombings have had a detrimental effect on tourist numbers and the local economy, efforts to rebuild and enhance its attractions, in an environment of continued stability, is likely to mean that Bali will recover and retain its status as a leading tourism destination, especially as a leading cultural tourist destination.

The Dutch colonised Bali in the early 1900s and the island subsequently became part of the Dutch-controlled East Indies. Major events since then include the fall of Indonesia to the Japanese in WWII and independence in 1949. Evidence of international tourism in Bali is noted as early as the mid 1920s to early 1930s when the Dutch operated five day tours to the island as a result of favourable reactions stemming from a Balinese orchestra performance in Paris (McKean, 1989). But it was not until the late 1960s and early 1970s that the Indonesian government actively began to capitalise on Bali's famed culture by promoting Bali as a mass tourist destination through the development of infrastructure and the implementation of a tourism master plan that emphasised the promotion of cultural tourism (Picard, 1995).

Today, Bali is still renowned for its rich and unique culture. According to a tourism survey undertaken by the Bali Tourism Office in 1997, more than half (56%) of the foreign tourists surveyed were interested in the Balinese people and their culture (Wiranatha, 2001). Many foreign academics including anthropologists, ethnomusicologists and artists have also built their reputation by conducting research on the island. They have become known as 'Baliologists' and have helped to shape our general understanding or misunderstanding of the island. It could be argued that external commentators provide a privileged point of view that shapes the 'way of seeing' Balinese culture and provides voice to certain minority perceptions while silencing 'others'.

Particular attention has been given to Balinese dance performances, which constitute an important element of the cultural tourism trade.

Dance performances are a visible, outward manifestation of Balinese–Hindu culture (Carter, 2000) and constitute the main avenue through which the great majority of tourists are able to sample pieces of Balinese culture (Picard, 1996a). They also exemplify the exotic and cultural difference through the use of colourful costumes, rhythms and gestures (Daniel, 1996) and they have been used extensively in tourism promotions abroad and as a form of tourist entertainment in hotels, restaurants and specifically designated venues in Balinese villages (Carter, 2000).

Balinese Dance Performances

The diversity of dance performances in Bali is staggering (Eisenman, 1989). Dances can range from modest solo dances to elaborate troupe performances, but in almost all cases dances are accompanied by gamelan (orchestra) players. The rich diversity of dance can be partly attributed to villages having their own interpretations of particular styles.

In Balinese–Hindu society, dance performances have multiple layers of meaning. At religious temple ceremonies and rites of passage celebrations, dances are conceived as an individual and communal offering to the Gods (Askovic, 1998). As Dwikora and Hartanto (2001) note:

> A ritual dance is actually an invitation to the gods and ancestors to descend (tedun) from their holy place. When the dancers go into trance, this is a sign that the deities are in attendance at the rite.

The practice of these dances thereby helps to sustain and reinforce religious ties for Balinese people.

In close conjunction with the religious calendar, the most elaborate dance performances were often held at the royal palaces during precolonial times (Askovic, 1998; Picard, 1995). By investing, organising and training dancers and musicians, the royal courts were able to showcase the strength and splendour of their kingdom whilst affirming their ties to old kingdoms and, indirectly, to the Gods (Askovic, 1998). Dance performances therefore also have a political function. While the courts have been disempowered (Askovic, 1998), they continue to play an important role in the development of the performing arts. Similarly, modern-day political parties have also used dance and other art forms to further their interests and to ease recruitment of new party members (Dwikora & Hartanto, 2001). It is not surprising therefore, that apart from the religious and political functions dance has a universal social and entertainment function.

The Effects of Tourism on Balinese Dance Performances

As expressions of a living culture, dance performances are dynamic and open to interpretation and therefore change through time. Whilst various arguments have been proposed as to the extent to which tourism versus other modernisation and globalisation forces have impacted upon dance recitals, the fact remains that tourism is an agent of change. Rather the essence of the argument is 'the amount, the direction and the rate of change (that tourism has induced) and the degree of power communities have over these changes' Carter (2000: 3).

In a tourism context, dance performances are essentially a form of entertainment to be traded on the marketplace. Tourism has therefore added a capitalist element to a previously religious, social and political activity (Askovic, 1998). Economic forces that concentrate on fulfilling the needs of tourists have pressured dance troupes to adjust dance performances. For example, solo dances such as Topeng have been created by taking them from their religious and dramatic context; versions of court dances, such as Legong have been simplified; tourist specific dances have been created such as Panyembrama (Askovic, 1998); and various dances have been shortened and packaged to cater towards tourists tastes and attention spans (Picard, 1995).

However, much debate continues about the impacts of tourism on Balinese dance performances. In essence, this debate centres on whether or not tourism will enhance or destroy the object of its attention (Picard, 1995). Several authors have adopted opposing stances on this debate by either espousing the positive effects or by purporting the negative influences of tourism (e.g. Francillon, 1990). More recent accounts provide a more integrated perspective, viewing hosts as active participants in the construction of tourist experiences (e.g. Picard, 1996b).

Similarly, the incorporation of dances specifically adapted or created for tourists into ritual contexts has sparked much debate (Picard, 1996a). Picard (1996a) accuses Balinese people of confusing tourist and religious performances and thereby producing a 'touristic culture'. He retraces the history of the welcoming segment of the Legong dance package. In response to protest over the use of the Pendet dance (which has traditionally been used to pay reverence to divinities in temples) for tourist welcoming purposes, the Panyembrama was created. However, the tourist version eventually replaced the Pendet dance in temple ceremonies. It could be argued that the tourist version of the dance is more relevant and acceptable to present-day Balinese. Whether or not relevance equates to authenticity however, is debatable.

The Balinese actively began to voice their concern during the 1970s, but the provincial government of Bali did not provide a set of regulations until 1997. These regulations specified that:

- Dance troupes have to register and the condition of registration is that the individual dance troupe adheres to certain quality standards.
- Minimum wage standard is set at 20,000 rupiahs or about €2 per dancer for an hour's performance; and
- The type of dances that can and cannot be performed for tourists in hotels and restaurants are classified as either sacred or non-sacred performances.

Yet what often seem to be missing from the debate, or are not fully acknowledged in the foreign academic literature, are the perspectives of dance troupe performers. The sacred 'barong' dance will be discussed next to provide insight into the meanings associated with Balinese dance.

The Barong Dance

The barong dance-drama is popular amongst tourists and locals alike. The dance essentially represents the eternal struggle between good (the Barong) and evil (Rangda – the witch) (Carter, 2000). The main character of the dance, the Barong, is a mythical masked beast believed to date back to Bali's pre-Hindu era (Sanger, 1988: 91). The barong mask can take on the form of a mystical beast or a variety of animals. It requires two performers to hold the costume and frame together (made from bamboo and string) and through their performance of various movements, they are able to portray a wide range of emotions (Sanger, 1988). The dance-drama can be comprised of five acts or more, with a variety of supporting casts used to portray supporting figures in the story.

Towards the end of a full-length performance, which generally lasts for three or more hours, dancers enter a trance-like state and this can involve dancers stabbing themselves with daggers (Sanger, 1988). It has been said that on certain occasions, specific types of foods such as chicken and manggis fruit is needed to help them to snap out of this trance. It has been noted that tourists did not view dancers devouring several live chickens as the kind of 'traditional' culture they wished to experience (Sanger, 1988: 93).

In light of the above, I Madé Kredek, a famous dancer of Singapadu, designed a shortened, one-hour tourist version of the barong dance-drama for the village (Sanger, 1988). This contained a brief, well controlled, simulated trance section, minimal dialogue and the inclusion of humour to overcome cultural barriers (Sanger, 1988). Female dancers were also included to portray female characters previously performed by male dancers. Sanger reported that this basic barong format was still being used for tourist performances in Singapadu in 1988. Further, it is worthwhile noting that changes to aesthetics, particularly in relation to costumes, may be due to a deliberate attempt to suit the taste of the tourist market. For example, one of the case study participants has modified the appearance of the barong mask to more closely resemble the Chinese lion seen in other parts of East Asia to appeal to the growing number of tourists from this region.

Authentic or Commercialised?

As the above example indicates, differences between the traditional and tourist versions of the barong dance-drama are substantial. Whether the staged tourist version of the barong dance is a satisfactory experience for tourists remains uncertain. It may be that tourists are satisfied with shortened, simplified versions of Balinese dance performances that they view as being 'authentic' within a tourist context.

However, what about the impacts on the host? This remains hotly debated (McKean, 1989; Picard, 1996a; Wiranatha & Putra, 2000). Villages in Southern Bali tend to have at least one barong, as the barong has traditionally been used to protect villages from evil forces (Sanger, 1988). Whilst the barong may no longer be used to treat such evils as illnesses, it is still used in ceremonial performances (Sanger, 1998). As one performer relayed to us in more detail, sacred barong masks and costumes possess a spirit that can be awakened during performances:

> During the creation of a sacred barong, a special ceremony and offering is held to invite a holy spirit to enter and stay in the barong. When the barong dance-drama is performed in the appropriate time and place, during a special performance, the barong can look different. It is alive, it has spirit. Sometimes the spirit of a lion or a mythical bird is invited and the person will dance like a lion or a bird. (Balinese dance performer, interviewed June 2002)

Various views have been expressed in terms of the effects that tourism has had on barong spiritual powers for Balinese ceremonial rituals.

McKean (1982) mentioned that the power of a barong had diminished in one village due to its repetitious use in village tourist performances. Our interviews also indicated that tourist presentations in general are the most frequently performed, ranging from daily to twice a week performances, whereas dances performed purely for religious or ritual purposes are performed less frequently, between five times to once a month. This is not surprising, given that the dance troupes interviewed are commercially focused. However, this can indicate that frequently performed dances for tourists have the potential to impact upon their meaning during ritual purposes.

In the village of Singapadu, other barongs have been produced specifically for commercial tourist performances since 1962 to avoid desecration of their oldest and most spiritually powerful barong (Sanger, 1988). While one solution might be to use a different barong mask for ritual ceremonies, others suggest that performances should not be held within temples, to maintain their sanctity. Yet others believe that as long as ritualistic offerings are made beforehand, the context of the performance should not matter. Still other Balinese disagree with the use of barong in tourist performances altogether (Wiranatha, personal communication 1999, in Carter, 2000).

Of those dance troupes interviewed that were financially viable, positive benefits of tourism were expressed such as increased creativity and dynamism and the need for a politically stable and safe environment to make it more conducive for more tourists to visit. Those that were financially struggling and older respondents tended to express more cautious views and concern for sacred dances. This could indicate that those who benefit most economically support their source or that tourism does mainly have a positive effect for these respondents.

There is no doubt that tourism has brought some economic benefits, given the number of community and private dance troupes that have sprouted up in Bali, especially in the major tourist regions. According to Picard (1996a), of the 5000 troupes listed by the provincial cultural service, the tourist industry supports about a hundred dance troupes, which equates to about two to three thousand musicians and dancers, with most being located in the two principal tourist regions of the island – Gianyar and Badung. Some dance troupes solely specialise in barong dances and provide daily performances and have the ability to cater to a capacity crowd of over 300 people.

However, for all the investment that the Balinese put into their culture, and for all the concerns that have been raised about the commercialisation of dance, the question is raised whether the majority of Balinese dancers actually gain their just financial rewards from tourism. The minimum wage standard for a performing dancer in 1997 was set at 20,000 Rp per hour (The Provincial Government of Bali, 1997), which equates to only about €2 per hour. Many tourist businesses such as hotels, restaurants and travel agents (the majority of which are non-Balinese owned) deal through brokers, rather than with the dance troupes directly. The unequal power relations and the competitive economic environment created, especially in times of crises, are conducive to an environment where dancers are subjected to below minimum wage standards. As Wiranatha and Putra (2000) have noted previously, this is exploitation rather than promotion of culture for 'Balinese culture is used and misused, rather than the other way around'.

Conclusion

Tourism has attributed change to Balinese dance performances. The concerns that have been expressed, such as the development of a 'touristic culture' by Picard (1996a), should be heeded if tourism changes the fabric of Balinese dance performances. We cannot stress enough the importance of including local perspectives in the continued theoretical debates concerning the commercialisation and authenticity of Balinese dances performances. Ultimately Balinese dances and the changes to them are best understood by those who perform them and who attach cultural meaning to them. This requires the translation of existing Balinese work and the collation of more in-depth information on Balinese perspectives to inform the broader international debate. Not only will this allow for a more balanced interpretation, but it will also embed academic perspectives within local reality.

The current economic power distribution in the Balinese tourism industry has contributed to the low remuneration rates provided to Balinese dance performers. Below minimum wage standards for performers implies a power imbalance and a negative relationship between the amount invested in culture and the monetary rewards gained. Ramifications such as a decrease in the quality of dances performed are therefore likely to occur.

The work to date seems to suggest that there are diverging opinions amongst Balinese dance troupes and this could indicate that dance performers themselves are also grappling with the concept of authenticity, making it a hard concept to enforce. In order to protect Balinese customary performances, it is important that a common understanding amongst dance troupes is developed and adhered to.

In order to gain further insight into the demands of tourist performances and the meanings that visitors attach to Balinese dance recitals, it is also important to gain the perspectives of tourists, across the viewer spectrum from the 'package' tourists to the repeater 'connoisseur' tourists. Further, these perspectives should not just be confined to Western tourists, but should also encompass other tourist cultures, especially those from the growing Asian market, who are likely to place different demands and expectations on performances. One possible management strategy could be to target the high calibre end of the market, as opposed to promoting Bali as a cheap holiday destination. This will hopefully encourage and sustain the more authentic forms of Balinese dance performances.

References

Askovic, I. (1998) Creating modern traditions in Balinese performing arts. *Explorations in Southeast Asian Studies* 2 (1), 64–81. On WWW at http://www.hawaii.edu/cseas/pubs/explore/v2/v2n1-askovic.html. Accessed 7.02.02.

Carter, R.W. (2000) Cultural change and tourism: Towards a prognostic model. PhD thesis, University of Queensland.

Daniel, Y.P. (1996) Tourism dance performances: Authenticity and creativity. *Annals of Tourism Research* 23 (1), 780–797.

Dwikora, P.W. and Hartanto, H. (2001) Dance and power. *BaliEchoMagazine.com*. On WWW at http://www.baliechomagazine.com/features/dance_power.html. Accessed 17.10.02.

Eisenman Jr, F.B. (1989) *Bali: Sekala and Niskala Volume I: Essays on Religion, Ritual and Art.* Singapore: Periplus Editions.

Francillon, G. (1990) The dilemma of tourism in Bali. In W. Beller, P. D'Ayala and P. Hein (eds) *Sustainable Development and Environmental Management of Small Islands.* Paris: UNESCO & The Parthenon Publishing Group.

McKean, P.K. (1982) Tourists and Balinese. *Cultural Survival Quarterly* 6, 32–33.

McKean, P.K. (1989) Towards a theoretical analysis of tourism: Economic dualism and cultural involution in Bali. In V.L. Smith (ed). *Hosts and Guests: The Anthropology of Tourism* (2nd edn, pp. 119–138). Philadelphia: University of Pennsylvania Press.

Picard, M. (1995) Cultural heritage and tourist capital: Cultural tourism in Bali. In M.-F. Lanfant, J.B. Allcock and E.M. Bruner (eds) *International Tourism: Identity and Change* (pp. 44–66). London: Sage.

Picard, M. (1996a) *Bali: Cultural Tourism and Touristic Culture.* Singapore: Archipelago Press.

Picard, M. (1996b) Cultural tourism in Bali: The construction of a cultural heritage. In W. Nuryanti (ed.) *Tourism and Heritage Management* (pp. 147–164). Yogyakarta: Gadjah Mada University Press.

Richards, G. and Hall, D. (2000) The community: A sustainable concept in tourism development. In G. Richards and D. Hall (eds) *Tourism and Sustainable Community Development* (pp. 1–13). London: Routledge.

Sanger, A. (1988) Blessing or blight? The effects of touristic dance-drama on village live in Singapadu, Bali. In *Come Mek Me Hol — The Impacts of Tourism on Traditional Music* (pp. 89–104). Kingston: Jamaica Memory Bank.

The Provincial Government of Bali (1997) *The Management of Regional Arts*. Regulation no. 394 and 395.

Wiranatha, A.S. (2001) A systems model for regional planning towards sustainable development in Bali, Indonesia. PhD thesis, University of Queensland.

Wiranatha, A.S. and Putra, I.N.D. (2000) Sustainable tourism: In search of Balinese perspectives. Unpublished manuscript, University of Queensland.

Part 4

Interpretation

Chapter 15

Interpretation in Cultural Tourism

LÁSZLÓ PUCZKÓ

Introduction

One of the rules of thumb in tourism is that visitor demand depends on and is based on attractions. That is the key element of supply. Despite this statement being true and well accepted both by academics and practitioners, there is no agreement on how attractions should be managed, and more fundamentally, how the interpretation of attractions should be put into practice.

Talking about attractions and interpretation necessitates considering why a visitor at any time would like to visit a place, event, an exhibition or a site. People can have many reasons or motivations that would make them visitors. These include cultural appreciation, education, entertainment and social interaction. The number and variety of motivations making people become visitors are just about innumerous. All of the above-mentioned motivations, or maybe even more, could be mapped at any time at an attraction, i.e. different people with different backgrounds and needs are together at the same time. This chapter will, therefore, pay special attention to the attraction–visitor–interpretation triangle.

The factors behind tourism demand have been analysed in great detail. As motivation has always been at the core of applied and theoretical tourism research, several demand models have been developed (e.g. Holloway & Robinson, 1995; Horner & Swarbrooke, 1996; Kotler, 1992; Maslow, 1943; Middleton, 1994). Types of tourists and their likely preferences have also been the focus of attention for numerous authors, as well as variation, forms and trends of attractions.

Interpretation, especially its psychological background, can, however, be considered to be the least likely part of mainstream tourism research. With the help of the four case studies in this section, the aim is to raise some principal questions of interpretation and applied psychology.

227

Interpretation as Communication

The most common approach to describe the role and meaning of interpretation is to define it as a form of communication, in which information flows between the parties involved (Figure 15.1). Information as a very valuable raw material has become an integrative part of our life. From the point of view of interpretation, information flow means communication between the visitor and the interpreter or the attraction itself (Ham, 1992). Of course, interpretation has very close links to information flows, as one of its main roles is to transmit certain messages to the receivers, i.e. in this context, to visitors (Hooper-Greenhill, 1994).

According to definitions of information flow, information, data and messages can be transmitted from the sender to the receiver by different kinds of media. This process, however, can often become biased. The reasons are manifold, e.g. because of the type of media used, the noise occurring during the transmission or perception and information gathering difficulties at the receiver's end. In the process of communication the sender codes the message. In an ideal situation and in ideal conditions the receivers can decode the message and can understand the meaning of it. Pieces of information or data transmitted are put together by the receiver. Without his or her capability or the intention to do so, the message will remain hidden.

The success of communication depends on a few, well definable factors:

- coding of original message,
- selection of media,
- noise during transmission,
- receivers' capabilities of information gathering and understanding (after Prince, 1982).

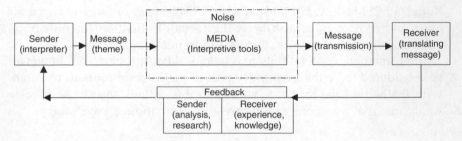

Figure 15.1 The process of interpretation

The so-called noise can be materialised in many forms, e.g. (1) crowding, (2) distorted signs, (3) mental or physical fatigue of visitors, or (4) noise of traffic from outside. The application of interpretation tools (and that of visitor management) is necessitated by the primary goal of reducing sources of noise to a minimum. To overcome these difficulties not only the professionalism and experience of interpreters or curators are necessary, but equally, the knowledge and understanding of information gathering and perception process of visitors.

The approach to the style of information transmission is twofold:

(1) informative style;
(2) interpretative style.

The difference lies in the 'how' and not in the 'what'. While the informative style limits itself to the transmission of information, the interpretative style often attempts to tell a story and to create and transmit complex messages (Aldridge, 1975).

In the following chapters the main focus is given to the core behind this model, i.e. why and how people can decode and understand messages (or themes). What kinds of factors make interpretation art and can create such heated debates between interpreters, curators and visitors?

The Definition of Interpretation

Researchers have developed many, rather similar, definitions and descriptions of interpretation, some of which are summarised below.[1] It should be noted, however, that interpretation cannot be limited to the use of one or more tools. Instead, it is understood to cover the whole process of information transfer, and in its broadest understanding interpretation can also be seen as an amalgam of various elements, i.e. education, entertainment, exhibition, information and enrichment.

Researchers and practitioners have formulated many definitions of interpretation, for example 'Interpretation is a communication process designed to reveal meanings and relationships of our cultural and natural heritage to the visitors through first-hand experiences with objects, artefacts, landscapes, or sites' (Interpretation Canada in Veverka, 1994: 19).

---

[1] Already in Ancient Greek cities visitors could find written commentaries describing a place, i.e. a form of travel guide, known as periegesis (Stewart *et al.*, 1998: 257).

According to Rennie (in Knudson *et al*., 1995: 13) interpretation seeks:

- to increase the visitor's understanding, awareness and the appreciation of nature, of heritage and of site resources;
- to communicate messages relating to nature and culture, including
  natural and historical processes, ecological relationships and human
  roles in nature;
- to involve people in nature and history through first-hand (personal) experience with the natural end cultural environment;
- to affect the behaviour and attitudes of the public concerning the
  wise use of natural resources, the preservation of cultural and
  natural heritage, and the respect and concern for the natural and
  cultural environment;
- to provide an enjoyable and meaningful experience; and
- to increase public understanding and support for the agency's role,
  its management objectives and its policies.

The main objectives of interpretation relate to assisting visitors in developing a keener awareness, appreciation and understanding of the areas they are visiting, the accomplishment of management goals and the promotion of public understanding of an organisation's objectives (Sharpe, 1976).

The research and practice of interpretation in the context of visitor attractions are the most advanced in North America. In the beginning of the 20th century, during the early years of interpretation research, Enos Mills, and during the mid-1900s Freeman Tilden, were the two researchers with the most significant impacts on interpretation theory. Analysing and synthesising what had been developed before, Tilden published his book *Interpreting Our Heritage*, which ever since has been considered to be one of the fundamental titles in interpretation theory (in nature interpretation especially). According to Tilden (1977), interpreta-tion should have the following objectives:

(1) Any interpretation that does not somehow relate what is being
    displayed or described to something within the personality or
    experience of the visitor will be sterile.
(2) Information as such is not interpretation. Interpretation is revelation
    based upon information. But they are entirely different things.
    However, all interpretation includes information.
(3) Interpretation is an art, which combines many arts, whether the
    materials presented are scientific, historical or architectural. Any art
    is to some degree teachable.

(4) The chief aim of interpretation is not instruction, but provocation.
(5) Interpretation should aim to present the whole rather than a part, and must address itself to the whole person rather than any phase.
(6) Interpretation addressed to children (say, up to the age of 12) should not be a dilution of the presentation to adults, but should follow a fundamentally different approach. To be at its best it will require a separate programme.

Time and, more importantly, changes in society as well as technical development, however, have not left interpretation theory unchanged. Tilden's six principles have been challenged many times and interpretation theory has extended its focus to other aspects of communication and psychological processes. In the very beginning, especially in the years of Tilden, interpretation almost exclusively was formulating recommendations about the interpretation of nature (his approach was not built on empirical evidence, but more on his personal experiences).

Since Tilden, researchers, curators and managers have been testing and challenging those six principles. Based on their experiences and on the results of thorough research studies and, furthermore, based on sometimes heated debates, the list of objectives has been refined and added to (Beck & Cable, 1998). For instance, interpretation should be targeted toward specific visitor groups and their interests, made entertaining as well as informative, and employ state-of-the-art technologies. As a very simple summary we can say that interpretation is understood to be a tool to enhance the visitor experience as well as to make the operation of the attractions successful.

As interpretation often wants visitors to follow certain behaviour patterns, the theory of Ajzen and Fishbein (in Cassidy, 1997: 208) can be interesting to consider. In their theory researchers identified three major factors that would have an impact on behaviour (Figure 15.2).

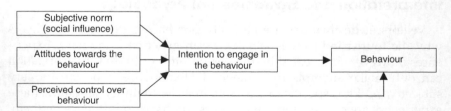

Figure 15.2 Factors affecting behaviour
Source: Cassidy (1997: 208)

Subjective norms are a set of values that are formulated by the social environment. Most people want to comply with and live up to certain social norms. It is predicted in the model that people are more likely to engage in certain behaviour if it is socially approved by others, whose views and opinions one values, i.e. values of the so-called reference group. The attitudes towards the directly or indirectly enforced behaviour, together with the perceived control over that behaviour, are very much dependent on the personal characteristics of the person in question. Interpretation, therefore, has to pay special attention to different visitor groups with different needs and backgrounds. Teenagers, for example, find controlled situations especially stressful. This is why media that involve them in the delivery of experience (e.g. doing some activities in a designated space) have a better impact than applying passive tools, such as railings to keep them away from areas.

Psychology of Interpretation

Interpretation theory has its roots in many other sciences, such as sociology, social and environmental psychology, and educational psychology. According to the principles of interpretation, the person has the central role in the process, as messages or themes are targeted at visitors. Without visitors, interpretation is nothing more than a beautiful but empty shell.

Interpretation, by definition, can or should have an impact on visitors in such a way that they react to the stimuli in the desired form (e.g. appreciation, enjoyment and understanding). It is anticipated, however, and this is one of the key hypotheses of interpretation, that the reactions of visitors can be managed or at least influenced. Of the many theoretical schools, the key findings of environmental and cognitive psychology are introduced in greater detail, as the approaches of these two schools are relatively easily translated to tourism or leisure terms.

Interpretation and Environmental Psychology

Visitors at destinations are basically purchasing experiences. This is why the tourist industry is labelled as an experience industry. Experiences, however, are created by the person him- or herself. Interpretation can only make attempts to influence it. Experience is or can be very subjective and it is specific to a person. In order to understand how these experiences are created and what factors can have an influence on them, it is necessary to understand the information-gathering and experience-building process of human beings. This is why principles of psychology are fundamental to successful interpretation. It has to be noted that psychology literature hardly ever refers to people as visitors. Therefore, the translation and application of psychological principles are necessary.

According to Borroughs (in Cassidy, 1997: 2), environmental psychology is the study of the inter-relationships between the physical environment and human behaviour. Practitioners in interpretation can find applicable elements of environmental psychology, as it is key to interpretation to understand why certain relationship patterns are developed between visitors and the attraction.

One of the key principles of environmental psychology was formulated by Lewin in 1951 (in Cassidy, 1997: 4), i.e. reactions of people should not be taken out of their environment, but should be analysed in relation to it. This is the so-called person-in-context principle. According to Lewin's approach, the behaviour and experience of people can be understood within an interactional framework or described with the function $B = f(P,E)$, where B is behaviour, P is person and E is Environment. It assumed that human beings, who presumably are always looking for a balanced environment, would somehow react to the stimuli stemming from the environment surrounding them.

Taking Lewin's principle and thinking about the selection of interpretation approaches and tools at an attraction, designers should not forget that environmental stimuli are categorised by visitors, such as ones causing extreme reactions and ones that would not cause any extreme reaction. Too much or too little of something, e.g. noise/sound or too much complexity or not enough content can equally create unpleasant experiences, and can cause stress or fatigue. Warr (in Cassidy, 1997: 34–36) describes this theory by the so-called vitamin model of the relationship between environmental events and mental health: additional decrement effect, i.e. like vitamins A and D, both too little and too much are damaging.

What is too much, or what is too little? It is rather difficult to give definite answers or definite numbers. Visitors perceive environmental stimuli differently and depending on their attitude, previous knowledge, physical state, etc. they can react very differently. Some people like loud music, others prefer quiet environments. Some people like to be surrounded by other people, i.e. fellow visitors; others would like to enjoy the attraction without too many other visitors around. Of some environmental factors or stimuli, such as temperature, both too much and too little would be inconvenient. This again underlies the complex nature of interpretation. To make the situation even more difficult, the preferred level of stimulus of the same person can also be different from time to time (e.g. at a concert of his or her favourite pop star loud music is very welcome, whereas the same volume is thought to be annoying if it was caused by a group of other tourists).

Some rather basic tools of interpretation, i.e. signs, can also be analysed through the person-in-context principle. Some signs are not there to add anything to the experience, but to stop the visitor doing something. The equation of Lewin ($B = f(P,E)$) can set a very interesting research question, i.e. what is the reaction of the visitor to a message that forbids something or to a message that implies certain action indirectly (i.e. NO TRESPASSING – Violators are prosecuted, or Photographing is forbidden! or Smile! CCTV is in operation).

With thoughtful and creative interpretation, the fundamentals of which are rooted in the understanding of assets, interpreters, for example, can predict how visitors would react to certain environmental stimuli (e.g. change in colour scheme). One can learn from Barker's principle that knowledge about the behaviour setting is more useful in predicting behaviour than knowledge about the characteristics of the individual in the setting, i.e. there is much more consistency between individuals in the same behaviour setting than there is within the same individual in different behaviour settings (Barker in Cassidy, 1997: 47).

Interpretation and Cognitive Psychology

The cognitive approach to psychology focuses on perception. It presumes that individuals relate themselves to the world they construct through experience (Prince, 1982). Furthermore, according to the principles of Gestalt psychology, the whole is greater than the sum of its parts.

Information or stimuli come in through the perceptual system and are saved in the visual or audial stores. The information is then transferred to short-term memory, in which it activates items (information, experiences, views, etc.) saved in long-term memory (Figure 15.3). These saved items can either be memories of previous visits, traces of what was learnt in school or elements of social norm, etc. Stored and new information then are linked and understood by the steps described by the concept of 'chunking' (after Alter & Ward, 1994).

Understanding and storing information does not happen at the same time, but in chunks or clusters. Similar or somehow similar looking information is synthesised and stored in the same clusters. Sensitive tour guides for example, maybe without intention, apply this chunking when they alter their speech according to the nationality of their visitors. No reason to flood visitors in a foreign country with dates or names, since

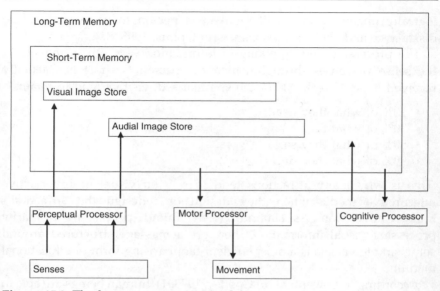

Figure 15.3 The human processing model
Source: after Alter and Ward (1994: 206)

these would not really mean anything to them. If a tour guide relates an event or person in the visited country, to an event or person from the home country of the visitor, it is more likely that visitors can find the chunk that can make the story understood.

Visitors do not intend to spend too much time with their visits or with trying to understand the text. That leaves interpreters with the only option of trying first to find elements in the story, and then tools of the interpretive media that can then somehow be related to what visitors already know. With this approach, interpretation builds on already existing and stored knowledge. This can then lead to the creation of a new chunk or to the extension of an old one stored in long-term memory. These stored information chunks form the so-called cognitive maps of any visitor (Bartlett in Prince, 1982a; Kaplan, 1987; Kaplan *et al.*, 1998).

According to Festinger's theory, one's learning process is described in terms of the relationships between different cognitive elements. An individual's perception of any two elements are in consonance if they are consistent or supportive of one other, i.e. the theory categorises situations, statements or messages as being dissonant, consonant or irrelevant. As Festinger said, the existence of dissonance, being psychologically uncomfortable, will motivate a person to try to reduce the dissonance and achieve consonance (in Orams, 1995: 87).

The processing and chunking of information very much depend on the sense or senses through which the person (visitor) has actually received it. As Veverka (1994: 25) summarised, visitors tend to retain:

- 10% of what they hear,
- 30% of what they read,
- 50% of what they see,
- 90% of what they do.

This is why many attractions tend to rely on visual or (inter)active interpretive media when they design or redesign the attraction's interpretative plan. As Hammitt (1984) found, people are primarily processing visual information, therefore a message structured around some simple visuals is a most efficient familiarising form of educational medium.

According to Lowenthal (in Goodey, 1973: 1), human beings are able to recognise up to 18 visual elements in a second. This fact makes visitors very demanding. They will filter out most of the stimuli and will pay attention to only those that are somehow related to their existing knowledge, i.e. one or more chunks of their memory.

It is presumed that human beings (including visitors) can think six to seven times faster than they can talk, i.e. most of the time we are talking to ourselves. This is why visitors switch off so easily, especially if the information or more likely the interpretation is not relevant to their interests or previous experiences. This is what can be called external–internal shift (Beck & Cable, 1998: 17).

If interpretation fails to provide visitors with a recognisable flow of themes and the media used are not appropriate or relevant, visitors will step out from the context (e.g. they will observe other visitors passing by). Guided visits facilitated either by a person or some other medium, e.g. sound-guide, can have a better impact on information gathering. But again, it should be noted that interpretative media are only tools and not the purpose of interpretation. Boring guidance, trivial messages or too complicated to operate sound-guides will have exactly the same impact as visits without any guidance. Researchers analysing the information recognition and understanding capabilities of people have found that conceptual frameworks provide a useful mechanism for the processing of information.

Interpretation and Education

Interpretation as a form of education provides visitors with information, data, stories, etc. about natural, cultural or other assets (attractions). However, interpretation should not be seen as an equivalent of education. As Hammitt (1984: 11) said, '...environmental education involves students while environmental interpretation involves visitors ...'.

Education is provided in a well structured, preorganised and relatively inflexible form, which is, or is perceived to be, obligatory by the receivers (students). On the contrary, effective interpretation applies a more flexible and joyful approach when delivering structured messages. The other well appreciated quality of interpretation is its nonobligatory nature. While interpretation, similarly to education, aims to transmit certain messages and for visitors to remember these messages, it can achieve its goals without the school-like atmosphere. Similar to interpretation, humans use four principal modalities as they are learning through:

- visual means – e.g. visual arts or maps;
- auditory mode – e.g. speaking, music, rhythm;
- kinaesthetic – e.g. movements;
- abstract codes and symbols – e.g. reading, writing and imagination (Christensen in Knudson *et al.*, 1995: 166).

The emergence of the 'edutainment approach' is a direct consequence of what has been introduced so far. Visitors prefer sites and interpretations that are informative, use understandable (and chunkable) vocabulary and at the same time create new, entertaining, relaxing, etc. experiences. Creating combined stimuli and applying various modalities of learning can really make interpretation different from education.

Formal education, however, from a delivery and management point of view, has many advantages over interpretation. We need to think especially of the well definable audience of education, i.e. the age, background or major interests of students are more alike in the same group, than that of visitors at the same attraction. This fact leaves interpreters with the options of either providing many lines of interpretation parallel to each other, or looking for the common denominator of their visitor segments. In the latter case interpretation can become neither too exciting or innovative, nor too basic, i.e. just average, which is not fully satisfactory for any visitor segment.

Interpretation often uses the same interpretative media, tools or messages as formal education, but attempts to achieve similar information transfer or behavioural change without sanctions or stress. One can argue however, that interpretation does put in place soft or well hidden sanctioning tools. Good interpretation can aim to prevent situations that should be sanctioned, e.g. creative queue or flow management techniques, or with interpretative texts.

Carter (1996: 361) raises the question of time-line difference between (environmental) education and interpretation. Interpretation, especially heritage interpretation, is site-specific, related to the past and designed to meet almost entirely the needs of the management. Therefore there is risk of transmitting biased or subjective messages. Environmental education, on the contrary, tends to be more closely related to the person and his or her needs, and assists visitors (or students) in reaching personal views of past, present and future.

Education and interpretation differ in the type of site or location where they take place. Education tends to be located in purpose-built and functional buildings or places, whereas interpretation often has to meet many restrictive measures, as it is located in listed buildings or at sites where the primary function used to be very different. On the other hand, visitors often prefer sites (attractions) that have a special atmosphere or sense of place.

In spite of all these differences, education and interpretation are not antagonistic enemies, as many objectives can be found in common, for example, the special courses or classes provided by attractions to schools or other segments with special interests.

Tools of Interpretation

Applying and extending Falk's analogy of museum visitors to a broader scale (in Bicknell & Mann, 1994: 197), '. . .visitors being like people who are out window shopping – when something catches their eye they stop and look, and may eventually take away a purchase, i.e. take away ideas and information'. Tools of interpretation are aimed at the stopping-and-purchasing element of the visit. One of the main objectives of any interpretative plan is to make visitors stop as often as they can and these stops should take place at the desired location (not just anywhere).

Researchers found that those visitors who visit museums on an irregular basis typically engage themselves with the following activities during their visit (in Falk & Dierking, 1992: 58):

(1) information search, wayfinding (3–10 min),
(2) intensive attention (15–30 min),
(3) cruising (20–45 min),
(4) departure (3–10 min).

Because they lack experience, they will look for other more experienced visitors and copy their behaviour; because as we have seen before, people intend to comply and do not like the stress of not knowing what to do. The wide variety of interpretive media provides alternative ways in which visitors can engage themselves with the theme. Cruising happens when interpretation fails to provide what visitors want or are capable of taking. In this case visitors become people who just happen to be surrounded by, but are not involved in, interpretation.

The media used in interpretation can be of paramount importance. The spectrum of interpretative media is endless, ranging from simple panels of printed texts to 3D virtual experiences:

(1) passive methods providing visitors with one way communication (e.g. self-guiding trails), or
(2) active methods with the option of two-way communication (e.g. guided trails, touch-on media) (after Prince, 1982b).

Taking the form of visitor involvement to the delivery of the experience into account interpretative methods are either:

(1) personal, such as

   • demonstrations,
   • personalisation, enactments, and
   • guided trails; or

(2) impersonal, such as

   • signs,
   • displays,
   • self-guided trails,
   • (animated) models, and
   • computer-aided displays.

The Case Studies

Four very different case studies were selected for this chapter. As interpretation is seen as a kind of art, the cases represent some of the often argued complexity.

As stated before, opinions of interpretation or personal preferences do depend on the context and on the person in question. The case on museum interpretation in the UK highlights the main points of the argument one can face between curators, officials, interpreters and the general public. Appleton formulates strong opinions that do not always favour recent interpretation trends and also raises concerns about the disappearance of traditional museums.

Interpretation can be understood on many levels. We can and should talk about interpreting cities, which in a broad sense relates to the interpretation of atmosphere or sense of place. One understanding of a sense of place theory stems from the geographical works of Tuan (in Stewart *et al.*, 1998: 258), i.e. place may be said to have a spirit or personality, but only human beings can have a sense of place. People demonstrate their sense of place when they apply their moral and aesthetic discernment to sites and locations. When applying the theory to practice, it can be relatively easy to understand why there is a difference between the approaches to assets of a city or the attraction of local people versus visitors. Most locals have been raised in that environment and therefore help to create and absorb the sense of place, whereas visitors have to develop an understanding and appreciation within a short period of time. Stuart-Hoyle and Lovell in their case study of Canterbury, UK discuss the management approaches that the municipality and other organisations apply to make the city more attractive, better interpreted and to protect its sense of place.

Standardisation of attractions, or more likely the standardisation of interpretative tools used in attractions, is discussed in Diekmann's case study. There is a tendency for similar attractions, such as caves, to rely on the same set of interpretive tools, which can lead to the creation of unified experiences. Both attraction managers and visitors find it difficult to differentiate sites of a similar kind. However, it can be argued that similarity to a certain degree makes understanding easier for visitors.

Rátz's case study on a purpose-built attraction, i.e. the House of Terror (Budapest, Hungary) highlights the risks associated with the interpretation of heritage sites and themes that are of an especially sensitive nature. This sensitivity stems from the historical, cultural and political environment and can have a strong influence on the story or theme, as well as on the tools installed.

Conclusion

Learning from the case studies in this chapter, one can develop rather inconsistent views about interpretation. Interpretation is art. Interpretation is a way of commodifying values and degrading assets. Interpretation brings attractions alive. The introduction of arguments about different methodological approaches or the psychological backgrounds of interpretation can refer to the complexity and difficulties of interpretation. The very different case studies, i.e. interpretation at destination level; tools and approaches used in similar attractions; and interpreting heritage attractions, focus on various aspects of interpretation. But still, they share largely the same questions and issues: that is, how to tell a story. There is no unified answer to this question. Sites, themes, people, approaches, etc. are different and this is how it should be. Having said that, however, anyone who is involved in interpretation should consider that it is aimed at people, i.e. visitors, who have expectations, their own perceptions, capabilities and attitudes, etc., and develop their opinion about the attraction, too. It is up to managers, interpreters and curators, etc. to decide whether they care about these opinions or not.

References

Aldridge, D. (1975) *Guide to Countryside Interpretation, Part One*. Edinburgh: HMSO.

Alter, P. and Ward, R. (1994) Exhibit evaluation: Taking account of human factors. In E. Hooper-Greenhill (ed.) *The Educational Role of Museums* (pp. 204–211). London: Routledge.

Beck, L. and Cable, T. (1998) *Interpretation for the 21st Century, Fifteen Guiding Principles for Interpreting Nature and Culture*. Champaign, IL: Sagamore Publishing.

Bicknell, S. and Mann, P.(1994) A picture of visitors for exhibition developers. In E. Hooper-Greenhill (ed.) *The Educational Role of Museums* (pp. 195–203). London: Routledge.

Carter, G. (1996) Heritage interpretation and environmental education. In R. Harrison (ed.) *Manual of Heritage Management* (pp. 359–368). Oxford: Butter-worth-Heinemann.

Cassidy, T. (1997) *Environmental Psychology, Behaviour and Experience in Context*. Hove: Psychological Press.

Dann, G., Nash, D. and Pearce, P. (1988) Methodology in tourism research. *Annals of Tourism Research* 15 (1), 1–28.

Falk, J.H. and Dierking, L.D. (1992) *The Museum Experience*. Washington DC: Whalesback Books.

Goodey, B. (1973) Perception of the environment, an introduction to the literature. Birmingham: University of Birmingham, Centre for Urban and Regional Studies, Occasional Paper No. 17.

Goodey, B. (1974a) Images of places, essays on environmental perception, communications and education. Birmingham: University of Birmingham, Centre for Urban and Regional Studies, Occasional Paper No. 30.

Goodey, B. (1974b) Urban walks and town trails, origins, principles and sources. Birmingham: University of Birmingham, Centre for Urban and Regional Studies, Research Memorandum 40.

Goodey, B. (1991a) God's market place: The interpretation of cathedrals. In B. Goodey and I.A.C. Parkin (eds) *Urban Interpretation–Techniques and Opportunities* (Vol. 1, pp. 137–154). Oxford: Oxford Polytechnic School of Planning, Working Paper No. 128.

Goodey, B. (1991b) Interpreting with change: Future areas for practice. In B. Goodey and I.A.C. Parkin (eds) *Urban Interpretation – Techniques and Opportunities* (Vol. 2, pp. 122–139). Oxford: Oxford Polytechnic School of Planning, Working Paper No. 128.

Goodey, B. (1991c) Language and layout in interpretation. In B. Goodey and I.A.C. Parkin (eds) *Urban Interpretation – Techniques and Opportunities* (Vol. 2, pp. 14–26). Oxford: Oxford Polytechnic School of Planning, Working Paper No. 128.

Goodey, B. (1991d) Urban trails: The early years. In B. Goodey and I.A.C. Parkin (eds) *Urban Interpretation – Techniques and Opportunities* (Vol. 2, pp. 39–75). Oxford: Oxford Polytechnic School of Planning, Working Paper No. 128.

Goodey, B. (1991e) Why interpretation? In B. Goodey and I.A.C. Parkin (eds) *Urban Interpretation – Techniques and Opportunities* (Vol. 1, pp. 32–40). Oxford: Oxford Polytechnic School of Planning, Working Paper No. 128.

Goodey, B. (1991f) Interpreting with change: Future areas for practice. In B. Goodey and I.A.C. Parkin (eds) *Urban Interpretation – Techniques and Opportunities* (Vol. 2, pp. 122–139). Oxford: Oxford Polytechnic School of Planning, Working Paper No. 128.

Goodey, B., (1991g) Introduction: Why the urban heritage industry? In B. Goodey and I.A.C. Parkin (eds) *Urban Interpretation – Techniques and Opportunities* (Vol. 1, pp. 1–13). Oxford: Oxford Polytechnic School of Planning, Working Paper No. 128.

Goodey, B. (1994) Art-full places: Public art to sell public spaces? In J.R. Gold and S.V. Ward (eds) *Place Promotion, The Use of Publicity and Marketing to Sell Towns and Regions* (pp. 153–179). Chichester: Wiley & Sons.

Goodey, B. (1996) Interpretive planning. In R. Harrison (ed.) *Manual of Heritage Management* (pp. 303–319). Oxford: Butterworth-Heinemann.

Ham, S.H. (1992) *Environmental Interpretation, A Practical Guide for People with Big Ideas and Small Budgets*. Golden, CO: North American Press.

Hammit, W.E. (1984) Cognitive processes involved in environmental interpretation. *Journal of Environmental Education* 15, 11–15.

Hooper-Greenhill, E. (1994) *Museums and their Visitors*. London: Routledge.

Horner, S. and Swarbrooke, J. (1996) *Marketing Tourism, Hospitality and Leisure in Europe*. London: International Thomson Business Press.

Kaplan, S. (1987) Aesthetics, affect, and cognition: Environmental preference from an evolutionary perspective. *Environment and Behavior* 19 (1), 3–32.

Kaplan, R., Kaplan, S. and Ryan, R.L. (1998) *With People in Mind, Design and Management of Everyday Nature*. Washington, DC: Island Press.

Knudson, D.M., Cable, T.T. and Beck, L. (1995) Interpretation of Cultural and Natural Resources. State College: Venture Publishing, Inc.

Kotler, P. (1992) Marketing management. *Elemzés, tervezés, végrehajtás és ellenőrzés* (3rd edn). Budapest: Müszaki Könyvkiadó.

Middleton, V.T.C. (1994) *Marketing in Travel and Tourism* (2nd edn). Oxford: Butterworth-Heinemann.

Orams, M.B. (1995) Using interpretation to manage nature-based tourism. *Journal of Sustainable Tourism* 4 (2), 81–94.

Plog, S.C. (1974) Why destination areas rise and fall in popularity? *Cornell Hotel and Restaurant Quarterly* 14 (4), 55–58.

Prentice, R.C. (1989) Pricing policy at heritage sites: How much should visitors pay? In D.T. Herbert, R.C. Prentice and C.J. Thomas (eds) *Heritage Sites: Strategies for Marketing and Development* (pp. 231– 271). Aldershot: Avebury.

Prentice, R. (1990) Spatial promotional markets of Tourist Information Centres. *Area* 22 (3), 219– 233.

Prentice, R.C. (1993a) *Tourism and Heritage Attractions*. London: Routledge.

Prentice, R. (1993b) Measuring the educational effectiveness of on-site interpretation designed for tourists: An assessment of student recall from geographical field visits to Kidwelly Castle, Dyfed. *Area* 23 (4), 297– 308.

Prentice, R.C. (1995) Heritage as formal education. In D.T. Herbert (ed.) *Heritage, Tourism and Society* (pp. 146– 169). London: Mansell.

Prince, D.R. (1982) Evaluating interpretation: A discussion. Birmingham: University of Birmingham, Centre for Environmental Interpretation, Occasional Papers: No. 1.

Prince, D.R. (1982) Countryside Interpretation: A cognitive evaluation. Birmingham: University of Birmingham, Centre for Environmental Interpretation, Occasional Papers: No. 3.

Sharpe, G.W. (1976a) Exhibits. In G.W. Sharpe (ed.) *Interpreting the Environment* (pp. 285– 303). New York: Wiley & Sons.

Sharpe, G.W. (1976b) Information duty. In G.W. Sharpe (ed.) *Interpreting the Environment* (pp. 123– 140). New York: Wiley & Sons.

Sharpe, G.W. (1976c) Selecting the interpretive media. In G.W. Sharpe (ed.) *Interpreting the Environment* (pp. 81– 101). New York: Wiley & Sons.

Sharpe, G.W. (1976d) Self-guided trails. In G.W. Sharpe (ed.) *Interpreting the Environment* (pp. 247– 269). New York: Wiley & Sons.

Stewart, E.J., Hayward, B.M., Devlin, P.J. and Kirby, V.G. (1998) The 'place' of interpretation: A new approach to the evaluation of interpretation. *Tourism Management* 19 (3), 257– 266.

Tilden, F. (1977) *Interpreting Our Heritage* (3rd edn). Chapel Hill: The University of North Carolina Press.

Uzzell, D.L. (1989a) Introduction: The natural and built environment. In D.L. Uzzel (ed.) *Heritage Interpretation* (Vol. 1, pp. 1– 14). London: Belhaven Press.

Uzzell, D.L. (1989b) The hot interpretation of war and conflict. In D.L. Uzzel (ed.) *Heritage Interpretation* (Vol. 1, pp. 33– 47). London: Belhaven Press.

Uzzel, D.L. (1989c) Introduction: The visitor experience. In D.L. Uzzel (ed.) *Heritage Interpretation* (Vol. 2, pp. 1– 15). London: Belhaven Press.

Uzzell, D.L. (1996) Heritage interpretation in Britain four decades after Tilden. In R. Harrison (ed.) *Manual of Heritage Management* (pp. 293– 302). Oxford: Butterworth-Heinemann.

Veverka, J.A. (1994) *Interpretive Master Planning*. Helena MO: Falcon Press Publishing Co.

Chapter 16
Interpretation in the House of Terror, Budapest

TAMARA RÁTZ

Introduction

'May you live in interesting times' says the proverbial curse, and a longing for simple, peaceful times is a basic human instinct. For cultural destinations, however, a turbulent and rich history is a major resource. Heritage attractions based on historic events, persons or periods are popular with contemporary tourists who wish to directly experience the past of the visited areas (Chhabra *et al.*, 2003). While it is clear that history is a series of accepted judgements instead of being a factual truth (Barraclough, 1984) and the development of the heritage product means subjective selection and explanation of facts, most tourists accept the presented facts as reality and do not search for alternative interpretation.

Image is a serious attraction in tourism and a significant part of Hungary's international image is its Communist past together with its historic attractions. Considering the domestic image of Budapest, the major elements are the crowds, the sights and the shopping possibilities (Michalkó, 1999). Hungarians, when planning to visit Budapest, would easily forget about political history, were they not reminded by the existence of the House of Terror, an almost compulsory sight for all domestic tourists.

The Heritage of Atrocity

Heritage in its broader meaning is 'something transferred from one generation to another' (Nuryanti, 1996: 249). The word heritage includes both cultural and natural elements. In the cultural context, heritage describes both material and immaterial forms, e.g. artefacts, monuments, historical remains, buildings, architecture, philosophy, traditions, cele-brations, historic events, distinctive ways of life, literature, folklore or education. In the natural context, heritage includes landscapes, gardens, parks, wilderness, mountains, rivers, islands, flora and fauna. Natural heritage also has cultural components, as its value is dependent on subjective human assessment.

The word 'heritage' is applied in a wide variety of contexts (Tunbridge & Ashworth, 1996). It is used as a synonym for objects from the past or for sites with no surviving physical structures but associated with past events. It is also extended to nonphysical aspects of the past, like cultural and artistic productivity. Heritage is a cultural, political and economic resource. Because heritage is seen as a value in itself, heritage artefacts are suitable for collection, preservation and presentation. National heritage based on national history 'explains the distinctiveness of a nation through time' (Tunbridge & Ashworth, 1996: 46), thus it is a valuable tool in increasing national unity and pride, or creating a national image.

The attraction of death and tragedy has always been a powerful motivation for travel (Kazalarska, 2002). Today however, the heritage of atrocity and the sites associated with disaster such as concentration camps, battlefields, prisons, torture chambers or assassination sites are routinely developed as popular and profitable tourist attractions (Michalkó, 2004). The consumption of the disturbing past is driven and shaped by tourists' needs, but it is also subject to changes in political and cultural climates (Seaton, 1996). Thus, on the one hand, the selection of culturally significant themes and the interpretation of sensitive political issues depend on the socioeconomic framework that heritage and cultural tourism exist in. Heritage interpretation, on the other hand, is a resource regularly used as a political instrument in shaping national identities or legitimising a dominant regime. The heritage of atrocity may be a powerful political tool, as controversial events are often effective in creating a sense of division between victims and oppressors, involved and uninvolved.

Interpretation in Cultural and Heritage Tourism

The central challenge in heritage tourism is the way of reconstructing the past in the present through interpretation (Nuryanti, 1996). Interpretation does not only describe historic facts, but creates understanding or emotional response, increases appreciation, awareness and enjoyment (Herbert, 1989). Thus interpretation should involve much more than information provision, according to the following six main principles (Tilden, 1977 in Nuryanti, 1996):

- Interpretation should relate the presented heritage to the personality or experience of the visitor.
- Interpretation includes, but is more than, information.

- Interpretation is an art, combining many art forms.
- The major aim of interpretation is provocation, not instruction (though the educational role of interpretation is not negligible).
- Interpretation should aim to present the whole rather than a part.
- Interpretation should be designed with different visitor segments in mind, following a fundamentally different approach in the case of each segment.

It is important to recognise the scale of heritage attractions concerning possible market segments: only a minority of heritage sites can be considered as international attractions, the rest appeal to national, regional or local visitors only (Puczkó & Rátz, 1999). Even on an international scale, there are two levels: primary international attractions generate visits from foreign countries on their own, while secondary attractions are not themselves the major determinant in the tourists' choice of destination, but have sufficient value to make tourists visit them once they have arrived in the given county (Jenkins, 1993).

Heritage interpretation is often endowed with political messages. A selective use of the past for current purposes and its transformation through interpretation is a widely experienced phenomenon in cultural and heritage tourism (Puczkó & Rátz, 2000). The interpretation of atrocity is a particularly sensitive and complex issue. Interpretation may contribute to the healing process for the survivors and their descendants, may be part of the reconciliation process between the communities involved (Hollow, 2001). It also affects the public memory of the atrocity – by interpreting the facts through a wide range of mediums, history is created and memories are established. The present determines what of the past is remembered and this collective memory reflects the power structure of a community (Novick, 2000).

The House of Terror

Museums may reveal more about the particular context in which they are set up than about what is actually on display (Golden, 1996). This statement is particularly true for the House of Terror, one of the most controversial Hungarian cultural institutions, which was created by a political decision and has been the subject of fierce criticism ever since. After the political changes of 1989–90, it took a decade in Hungary for the time to be appropriate to build a museum that commemorates the victims of terror in general and of Nazism and Communism in particular.

The building on Andrássy Avenue selected to house the institution was bought by the Public Foundation for Central and Eastern European Historic and Social Research in December 2000 in order to convert it to a museum of terror.

The elegant former apartment building housing the museum, 60 Andrássy Avenue, has a symbolic significance in Hungary. From 1940 it served as the headquarters of the Nazi-affiliated Arrow Cross party. In 1944, they used the building as a prison and torture centre. Following the Soviet liberation and occupancy of the country in 1945, it was taken over by the Communist Secret Police (the notorious ÁVH, later renamed as ÁVO), and it was the ÁVH's interrogation centre until the 1956 uprising. The House of Terror opened on 24 February 2002, on the eve of the memorial day of the victims of Communist terror. During the necessary reconstruction, both the building's exterior and interior have changed. All the interior design, including the interpretation system, as well as the unique façade, has been created by Hungarian and international architects. The exhibition's music is composed by a popular and renowned musician, an unusual factor that has increased the museum's attraction among young Hungarian visitors.

While promoted as such, the House of Terror is not a real museum in the general understanding of the term (Bloch, 1997). Although it has a varied collection of items such as clothes, weapons or personal objects from the 1940s and 1950s, the original objects on display would hardly be sufficient for a comprehensive exhibition on totalitarian terror, including wartime fascism and post-war Communism in Hungary. In addition, the House of Terror is more committed to education and research than to collections management, so it should rather be defined as a heritage centre. However, the House of Terror is a good illustration of the new kind of museum the function of which has gradually evolved from passive to interactive and from the authenticity of the object in the museum's collection to the authenticity of the visitor's experience.

While the official raison d'être of the House of Terror is being a memorial and a warning to young people, it is obviously meant as a tourist attraction as well, both for Hungarian visitors and for foreigners. Since its opening in 2002, the museum has been visited by more than 500,000 people. In addition to being a popular visitor attraction, the House of Terror is also respected professionally for its modern and creative interpretation system. In 2004, the institution was specially commended by the European Museum Forum in recognition of its excellence in conception, innovative approach to interpretation and attention to the needs of their visitors.

A significant part of Hungary's attraction as a tourist destination is its Socialist[1] past – however, the country is changing rapidly and the visible, intangible signs of the Socialist system are fast disappearing. In fact, many foreign tourists complain that Budapest is losing its 'exotic eastern' image and 'it's not like it used to be'. Therefore, the creation of a heritage centre as the House of Terror has seemed to be necessary for various reasons: in addition to preserving the memory of Nazi and Communist terror for Hungarian generations who are too young to remember, it also provides a unique opportunity for foreigners to get a glimpse of the country's past behind the iron curtain. It is actually ironic to overemphasise the impact of 45 years of Socialism on the 1000-year-old country's international and even internal image, nevertheless 'being a former Socialist country' is probably the most significant part of this image, so the destination must offer suitable visitor attractions. At the moment, Hungary is one of the few Eastern European countries that have decided to capitalise on their Socialist past in the process of tourism development: in addition to Budapest's Park of Socialist Statues and House of Terror, tourists may visit Lithuania's Stalin World or participate in Gulag tours in Russia, but the House of Terror experience is closer to the sense of tragedy felt in the concentration camps than to the amusement enjoyed in theme parks.

Interpretation in the House of Terror

As discussed above, the building of the House of Terror has been a symbol of terror and suppression for decades in Hungary. Although the ÁVO moved out in 1956 and the building served as an office centre for more than 40 years, its dark past has been remembered by millions of Hungarians. Consequently, for those who are familiar with its history, the House of Terror's location is itself part of the interpretative message. The memorial function of the edifice is emphasised and reinforced by the cornice hanging over the building: the word 'TERROR' is cut out of it and when the sun shines through these huge letters, it symbolises the

[1] Although the terms Communism and Socialism are sometimes used as synonyms in Western literature, they are significantly different concepts. In Marxist theory, Socialism is a stage on the way to the more advanced equalitarian system of Communism. In Eastern European post-war history, Communism was a theoretical and ideological notion, while Socialism was an established political and economic system. Although officially all Socialist countries strived to build Communism, this goal has not been achieved anywhere. In this chapter, all references to Communism are indicative of crimes committed or actions performed in the name of Communist ideology.

terror that was projected onto Hungarians for more than 50 years. The striking metal awning is in sharp contrast with the elegant, fin de siecle architecture of the World Heritage listed Andrássy Avenue and initially it caused an uproar in the city's architectural and heritage protection circles, but now it is generally accepted.

The logo of the museum is widely used in communication and it is an instantly recognisable and visually very powerful picture: it consists of a black arrow cross in red background together with a red star in black background, with the inscription of 'House of Terror' in Hungarian and in English. The balanced nature of the image – the background colours divide the space and the symbols of terror are of the same size – suggests a similar balance in the interpretative contents, an equal significance of Nazi and Communist terror.

Inside, on 2150 m², the multilevel exhibition is organised in a time frame with a thematic structure, following a chronological series of events. Modern audiovisual interpretation techniques are used to paint a dark, emotional picture of Hungary's past: the image presented here is less the friendly 'goulash communism' and more the cold war-style 'evil empire'. The music filling many of the rooms sounds like a film score – it is dramatic and slightly theatrical. The atrium of the House of Terror features a Soviet tank in a shallow pool of water, and a wall covered with haunting black and white portraits of the victims of the building: as the faces are reflected on the water, the visual effect is the tank rolling over the victims' faces. The exhibition begins with the short-lived but brutal German occupation of Hungary in 1944. Yet the main focus is on the early years of Communist rule, which began when the Soviet army defeated the Nazis and occupied the country.

The House of Terror has many memorable exhibits, including a labyrinth of pork-fat bricks reminding visitors of the harsh conditions of the 1950s, when mostly lard spread on bread, the simplest and cheapest food in country, was available. In the room featuring Gulag life, a large-scale map of the Soviet Union stretches across the floor to give a sense of the distances between Hungary and the forced labour camps where hundreds of thousands of Hungarians were exiled after World War II. The wooden walls of the room resemble those of a cattle car, and the Russian steppe flashes by on video screens as if seen from a moving train. The room entitled 'Changing Clothes' presents the surprisingly smooth transition from Nazism to Communism. After World War II, the suddenly powerful Hungarian Communist Party was joined in great numbers by former members of the Arrow Cross. On the video screen of an old-fashioned locker room, common people are changing their clothes as well as their political affiliations. A slowly rotating, Janus-faced dummy – Communist uniform on one side, Arrow Cross uniform on the other – symbolises the continuity of dictatorships and the ease of 180° turns in political conviction.

The last section of the exhibition begins with a three-minute video of a guard explaining an execution played while you descend by elevator into the prison basement. The creatively furnished themed rooms that tell the story of terror in a professional edutainment-style do not prepare the visitor for the shock of this simple yet powerful interpretation tool. Locked in a slow moving elevator, having no choice but to listen to the emotional description of an execution, it is a chilling and slightly claustrophobic experience and a reminder that the victims of terror had no choice either. During the 1950s, the basement of the building was the scene of torture. Although the ÁVO moved out after the revolution of 1956 and the basement became a youth club for local Communists, the jail cells have been renovated to their mid-1950s style and bear witness to the confinement and torture of the Communist system's political prisoners.

The last two rooms – with the only colour video clips – show the festive and exhilarating days in 1989 when the Soviet army departed Hungary. Scenes include the reburial of the martyr prime minister, Imre Nagy and the Pope's visit (a momentous event in a predominantly Roman Catholic country where religion was officially suppressed for decades). The closing element of the interpretation process is the Gallery of the Victimizers in the exit hall: a collection of pictures of Hungarians who served the Arrow Cross and the Communist dictatorship's secret police as torturers and executioners, many of whom are still alive and who were never brought to justice.

The House of Terror's souvenir shop offers a wide range of themed souvenirs, such as Communist worker's certificates, metal mugs used in prison or in the Gulag forced labour camps, wall plates and fridge magnets decorated with the Socialist Hungarian coat of arms, and candle busts of Lenin, Stalin or the dreaded political leader of the 1950s, Mátyás Rákosi. While burning the bust of Stalin or Rákosi may indeed give a certain satisfaction, it is surprising that only Communist icons are available for this postmodern voodoo ritual, as there is no candle bust of Hitler, Mussolini or the Hungarian Arrow Cross leader Ferenc Szálasi. Typical themed souvenirs such as key rings, bottle openers and T-shirts are also available in the shop, together with history books and fake 'lard bricks'.

Foreign visitors are required to pay twice as much for entry as Hungarians; a relic of Communist-era double pricing in which hard currency was scarcely obtainable, although unlikely a deliberate interpretation tool. Another, probably also unintentional reminder of the Communist regime's heartlessness is the inefficiency of the conventional single entry system: the queue is often long and while waiting inside, the same short video is shown repeatedly.

An Assessment of Interpretation in the House of Terror

The interpretation of terror and Hungarian history is creative and professional in the museum. The intense use of music, film and high-tech methods of narrative, combined with the careful control of lighting and the use of tight spaces result in a memorable experience. Information is available in both Hungarian and English, although the exact contents differ in order to provide foreign visitors with a more detailed background of the events and personalities of the presented eras.

Heritage is always one's inheritance of the past, should it be an individual's or a nation's possession. Understanding heritage without a personal or social affiliation is certainly possible, but there are differences in engagement. For Hungarian visitors, it might be extremely difficult to disregard the political connotations of the House of Terror. Since its foundation, the museum has received extensive coverage in left- and right-wing mediums alike, so almost all visitors arrive with a certain kind of preconceived opinion. Hungarian visitors, on the other hand, may more appreciate the varied high-tech exhibition than foreigners, who are more accustomed to purpose-built visitor attractions with high-quality interpretation systems.

From an international point of view, terror is a current and global issue. A cultural attraction based on political suppression, terror and a fight for democracy is like the modern version of popular historic sights such as medieval torture chambers or 17th-century slave castles. For most international travellers, the House of Terror is a modern edutainment experience, one of Budapest's contemporary cultural attractions: they can understand and imagine the tragedy of the victims, but they are not personally involved in the story.

The design of interpretation in the House of Terror has put Tilden's (1977) six principles into practice in quite an effective and efficient way. Although facts and figures are provided, the interpretative message is rational and emotional at the same time, and it is mostly conveyed by the dramatic effects of audiovisual art forms. As Hungarian and foreigner visitors are both targeted by the museum, several attempts have been made to relate the presented heritage to these visitor segments. As for the aims of interpretation, the House of Terror has definitely proved more successful in provocation than in instruction, although the educational role of the exhibit for schoolchildren is rather significant.

Concerning visitor attitudes and experiences, several distinct groups may be defined. Most international visitors arrive without preconceptions and without a deeper knowledge of modern Hungarian history. Among Hungarians, the major categorisation factor is age: a generation gap divides those whose lives have been affected by terror and those who are too young to have personal memories. The emotional involvement of the former group also depends on their self-identification as victims or criminals or as left- or right-wing supporters.

Probably one of the most difficult tasks of interpretation design is the requirement of presenting the whole story, the whole truth rather than a part. Limited space and resources together with a subjective understanding of history make the interpretative message inevitably incomplete. One of the most criticised issues in the House of Terror is the predominant focus on Communist terror as opposed to a balanced representation of pre- and post-war totalitarianism. While the official aim of museum is to memorialise all the victims of terror, the institution is considered by many as a symbol of the charged, right-wing atmosphere that has swept Hungary in the late 1990s. Due to the teleological progression in the narrative, the exhibition presents a certain understanding of history and there is little room for alternative readings (M. Metro-Roland, personal communication, 04.2004). Only the museum's official guides are allowed to show visitors around and they all provide standard information. Although this practice is a guarantee of reliable service quality, it may also be a source of conflict in cases when visitors believe in a different interpretation of the past.

Tours are available in both Hungarian and English. There are differences in engagement, particularly in the way that the headphones mark one off and in many ways separate one even further from the staged reality behind the displays. Uninvolved or unaffected visitors – particularly foreigners and young Hungarians with no personal experiences of terror – may have a sense of being an outsider and acting as a voyeur on someone else's suffering (M. Metro-Roland, personal communication, 04.2004).

Controversial Issues Concerning the House of Terror

The House of Terror has been under almost constant political attack since the birth of the concept. Although it has been widely accepted that a memorial of the victims of terror should be developed, the implementation of the idea has raised several concerns. Probably the most controversy arises from the House of Terror's alleged political motives. Between 2000 and 2002, the right-wing government of Prime Minister Viktor Orbán seemed to spare no expense in creating the museum, from the ubiquitous marble and high-tech multimedia exhibits, to the authentic Soviet tank parked in the atrium and the restored torture chambers in the cellar. The House of Terror was timed to open in the final stages of a heated election campaign, and it became a rhetorical weapon against the Socialist opposition. The main message was that the Socialists were a direct continuation of the Stalinist regime and the creation of a memorial to the victims of terror served as a warning to voters. Consequently, when the Socialist Party won the elections, the fate of the House of Terror became a subject of intense arguments, in spite of the principal concept's general acceptance.

A contradiction arises between the aim of the museum and the timeframe of the exhibition: while Communist terror in Hungary discontinued in 1956, chronologically the exhibition ends with the departure of the Soviet Army. A subconscious effect of this structural arrangement is the shift of responsibility from Hungarians to an external occupying power. Furthermore, as primarily Communist atrocities are presented, the country seems to be more connected to the East rather than the West (Nazism, however tragic and sad, is a Central and Western European phenomenon – an additional, though most probably unconscious reinforcement of Hungary's 'Communist country' stereotype).

As the museum focuses on the heritage of totalitarian terror, very little attention and space are given to any of the benefits of life in the Socialist system between 1945 and 1989 such as the provision of free education and health care or the development of basic but affordable social housing. Although most of the themes presented in the House of Terror's main exhibition are sensitive to the privacy rights of victims and executioners alike, probably the most controversial part of the exhibition is the Gallery of the Victimizers. In this passageway, dozens of black and white pictures cover the walls – with name, rank, and year of birth – of those Hungarians who served the Nazi and the Communist dictatorships as torturers and executioners or held high positions in the totalitarian systems' executive authorities.

Unfortunately, without a detailed description of each person's acts and responsibilities, the list of victimisers seems to be arbitrary. Although society's sense of justice obviously requires the condign punishment of the guilty, it is a rather unusual role for a designated museum to take on the responsibility of judgement. According to Tunbridge and Ashworth (1996), heritage may be considered as a hierarchy of scales where personal heritage is the most basic level. The museum's perceived need for involvement might be understood by attributing more importance to the heritage of a community or a nation than to personal heritage. However, society has again been divided over the issue: while many have welcomed the provoking acknowledgement of the past as a proof of democratic transition, others consider it as a further step towards the country's polarisation.

While the whole Hungarian society suffered under Nazism and Communism, certain social groups were more affected than others. In 1944–45, with the active cooperation of the Hungarian authorities, more than 400,000 Hungarian Jews were deported and killed in the Nazi concentration camps. Hungarian Jews have expressed concerns about the presentation of all victims as equal and all victimisers as equal, as this message may diminish the uniqueness of the Holocaust. By devoting only one room exclusively to the Holocaust, the House of Terror, in certain opinions, implies that Communism was far worse than Nazi terror. The permanent exhibition's structure may lead to the under-estimation of Hungarians' complicity in the Holocaust: as the first theme of the interpretation is Hungary's double occupation by external powers, most responsibility for the tragic events seems to be shifted to the Nazis.

Maybe as a response to these accusations, in commemoration of the Holocaust's 60th anniversary in 2004 the museum ran a special series of programmes entitled 'Hungarian Tragedy 1944'. One of the particularly moving temporary exhibitions was dedicated to the memory of the 1.5 million European and 190,000 Hungarian children murdered in the Nazi death camps. (The history of the Holocaust is also presented to the public by the recently inaugurated Budapest Holocaust Memorial Center. Cooperation between the two institutions may potentially provide visitors with a balanced picture of Hungary's 20th-century political heritage and may decrease the criticism directed at the House of Terror.)

Summary

Interpreting the past often provokes fierce controversy. Although in the last 15 years Hungary has undergone a transition from a Socialist to a democratic political system, the ghosts of the country's unsettled past still linger. Since it opened in February 2002, the House of Terror continues to foster a storm of debate, and it has become a major political issue in the country, a quite unlikely achievement for a heritage attraction. Of course, the institution is not simply a museum presenting the horrors of totalitarian terror; it also serves as a memorial for the victims and as a warning for future generations. Although the need for such a memorial is widely accepted in Hungary, currently the over-politicised nature of the museum seems to hinder the objective evaluation of its exhibitions.

Although Hungary's Socialist system was often perceived as free-wheeling 'goulash Communism', particularly compared to other members of the Soviet Bloc, the multimedia exhibition of the House of Terror presents a vivid tableau of a dark era in which terror affected everyone and everything. The interpretative methods often strike visitors with surprise or horror, but it is a deliberate policy of the museum to be blunt rather than diplomatic in the formulation of messages.

All the new democracies of Eastern Europe must come to terms with past atrocities from internal and external repression. Establishing peace through seeking a certain kind of restorative justice is one possible solution to reduce tension. Remembering the past is essential to re-establish the dignity and humanity of the victims and to allow for forgiveness and reconciliation. The House of Terror, although controversial and not necessarily fully objective, is a powerful heritage institution and may significantly contribute to democratic development in the region.

References

Barraclough, G. (1984) *History in a Changing World.* Westport, CT: Greenwood Publishing Group, Inc.

Bloch, S. (1997) Museums. *Insights.* London: English Tourist Board, D7–12.

Chhabra, D., Healy, R. and Sills, E. (2003) Staged authenticity and heritage tourism. *Annals of Tourism Research* 30 (3), 702–719

Golden, D. (1996) The museum of the Jewish diaspora tells a story. In T. Selwyn (ed.) *The Tourist Image? Myths and Myth Making in Tourism* (pp. 223–250). Chichester: John Wiley & Sons.

Herbert, D.T. (1989) Leisure trends and the heritage market. In D.T. Herbert, R.C. Prentice and C.J. Thomas (eds) *Heritage Sites: Strategies for Marketing and Development* Hants: Avebury.

Hollow, R. (2001) Massacre sites – How, and should we, interpret and present these sites? In 9th IAA Conference Proceedings. *Interpretation: Getting to the Heart of It*, 2001, Alice Springs, Australia (pp. 86–90). Collingwood, Vic.: Interpretation Australia Association.

Jenkins, C.L. (1993) Marketing culture in international tourism. In W. Nuryanti (ed.) *Universal Tourism: Enriching or Degrading Culture*, Proceedings of the International Conference on Culture and Tourism (pp. 171–179). Yogyakarta: Gadjah Mada University Press.

Kazalarska, S.I. (2002) 'Dark tourism': Reducing dissonance in the interpretation of atrocity at selected museums in Washington, D.C. Thesis, The School of Business and Public Management, George Washington University.

Michalkó, G. (1999) *A városi turizmus elmélete és gyakorlata*. Budapest: MTA FKI.

Michalkó, G. (2004) *A turizmuselmélet alapjai*. Székesfehérvár: Kodolányi János Főiskola.

Novick, P. (2000) *The Holocaust in American Life*. New York: Mariner Books.

Nuryanti, W. (1996) Heritage and postmodern tourism. *Annals of Tourism Research* 23 (2), 249–260.

Puczkó, L. and Rátz, L. (1999) Cultural attractions, interpretation and visitor management: Two cases of Hungary. In M. Korzay et al (eds.) *Heritage, Multicultural Attractions and Tourism* (Vol. 1, pp. 375–395). Istanbul: Boğaziçi University.

Puczkó, L. and Rátz, T. (2000) *Az attrakciótól az élményig. A látogatómenedzsment módszerei*. Budapest: Geomédia.

Seaton, A. (1996) From Thanatopsis to Thanatourism: Guided by the dark. *International Journal of Heritage Studies* 2 (4), 234–244.

Tunbridge, J.E. and Ashworth, G.J. (1996) *Dissonant Heritage. The Management of the Past as a Resource in Conflict*. Chichester: John Wiley & Sons.

Chapter 17

UK Museum Policy and Interpretation: Implications for Cultural Tourism

JOSIE APPLETON

Introduction

Four out of five of the top tourist attractions in the UK are museums receiving more than 100 million visits each year; more than the top sporting events combined (Manifesto for Museums, 2004). Over the past 10 years, there have been major shifts in the assumptions that lie at the base of museum policy and interpretation – with a shift in focus away from the collection and towards serving the visitor. Yet the paradox of this shift has been that the visitor is today less well served, and gets less out of the museum experience. The argument of this chapter is that museums tend to become indistinguishable from other entertainment/ welfare institutions, and serve up a thin soup for their 'customers' – rather than inspiring them with the wealth of the artefacts of nature and history.

During the screening of the UK TV programme *Big Brother*, an exhibition was built around the show in the newly opened Wellcome Wing of the Science Museum. The exhibition posed questions such as whether or not the contestants would be harmed by their experiences, then asked visitors: 'would you like to be a guinea pig in the *Big Brother* house?' Three options were given: Yes/No/Don't know. Votes were clocked up in large electronic numbers. Upstairs on the floor 'Who am I?', visitors could explore the principles of genetic fingerprinting on a mock fruit-machine, matching up the DNA bands of father, mother and offspring. On the floor 'Digitopolis' they could create digital music or set up their own website. The wing was semi-dark, bathed in spacey sounds and moving lights. Here was a museum: but not as we know it.

An interview with one of the Wellcome Wing project leaders, Heather Mayfield, illustrates the thrust behind the project. When some of the interactive machines broke down, Mayfield's direct telephone number was flashed up 'for all those dissatisfied visitors' (*Museums Journal*, 2000). The focus of the wing seems less on producing exhibitions with high-quality scientific or intellectual content, than on attracting and engage its visitors.

The exhibitions on the ground floor of the Wellcome Wing change frequently, according to whatever the curators think will excite interest at the time. Many of the interactive machines ask visitors what they think about current scientific controversies, such as the use of drugs to treat depression, foot-and-mouth disease or the male pill. The museum is anxious to assure its visitors that their views are important and will be taken very seriously by scientists, though what happens to all the Yesses/Noes/Don't knows is not clear.

The Wellcome Wing is not alone. In recent years, a new generation of museum professionals, backed by the New Labour government, has begun to create a new type of museum. In this people-centred museum, the visitor has become the focus of the museum's activity: everything, from the physical layout to the choice of exhibition to the organisation of the collection is assessed in terms of how it will appeal to and stimulate people. Museum officials' focus on the visitor has meant that the original purpose of museums, the collection, study and exhibition of objects, is now subordinate to a vast array of other social activities. The concern is not really to communicate the wealth of collections to the public – an admirable aim, which museums had sometimes neglected in the past. Instead, the aim of some in today's museums is to 'just connect', to reach museum visitors in any way possible.

Turning museums towards the visitor in this way is not just a change of direction or an embellishment of what went before. It is a total reversal of the meaning and purpose of the museum and puts in question the existence of museums as such. For 200 years, from the creation of the Louvre by the French republican government as the first national museum open to the general public, the central concern of curators was the collection, preservation, study and display of objects deemed to be of artistic, historic or scientific interest. The museum was organised around its collections. Because these collections were held in perpetuity on behalf of the public, museums have always had a concern with, and sense of obligation to, society at large. Whatever the ideological bent of those who ran the museum, the fact that it was bound by a clearly defined professional obligation gave its activity some rational purpose. The new museum, by contrast, organised around the ever-changing presumed needs of people, lacks any rational foundation whatsoever. Its function bends and twists to fit perceived demands, most of which are

arbitrarily chosen by the government or the museum authorities themselves, and which often have no connection with the original core activity
of the museum.

We can identify two key trends that have led to this state of affairs.
These trends can be summarised briefly as the ascendancy over a period
of 20–30 years of two seemingly opposed, yet ultimately compatible
ideologies: the ideology of the economic right on the one side, and of the
cultural left on the other.

Cultural leftism has gained supremacy in academic and intellectual
circles since the 1960s. The enduring legacy of the cultural left has been
its hostility to the idea of objectivity itself. For the cultural left, the claim
to objective knowledge was no more than an attempt by the establishment to assert its intellectual hegemony. Expressed in various forms –
postcolonial and feminist theories, postmodernism, Foucauldian theories
of power relations – the cultural left undermined every attempt at
objective truth and universality. Foucauldian theories had an especially
pernicious influence within the museum profession: the acts of collecting, categorising and interpreting objects came to be seen not as the
disinterested pursuit of knowledge, but as the striving for power on the
part of the Western elite. The very act of building collections was seen as
an affirmation of Western racism and imperialism. Collections were
deemed no longer to have any meaning distinct from the subjective
interpretations imposed on them by scholars and curators. The result
was a loosening of the bonds that tied the scholar and curator to their
objects. If all interpretations were subjective, then why privilege the one
that laid false claims to objectivity? Freed from the discipline of objective
knowledge, those in museums now had unprecedented scope for the
exercise of whim and fancy.

The intellectual nihilism of the cultural left was compounded by the
attack on traditional institutions from the economic right. Under the
Conservative government of Margaret Thatcher, public arts bodies were
forced to justify their existence by proving that they could give value for
money. Under the new market criteria, arts bodies started to became
service delivery organisations, indistinguishable from businesses or Star-
bucks. 'The customer always comes first' was the new mantra. If the arts
could not find customers, then they would have to go to the wall. Having
lost their intellectual bearings, museum professionals were now beginning to be pushed decisively in a new direction – towards the new
market ideology of customer satisfaction. At the same time, they could
justify this move in pseudodemocratic terms: 'The People have been
excluded from museums for too long – time to give them a say in what

we do'. Thatcherism saved the cultural left by giving a focus and a rationale to its activities: having lost the rigour (s)he once found in his/her professional work, the museum official could now fall back on one overriding criterion of judgement: 'does the customer like it?' The peculiar mixture of economic rightism and cultural leftism explains the odd jargon of the new official. He speaks with a leftish social conscience (the People, social inclusion, accessibility, raising self-esteem), but delivers all these as services that can be measured, audited and justified in hard-nosed market terms (such as 'benchmarking', 'best value' and so on). Just as the New Economy business speaks of meeting the diverse needs of its customers, so the new museum speaks of meeting the diverse needs of visitors.

This coming together of two seemingly opposed forces reached its apogee in the election of the New Labour government in 1997. For the first time, the state, big business and culture all spoke the same language – empowerment, inclusiveness, diversity and customer satisfaction. The new orthodoxy was churned out from the new super-ministry at the Department for Culture, Media and Sport (DCMS).

Most new museum professionals have grasped this moment with enthusiasm. No longer simple curators or scholars, now they are social campaigners, out there on the frontline, fighting for the people, raising health/environmental/gender/identity awareness. The heady effects of the new orthodoxy can be seen throughout the profession. David Fleming, director of Tyne and Wear museums and convenor for Group for Large Local Authority Museums (GLLAM), told the 2000 Museums Association conference: 'I came into museums because it was my way of trying to change the world'.

A GLLAM report on museums and social inclusion (GLLAM, 2000) offers some examples of museums that now function as composite health, education and social service centres. An Asian women's textile project at the Birmingham Museum and Art Gallery is run in collaboration with social services and targets isolated Asian women with mental health problems. Describing the benefits of the project, the report states: 'Not only does this project enable the women to improve their skills and self-confidence, but it also provides a safe space for mental health issues to be confronted and discussed'. Tyne and Wear Museum worked with Michael – 'a real tearaway [who] became involved in the production of a CD-ROM for the museum, and gained enormously in self-esteem'. Once museums are freed from the core obligation to their collections there are almost no limits to their functions. This is a problem.

Museums, which once concentrated on organising and classifying objects, now, with the active encouragement of government, are much more interested in classifying, segmenting and categorising the public. The visitor is always treated as a group-member, never as an individual. Artefacts are no longer seen to have universal appeal, but are divided up on the basis of the particular social group to which they are deemed to be of interest. Exhibitions on African art or slavery are seen to be of interest to Black British communities; the Science Museum constructed an exhibition on sport to appeal to teenage boys. This involves a narrow and patronising view of the audience.

Museums vie with each other in drawing in the key target groups: the young, ethnic minorities and the economically marginalised. The DCMS (2000) suggests that museums identify an 'excluded group' and their distribution, then 'engage them and establish their needs'. In keeping with the new market-driven spirit, all museums funded by the DCMS (1999) now have to publish access targets and detail measures by which they are 'widening access to a broad cross-section of the public for example by age, social class, and ethnicity'. Museum exhibitions, it suggests, should consciously attempt to appeal to the young as well as the old, Asian as well as White, working class as well as middle class. The diverse needs of all these different groups of people should be at the forefront of curators' minds, and inform every aspect of their work. Of course, everybody wants museums to be free and open to all, to come as they please. But this target approach involves categorising the public, rather than putting on exhibitions that will be of general interest.

Good for the Collection?

The collection in decline?

Once a museum puts the perceived needs of the people at the heart of its work, the collection will quite naturally lose its importance and value. A collection is no longer seen as valuable in itself – because it is rare or beautiful – or because it represents something important within a particular field. Instead, its value is embodied in the immediate relationship it is able to establish to the public, how it will help the museum and its officials connect with the public, or how it will lead to observable changes in the lives of visitors.

The loss of collections' value can be observed in many aspects of museum practice. Sometimes collections are left to gather dust while museums get on with more exciting and socially responsible activities. In the GLLAM case studies of best practice, museum projects involved awareness-raising about teenage pregnancy, or setting up a football team with young vandals. The report argues that a reorientation towards social ends will show why collections 'are worth having in the first place'. But in practice the desired social ends are more easily achieved without bringing artefacts into it. If they are used, the objects become no more than props for the wider social project.

Sometimes interactive exhibits replace objects. If the main concern of a museum is to engage the public in particular ways, these aims might be better achieved with animation or interactive technologies than with the raw object. The object allows for an open encounter with no predetermined outcome – the visitor can make of it what he or she likes. Interactive technology only allows for closed outcomes because the encounter is all programmed in advance by the museum. For museums geared towards building relationships with the people, an open-ended encounter between visitor and object leaves far too much to chance. Likewise, animated contraptions, which sometimes replace original specimens, are calculated to elicit a desired effect. The animated tyrannosaurus rex at the Natural History Museum, for example, elicits the 'Wow, scary' effect.

Forming links with specific communities is taken to its logical extreme by simply giving objects back. Influenced by similar cases in the USA, Glasgow Museums repatriated the Lakota Ghost Dance Shirt to a tribe of Native Americans. Mark O'Neill, of Glasgow Museums, told a Museums and Galleries Commission conference in 2000 that the loss of the shirt was outweighed by the benefits of 'bringing healing to a sad people'. This case reveals an important shift. Some museum professionals seem to value the demonstration of empathy and social responsibility more highly than they value the collections they are supposed to protect – even when these collections are supposedly held for the enjoyment and enlightenment of all of the public.

Curators and scholarship

Advocates of the people-centred museum argue that collections have no intrinsic value anyway. Their value lies instead in their relationship to the public. At best, this is a statement of the obvious. Without society, without thought and knowledge, there would be no museums and objects would have no value in any meaningful sense of the word. It is true also, that society's understanding and appreciation of objects changes through time. Charles Saumarez Smith (1989) has traced the V&A's treatment of the Mark Lane doorway, which started out as the carved wooden front for a late 17th-century London house. In the late 19th century it was acquired by the museum for the quality of its woodwork, and in the late 20th century was placed in the V&A shop. As time passed, the same object was seen by turns to have a decorative, historical, aesthetic and commercial value.

However, just because different societies might bring to light different or even conflicting aspects of the same object does not mean that the aesthetic or scientific value of those objects is arbitrary. Society might impose its tastes upon museum collections – classifying, organising and interpreting in its own way. But that is only one side of the relationship, because objects also impose themselves upon society. The Parthenon marbles did not gain their importance from the whim of Lord Elgin or the British Museum. They hold their place today because of their artistic greatness, the perfection of the craftsmanship and their unique historical significance.

It is the task of scholarship to assess the relative importance of objects, for what they are in themselves and for the broader artistic, scientific or historical context within which they are to be placed. Collections are *evidence* – of past societies, of different cultures, species of bird, forms of rock, etc. Collections are the raw material of our knowledge on so many subjects. Of course, collections require interpretation – they need to be approached with particular questions and theories, and interpretation will change over time. The study of works of art develops our ideas about art as such, just as the study of the products of nature develops our ideas about the natural world, or the study of the artefacts of past societies develops our ideas about history. Knowledge is not some arbitrary ideological construct within our minds. In the context of museums, knowledge comes from the critical encounter between the curator and artefacts.

It is rare for the core activities of curatorship and scholarship to be done away with altogether. Instead, they are swamped by an ever-expanding array of 'audience-related' activities. In the past 30 years there has been a remorseless growth in education, helpdesk and marketing functions. A survey on museum research and scholarship documented the sense among many curators that their research function was under threat. Eighty percent said that they were not as active in research as they would like to be, and most said the time available for research had declined in the past 10 years. However even these figures do not fully convey the depth of the malaise. Much of what now passes for research would have been done in the past by the marketing department (if there even was one). Many curators now spend an increasing amount of their time researching the public and the attitudes of the public towards their work.

Often a museum's small number of curators are expected to double up as PR officers and managers. True. But often this is due to lack of staff. Many museums emphasise the importance of management training – the Cultural Heritage National Training Organisation now produces courses in management for museum professionals.

Fewer people entering the museum profession today have the specialist training necessary to study and care for collections. Many enter the profession not by gaining a doctorate in art history or palaeontology, for example, but by doing a one-year Museums Studies MA (this is especially the case for those working in local and independent museums). A small proportion of the Museums Studies course is concerned with the conservation and interpretation of artefacts – most is concerned with the study of audiences and cultural theory analyses of power in exhibitions. In response to this training gap, University College London has created a separate Artefact Studies MA.

Even when curators have studied their collections, they are often asked to defer to nonspecialists when organising exhibitions – administrators, PR officers or members of the public themselves. Tyne and Wear museum has encouraged the display of works which 'may not necessarily be famous or highly regarded, but instead have been chosen by members of the public simply because they like them or because they arouse certain emotions or memories'. Of course, it is a difficult and admirable task for curators to try to communicate their knowledge to the public – it is tricky to squash years of research into a single display case. And many curators may be weak at doing this. But the answer is not to get rid of curatorial expertise entirely.

For curators to learn the most from museum artefacts, they must be allowed some degree of separation from the immediate demands of politicians, bureaucrats, and even from the public. They must be allowed to study their subject and to follow the demands of their own discipline without having to wonder all the time whether it is directly relevant to the public. The question of how to communicate the results of their research to the public will come at the stage of creating exhibitions – which is an equally important curatorial activity. But in the process of original research, concentration necessarily means the exclusion of external concerns.

If scholarship in museums is neglected, our knowledge will suffer. Museums cannot simply rest on the expertise they have built up over the years. There must be a constant replenishment of that knowledge by scholars who keep up with the latest research and who are ready always to reassess the significance and meaning of objects. If this task falls into neglect, it will be very difficult to repair the damage done. If, for example, the expert in fossil reptiles has been redeployed to study how people react to fossil reptiles, he or she is less likely to concentrate on new discoveries in the field. At worst, whole branches of knowledge could go into decline through wilful neglect.

The socially responsible museum

While the core function for which museums were created is down-graded to an ancillary activity, a vast range of spurious functions are loaded on to them for which they are entirely unsuited. For the new orthodoxy, museums must reflect the concerns and experiences of our society and of everyday life. They must become relevant, and inclusive, and should talk to 'real people'.

Museums try to make themselves relevant in two different ways. The first method is to cling to the appeal of mass entertainment. The logic here is crude, but occasionally effective: lots of people watch TV (for example), therefore museums should use TV in their exhibition to pull in the crowds. Exhibitions based around this principle include the Brand new exhibition at the V&A and the video games in the Wellcome Wing. The second approach is to target specific groups, such as women, youth or ethnic minorities. This strategy is far less effective because it almost always involves some massive presumption on the part of the museum as to what appeals to these groups.

Social inclusion is another crusade aimed at transforming the function of the museum. In his 1999 budget speech, the UK Chancellor Gordon Brown committed museums to the struggle against social exclusion. The DCMS had the vision of museums becoming 'centres for social change', improving people's self-esteem and improving community relations, while the GLLAM social inclusion report defined seven social ends to which museums should gear themselves, such as personal growth and development, community empowerment and tackling unemployment and crime.

More widespread concerns about social cohesion and the decline of the traditional bonds of church, family and political parties have led commentators to search for alternative sources of social bonding. This concern was no doubt heightened by the apathy implied by the historically low turnout in the 2001 general election. Museums are seen as 'cultural meeting places' that could fill the gaps left by the decline of the old institutions and bring cohesion to a fragmented society. New Labour thinkers Charles Leadbeater and Kate Oakley (1999) write that 'art, culture and sport create meeting places for people in an increasingly diversified, fragmented and unequal society', meeting places that were once 'provided by work, religion or trade unions'. This explains the interest with which government watched the crowds bustling at Tate Modern when it first opened.

There is nothing new about using museums and cultural institutions for social purposes. In the early 19th century Prime Minister Sir Robert Peel stated that one of the purposes of the new National Gallery would be to 'cement the bonds of union between the richer and poorer orders of the state'. The difference was, however, that the 19th-century elite tried to achieve its social aims by setting up public museums full of the artefacts of art, science and history. As a result, visitors were freer to dispense with the ideological intentions of the founders, and enjoy and learn from artefacts as they pleased. The Victorian elite may have believed that art would refine the unruly masses and make them less likely to rebel – however, whatever they may have thought, a desire for social revolution and a liking for Titian are not incompatible.

In the people-centred museum, however, social ends tend to take over. Much of the activity of museum staff is now indistinguishable from that of a host of social, health or educational services. Most of the DCMS or GLLAM case studies of best social inclusion practice could have been performed by any charity or social service. The collection and the specialist knowledge required to understand it are pushed to the margins. In its efforts to provide every sort of service, from health to social support, the people-centred museum tends to undermine the distinctive character and eventually the very rationale of the museum. This is compounded by efforts to dissolve the museum into its community, to break down any barriers with the world around. Outreach programmes, attempts to involve local communities in the museum's activities, and the outright dispersal of the collection into community centres; all these blur the museum out of existence. When the newly appointed head of Resource Matthew Evans suggested in February 2000 that museums get away from the idea that they are constrained by physical walls and that they should get their collections into shops, clubs and pubs, many in the profession reacted at first with surprise. 'We're already there, we're doing it', said Simon Thurley, then director of the Museum of London.

Good for Visitors?

Advocates of the new museum say that because museums are public institutions funded by public money, they must answer to all the people and not just to a cultural elite. This seems a reasonable argument. So let us examine how well the people-centred museum fulfils its obligations.

In the case of the new museum, the people that they are so anxious to follow are a pure projection, a creation by the museums themselves. Nobody outside the cultural elite ever demanded that museums become more accessible, relevant, inclusive, diverse and interactive. All these views were hatched within government and the museum world itself and then projected out onto the public.

The consequences of orienting the museum towards visitors are twofold. As the Dome proved beyond doubt, when the new cultural elite start second-guessing what people want, they invariably underestimate them and try to go for the lowest common denominator. Reaching for the lowest common denominator explains the growing tendency in museums to treat all visitors as children. Secondly, the people focus also leads museums to build manipulative and invasive relationships with their visitors. When the purpose of an exhibition lies in its relationship to the visitor, the museum will, quite naturally, want to check to see if the relationship is working. People become the objects of study, their interests and responses catalogued and catered to.

Direct address and forced chumminess are favoured to assist the visitor; impersonal and abstract terms are now considered too cold and too user-unfriendly. Both the Science Museum and the Natural History Museum use the second person in their exhibitions on human biology: 'This is your brain', 'Have you ever wondered where your relatives came from?', as if people would not be interested if the model was of the human brain, in the abstract. At a Natural History Museum exhibit on leaf structure and function, a voiceover announces: 'Welcome to the leaf factory. You are an 8000th of your normal size and are inside the leaf.' An intellectual regression seems to be taking place here. Making the abstraction from the particular 'me' to the general human is not only fundamental to thought itself, but is something that children grasp at school. On a visit to the High Street Londinium exhibition in the Museum of London, I overheard the following exchange between a member of staff dressed in a toga and a visitor:

Actress: My husband has gone to the amphitheatre. Come in and help yourself to food. There's some nice cheese over there. . .:
Visitor: How do you know they made cheese?:
Actress: What do you mean *they*? This is *me* you're talking about.:

'Me', 'you', not 'they'. Don't question, don't try to stand back, says the new museum.

The new museum aims to help people understand through fabricated feelings and experience rather than by reason. Full-scale reconstructions such as the Jorvik Viking Centre and High Street Londinium at the Museum of London are presented with the claim that visitors gain an authentic experience of the past. 'Visit the Jorvik Viking Centre, step aboard a time car and be whisked back through the centuries to real-life Viking Britain. You can experience in sight, sound and smell exactly what it was like to live and work in Viking-age Jorvik'. 'Leave year 2000, and enter High Street Londinium, first century AD. You enter Londinium early in the morning.' Both of these reconstructions are based on actual archaeological digs; they are representations and interpretations of the evidence uncovered. Why does this evidence need to be presented as a 'real' picture of the past, rather than what it is, archaeological evidence? Any opportunity for the visitor to exercise imagination is severely curtailed.

Many museums seem to think the public has the most limited capacity for concentration and little need for quiet. The proliferation of gadgets and interactive displays, flashing lights, talking exhibits, music and sound effects tell us more about museums' view of the public than it does about the public itself. Children have limited concentration and are still at the stage of 'learning through play'. But adults can read books for hours on end; they can sit and concentrate on ideas without moving their body in any way.

A common refrain from the new museums and their government backers is that many of the visitors they want to attract are from marginalised social groups and are therefore easily intimidated – a patronising and rather strange perception of the public. One of the 'barriers to access' identified by the DCMS (1999) is 'attitudinal', that is 'museums not making all of their visitors feel welcomed and valued'. To draw in the shy masses, museums now create spaces for public participation. In order to bolster people's confidence, some museums – such as the Castle Museum in Nottingham and the People's Gallery in Birmingham – show community exhibitions chosen and curated by local people. Other museums help their visitors to feel valued by asking their opinion in the exhibition, such as the 'Tell us what you think' exhibits in the Science Museum's Wellcome Wing.

In their every move the public are watched and examined, giving the relationship of museums to their public a predatory aspect – museums feed off the shifting source of public opinion and reaction. Officials debate how architecture affects the way visitors move around buildings. Questionnaires and focus groups analyse visitor response to exhibits, or their understanding of a particular label. Visitor figures are monitored to see what ethnic group, what age or gender group is under-represented and the missing groups can then be targeted.

While making few intellectual demands, exhibitions set up to engage visitors can be very demanding in other ways. People are not left to wander through the museum with their own thoughts, looking at an object or reading a label as they choose. To obtain information visitors often must press a button. This seems less a means to an end than an end in itself – the temperature and pressure of the planets of the solar system, for example, could be printed on a card, yet the Natural History Museum has interactive exhibits that provide these basic facts. Action is often demanded just to see an object. In the Jersey Maritime Museum some of the text accompanying exhibits is hidden away in models of shells, boats and bottles that the visitor must open up if they wish to see it.

We arrive then at a paradox. The curator who loudly professes his respect for every ethnic, class, age and gender group and who builds his exhibition around what he perceives to be their needs, almost inevitably ends up expressing disdain for the public. On the other hand, the curator who is concerned above all with his collection, is more truly respectful towards the public, and better serves their needs.

Conclusion

Museums should arguably stick to what they do best – to preserve, display, study and where possible collect the treasures of civilisation and of nature. They are not fit to do anything else. It is this single rationale for the museum that makes each one unique, which gives each its own distinctive character. It is the hard work of scholars and curators in their own areas of expertise that attracts visitors. It is museums' collections, and the enlightenment and pleasure that they can bring, that are more likely to attract visitors.

References

DCMS (2000) *Centres for Social Change: Museums, Galleries and Archives for All*. London: DCMS.

DCMS (1999) *Museums for the Many*. London: DCMS.

GLLAM (2000) *Museums and Social Inclusion*. London: MLA.

Gunn, A.V. and Prescott, R.G.W (1999) *Lifting the Veil: Research and Scholarship in United Kingdom Museums and Galleries*. London: Museums and Galleries Commission.

Leadbeater, C. and Oakley, K. (1999) *The Independents*. London: Demos.

Museums Journal (2000) Interview with Heather Mayfield.

National Museums Directors Conference (2004) *A Manifesto for Museums: Building Outstanding Museums for the 21st Century, National Museums Directors Conference*.

Saumarez Smith, C. (1989) Museums, artefacts and meanings. In P. Vergo (ed.) *The New Museology*. London: Reaktion Books.

Chapter 18

Caves in Belgium: Standardisation or Diversification?

ANYA DIEKMANN, GÉRALDINE MAULET and STÉPHANIE QUÉRIAT

Introduction

Standardisation is a phenomenon that comes originally from the manufacturing industry. In order to increase the speed and efficiency of production, products are reproduced. The standardisation of the presentation of sites is one key to the so-called 'tourism industry' (Hewison, 1987). It does not only affect all types of tourism sites, but its characteristics can be observed worldwide. Indeed, standardisation can be found in different elements of a tourism site. For instance, the choice of materials shows similarities: the same pebble stones throughout Europe, the same litter bins and the same type of support and 'scene setting', such as classical music in castles.

> Like all processes, which act at national or international scales, tourism contains within a set of forces, which lead to increasing uniformity. Whether it is the house style of an international hotel chain, or something as simple as a national market for street furniture, tourism erodes differences but markets passes for individuality. (Newby, 1994: 225)

There are two main aspects to this standardisation. Firstly, standardisation is the application of preconceived standards, required for the safety and health of visitors, which are well known in tourism-related business, for instance, hotels, restaurants etc. They are to be considered as positive as they aim to guarantee appropriate conditions on site for the visitor.

Secondly, standardisation provides easily understandable and uniform information to visitors on tourism sites. In that sense, standardisation can be a threat to the individuality of a tourist attraction. This kind of standardisation refers to all communication types, such as promotional tools and contents, as well as items for sale in the shops.

Standardisation as an underlying issue of the 'heritage industry' (Hewison, 1987) and the heritage 'product' (Ashworth & Howard, 1999) has not received the attention it should have. Until recently, the determination of standardisation has lain essentially in the hands of practitioners (West, 1999). Even though they declare this as a risk, neither managers nor politicians seem to be preoccupied by the risk of standardisation. Standardisation depends to a certain extent on fashion. For instance, presentation tools considered to be modern (fashionable), such as new technologies, tend to be introduced in most sites, leading inevitably to standardisation.

This chapter focuses in particular on the second aspect of standardisation. It understands standardisation as a uniformisation of the presentation and interpretation of tourism sites, whereby characteristics of a site are reduced to a set of characteristics easily recognised by the visitor (MacCannell, 1989). These recognisable characteristics and common explanations are assumed to deliver the basis of a satisfying visit of the site to a large public.

The loss of rich information, individuality and identity through standardisation of the site is obvious. The consequent loss of individuality leads inevitably to a loss of authenticity. Indeed, standardisation increases the risk of 'staged authenticity' (Cohen, 1979) and 'falsifies' to a certain extent the visitor's experience. But who is responsible for the standardisation of the tourist site? MacCannell (1979) argues that tourism tends to favour generalisation, and that on the product development side, tourism requires simplicity to the point of banality. In a similar sense, Cohen (1979) points out that some uses of heritage favour generalisation, and that mass tourism often reduces the rich and complex past to a set of easily recognisable characteristics.

The way a site is presented and interpreted generally lies however in the hands of the site manager. It is questionable how far the interest and demand of the visitor are taken into account. It would be interesting to see whether visitor numbers increased dramatically after standardisation and fashionable presentation of a site. To a certain extent, standardisation seems to be the result of a transfer of a recipe from other successful (in terms of visitor numbers) sites. Some managers appear to consider the 'standardisation' or 'fashionable presentation' as a warrant for continuing visitor interest. Yet it has been proven that generalisation can be responsible for decreasing visitor attention (Moscardo, 1996). It may however be assumed that site managers are not consciously opting for standardised products.

The aim of this chapter is to determine standardised elements, locate them within cave sites and tackle eventual distinctive features aiming to avoid standardisation. In order to achieve that goal, the visitor's tour is followed. The authors are aware that the visitor perception and appreciation of standardisation is another important question that would deserve further research and cannot be addressed in this context.

Why Caves?

The natural setting of caves makes this tourist attraction an easy victim of standardisation of presentation and interpretation. It is difficult to avoid the *déjà vu* experience for this kind of site. Evidence will be given that even the wish for diversity can be seen under a 'standardised' light. The choice of caves for illustrating standardisation has furthermore been determined by the historical role that caves play in tourism history. Caves were among the first sites that were opened to visitors with an economic purpose, charging an entrance fee. Standardisation in the presentation of caves goes back as far as the first tourist activities in caves for the public in the middle of the 19th century (Quériat, 2002). They present, already in the earliest time of public access, similarities in their development plans, presentation and interpretation. Furthermore, the choice of the names of spaces and rooms within the caves shows the impact of the sociocultural tendencies (fashion). The 19th-century styles, such as Classicism, Romanticism and Orientalism influenced substantially the determination of these names: *Boudoir de Proserpine* (Han), *Détroit de Rhodes* (Tilff), *Palais de Bagdad* (Rochefort), *Salle de la Mosquée* (Han).

Caves were furthermore connected to satanic worship and witchcraft. These popular beliefs were translated by the names given to a number of rooms, such as the room of the dwarf, the room of the witch Sabbath (Rochefort), etc.

In the 19th century, people in charge of caves tried to attract their visitors through particular components of their site. As a matter of fact their diversity consisted in the rather uniform presence of particularly large spaces, called cathedrals, mosques etc. in order to express and promote their greatness.

At the same time, site managers were making caves safer and facilitating the flow of visitors: passages were made, tunnels enlarged, stairs and protection bars were installed. With technical development, electric light was introduced in most sites. The cave of Han was the first to create visitor facilities. In order to stay competitive, the other caves followed closely. In the beginning of the 20th century, the uniformisation of visitor facilities in caves increased security to a large extent, but also provoked criticism, talking about the *haussmanisation of the underground world* (d'Ardenne, 1897). Articles in tourist magazines (*Bulletin du Touring Club de Belgique*, 1914) promoted the natural, noncommercial exploited sites.

Promotion campaigns started mainly at the end of the 19th and beginning of the 20th century. Just as they are today, distinctive characteristics of each cave were promoted. They were described using fairly standard and similar superlatives. Each cave had the 'highest room', 'longest river' or 'nicest stone formation'. Publicity posters were equally subject to certain standardisation at that time. They used – as nowadays – a distorted vision of reality aiming to promote the cave through distinctive qualities: unreal light, multiplication of concretions and modification of their dimensions and artificial creation of larger spaces through false presentation of the size of people.

Case Studies

The following case studies are based on a survey undertaken with site managers and the site experiences of the authors. In order to analyse eventual standardisation purposes in Belgian caves, an indicator list integrating not only the cave and its presentation, but also all visitor facilities and services following the tour of the visitors were established to review the following:

- reception area and shop;
- presentation and interpretation;
- promotion; and
- supplementary offers.

The cases concentrate on caves with speleothems (or cave formations) and all caves are situated in rural surroundings in Wallonia (see Figure 18.1).

The caves under investigation were selected according to their visitor numbers and the existence of visitor management policies, such as reception spaces, organised visits, etc. Caves with less than 10,000 visitors each year have not been taken into account as they generally do not present any specific visitor management policies. The result consists of eight caves with annual visitor numbers of up to 300,000 for the caves of Han.

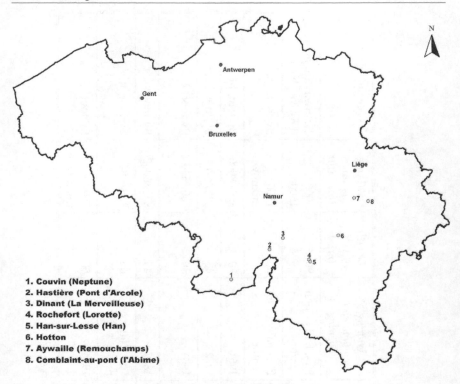

1. Couvin (Neptune)
2. Hastière (Pont d'Arcole)
3. Dinant (La Merveilleuse)
4. Rochefort (Lorette)
5. Han-sur-Lesse (Han)
6. Hotton
7. Aywaille (Remouchamps)
8. Comblaint-au-pont (l'Abime)

Figure 18.1 Location of the main caves in Belgium

Han and Remouchamps, the two most visited caves, were also the first to open to the public. Han is one of the emblematic sites of Belgium (a site with one of the highest visitor numbers in the country) and specifically of Wallonia. Frommer's guide considers the cave as 'probably one of the most spectacular and worth visiting sites in Belgium'. Remouchamps presents, according to the guide *Le petit futé*, the longest underground navigation of Europe. Hotton is generally known for its 'beauty'. It is the only cave listed as a natural heritage site. The characteristic features of the cave of Neptune are the waterfall and the different levels within the cave. 'La Merveilleuse' attracts visitors with its varied types of speleothems. The cave of Lorette is known for its 'wild and threatening' atmosphere (Blue Guide) while the cave of Abîme is characterised by high spaces. Except for Hotton and Neptune, all other caves opened either in the 19th century or the beginning of the 20th century (Table 18.1).

Table 18.1 Identification of selected caves

Cave name	Location	Number of visitors (2002)	Beginning of commercial opening	Length of visit (min)	Walking distance, total (m)	Means of visit
Han	Han-sur-Lesse	300,000	First half of 19th century	90	3000/ 16000	Tramway (to arrive at the cave), by foot, boat
Remouchamps	Remouchamps	100,000	First half of 19th century	60	1500/ unknown	By foot, boat
Hotton	Hotton	50,000	1961	70	300/8000	By foot, lift
Neptune	Couvin	40,000	1972	45	330/670	By foot, boat
La Merveilleuse	Dinant	40,000	1904	50	600/630	By foot
Lorette	Rochefort	22,000	1867	45	800/6000	By foot
De l'Abîme	Comblain-au-Pont	15,000	Late 20th century	60	365/684	By foot
Pont d'Arcole	Hastière	10,000	1924	50	750/ unknown	By foot

Within the eight caves under investigation, four are owned by the public sector (l'Abîme, Remouchamps, Pont d'Arcole, Lorette). The other ones (Han, Hotton, Neptune, La Merveilleuse) belong to private owners. The four public caves are managed by either private societies or associations depending at different levels on the public authorities or by a combination of both (Pont d'Arcole). The consequences of these diverging types of management are the different funding they receive.

It should be stressed that, although, as shown later, the contents of the visit are quite similar in each cave, walking distance and time spent in the caves are not linear due, amongst others, to the means of transport.

The Reception Area

The reception space constitutes the first contact for the visitor with the site and also forms the first impression. In all analysed caves, the reception areas follow a main scheme: flat buildings, sometimes in natural stone contain the ticket office, the shop, toilets and sometimes a coffee shop or a bar (Table 18.2). The reception area also includes the area where the visitors have to wait to enter the cave. Apart from Hotton, in all analysed sites these two spaces are separated.

After queuing for tickets, the visitor is led by signage to the area where (s)he has to wait for the guided tour. Large open spaces, or, in the case of Hastière a big room downstairs, allow the waiting visitors to gather. Even in recently restored sites, the public has to wait mainly standing without any distraction. Only one exception, the cave of l'Abîme, contains boards presenting the caves and showing small discovered items. In most of the visited caves the reception spaces are not used for providing detailed information on the site. Furthermore, visitor facilities such as toilets are limited, with the consequence of queues and at peak times the risk for visitors of missing their tour.

Receptions and waiting spaces could consequently be considered as standardised for the facilities they offer. It should however be stressed that facilities, such as toilets and ticket offices, are necessary basic elements of any tourist attraction. The standardisation tackled in this context relates more to the absence of distraction and information on the site that the reception area could offer to the visitor.

Furthermore, similarities within the choice of furniture and decoration have been tackled. For instance, the overall presence of bat items within the reception areas is rather common. Bats are frequently associated with caves and are used to create an attractive atmosphere within the site. Several reception areas have been restored within the last 5 years, with

Table 18.2 Facilities within reception area

	Han	Remouchamps	Hotton	Neptune	La Merveilleuse	Lorette	Abîme	Pont d'Arcole
Ticket office	X	X	X	X	X	X	X	X
Shop	X	X	X	X	X	X	X	X
Coffee shop/bar	X	–	X	X	X	X	X–	X
Open space	X	X	X	X	X	X	–	X
Toilets	X	X	X	X	X	X	X	X

the aim of modernising the site and in order to attract a higher number of visitors. Site managers were questioned during the survey whether the almost simultaneous restoration plans as well as the very comparable plans were a coincidence. Only one site manager admitted that restoration works may be influenced by similar sites and be subject to fashion or at least tendencies. Another manager considered visitor flow management as the only aspect taken into account for renovation. The responsibility is, in most cases, left in the hands of the architect and similar choice of colours or particular redundant arrangements within the reception areas are, according to the site manager, purely coincidental.

The Shop

In all the caves under investigation, the shop is located within the reception area. Visitors have the choice of visiting it either at the beginning of the visit or upon departure. The shops are managed by the site itself and the choice on offer lies in the hands of the site manager. The range of products sold by the shops is to a large extent standardised. One reason for this is the high cost of any individual production. Yet, the shop of the cave of l'Abime offers several items containing the logo of the cave. The typical cave shop sells local handicrafts and products, textiles, minerals and all sorts of stones. Tendencies to standardisation affect specifically this last group of items. The available stones are almost never from the site itself or even of local origin. They are imported from other countries or continents. Visitors are not necessarily informed about this fact. Only in the shop of Hotton is an information board is located near the minerals, which explains the reasons for this situation: fragility of the local environment and loss of beauty of the broken stone formations within the caves. The difference between the shops is evident in the quality of the products. A trend to increase the quality of the latter can however be observed throughout all visited shops. The consequence is a standardised market that due to its industrial production loses its individual connection with the site. Apart from exquisite local products ('produits du terroir') mainly consisting of typical beers and cheese, most products sold are imported.

Standardisation can equally be stated for the presentation of the products within the shops. Yet these tendencies go beyond the cave sites and are due to the general fashion of contemporary shop design. Standardised shop presentations can be observed throughout most of the recently restored sites throughout Belgium.

Table 18.3 Shop articles

	Han	Remouchamps*	Hotton	Neptune	La Merveilleuse	Lorette	Abîme	Pont d'Arcole
Mineral stones	X	–	X	X	X	X	–	X
Bat items	–	–	–	–	X	X	X	–
Textiles	X	–	–	X	–	–	–	X
Stationery articles	X	–	X	–	–	X	–	–
Books	X	–	–	–	–	X	X	–
Postcards	X	–	–	X	X	X	X	X
Food	X		X	X	X	X	X	X
Drinks	X		X	X	X	X	X	X
Local products	X		X	X	–	X	–	X

*The shop is closed for the time being.

The overview of the shop's articles (Table 18.3) shows that the majority of items are 'souvenir' articles. Only two shops offer books for sale. It is notable that the most standardised articles sold in cave shops are mineral stones.

Presentation and Interpretation of the Caves

Site visit

Visitor flow management starts only within the cave. Groups are organised in the waiting spaces according to the carrying capacity of the cave. The overall use of guided tours is motivated by security needs for the visitors and preservation requirements for the fragile ecosystem. In most caves visits are available in at least two languages. Within the caves, the guides are the only source of information for the visitor. As a matter of fact, the similarities of the visit between the different caves are quite obvious. Indeed, the authors have identified a similar structure in the contents of the guide comments of all caves. Site managers are aware of the risks of similarities of the guided tours. As exposed later in this chapter, some cave managers attempt therefore to diversify the visit by adding something particular to distinguish their site from the others.

Elements of the visit

In the Cave of Neptune, a warden accompanies the visitors and comments are prerecorded and provided by loudspeakers. In all other caves, guides are generally locals, having worked for quite a long time as guides and knowing each inch of the site. In some caves, students are employed in peak periods to increase the quantity of guided tours. The comments, information and interpretation are to a large extent standardised (Table 18.4). This seems to represent the desire to provide easily understandable information to a large public.

The guided tour starts in each cave in the waiting area. Before entering the cave, the guide announces general information, such as how far the group will walk and how deep the visitor will be underneath the ground. Other technical details including the temperature of the cave in summer and winter are given.

After entering the cave, the introduction is followed by a generally short but interesting story of the discovery of the cave and the fundamentals on the underground world and its speleothems. The most known cave formations are stalagmites and stalactites. Each language has its own associations made up to describe the difference between the two types of speleothems. These associations are the same in

Table 18.4 Elements of the visits

	Han	Remouchamps	Hotton	Neptune	La Merveilleuse	Lorette	Abîme	Pont d'Arcole
Technical information (km, depth, number of steps etc.)	X	X	X	X	X	X	X	X
General explanations on stalagmites and stalactites	X	X	X	X	X	X	X	X
Wildlife	X	X	X	–	X	X	X	X
Names of spaces	X	X	X	X	X	X	X	X
Anecdotes	X	X	X	X	X	X	X	X
Nicknames	X	X	X	X	X	X	X	X
Superlatives	X	X	X	X	X	X	–	X
Advanced scientific information (formation of the cave, speleothems, etc.)	–	–	X	X	X	–	X	–

all visited caves. For instance, in French the common explanation on stalagmites and stalactites consist of telling visitors that stalagmites are the ones that go up ('m' like 'monter'), and stalactites the ones that go down ('t' like 'tomber'). In English, associations are that stalactites hang 'tite' while stalagmites hold 'mite'.

These explanations are followed by a short description of the wildlife within the cave, an explanation of the names of the spaces, who chose them, when and why. In all caves, particularly this last aspect is highlighted with anecdotes. A redundant way of presenting specific cave formations is the use of nicknames. Names are chosen from current life such as cartoons or religious characters. For instance, Casper the phantom, Jumbo or Buddha as well as the Simpsons are quite common. They are symbols coming from a widespread common social environment without referring to any sociocultural connections related to the site itself.

Superlatives, such as the highest room, the biggest stalagmite etc. are highlighted throughout the whole visit. Only in three caves is more detailed scientific information provided about the geological aspects of the cave.

Technical support

As mentioned previously, technical developments were of major importance for the accessibility of caves. *Sound and light* and special light effects are frequently used tools to emphasise or expose specific speleothems and settings of a cave. These tools, in the cases of *sound and light*, accompanied by music have a great responsibility for the emotional experience of the visitor. Visitor surveys in Han showed that the 'sound and light' was often considered to be the best component.

The first *sound and light* was implemented in 1972 and is still a growing presentation tool in caves. In three of the examined caves (Han, Neptune, Lorette) the tour includes a *sound and light* presentation. The other caves use special light effects (e.g. different coloration) as a presentation tool for presenting specific speleothems and interesting cave formations. The overall use of *sound and light* and/or special light effects as part of the caves' presentation tends to confirm the tendencies for standardisation. However, it would be a biased conclusion to consider these presentation tools as negative and lacking individuality. It is however a reality, that the introduction of the latter has been a succession of 'copying' other caves.

Table 18.5 Promotional tools

	Han	Remouchamps	Hotton	Neptune	La Merveilleuse	Lorette	Abîme	Pont d'Arcole
Leaflets	X	X	X	X	X	X	X	X
Poster	X	X	X	X	–	X	X	–
Television spots	X	Unknown	–	X	–	–	–	–
Radio spots	X	Unknown	–	X	–	–	–	–
Guide books	X	X	X	–	X	X	X	X
Internet	X	X	–	X	X	X	–	–

Promotion and marketing

All caves under investigation use similar promotion tools (Table 18.5). Leaflets are the most common ones and each of the caves has one distributed in different places, such as other tourist attractions or tourist information offices and the national tourist organisation. Apart from the Neptune cave, they all can be found in different guidebooks, such as Baedecker, Michelin etc. Internet sites and posters are another marketing tool, yet three of them (Hotton, Abïme and Pont d'Arcole) do not have websites yet. Radio and television campaigns are rare and only used by two caves, Han and Neptune. The choice of marketing and promotional tools is obviously not necessarily related to the number of visitors.

Though certain choices of promotion and marketing tools depend on financial possibilities of the cave management, the promotional language is not influenced by financial means and can be tackled as a form of standardisation. The contents of cave promotion and marketing indeed has not changed since the beginning of cave promotion in the 19th century: promotion campaigns emphasise the distinctive characteristics of the caves. In order to highlight the difference of a particular cave in contrast to others, all cave managers choose the same strategy. Each cave has a unique superlative: you can either take an elevator (Hotton), boat trip, visit the only attraction in Belgium with 3 stars in the Michelin guidebook (Han), or attend an unusual 'music and light' display, unique in Europe with the music of Vangelis (Neptune) etc.

Yet, in a guide edited in 1885, the author already affirms that 'if the visitor has seen one cave, he has seen them all' (Conty, 1885). In order to avoid this impression, site managers insist in their promotion campaigns on the new products added to the cave: e.g. free visit to the Calestienne garden of walks (Hotton), caves museum (Remouchamps) or a new visitor centre with a new film, videokarst, on tectonic phenomena (Rochefort).

According to the site managers, promotion does not address specific segments of the public but the widest range possible. Very few visitor surveys (mainly in Han) have been conducted in order to learn about the visitor motivation and profile. Unlike for other cultural heritage attractions, it is difficult to establish a specific segment of cave visitor. The only available information from the visitor surveys is that the percentage of individual visitors is higher than groups.

At Han, of the 366,000 visitors in 2003, only 645 bought combined tickets with another smaller (± 10 km) cave nearby. It would however be wrong to conclude that the average cave visitor is not a cave enthusiast. It might simply indicate that most of the visitors are visiting a specific cave only once and therefore do not choose the combined ticket. The site management is equally aware that most of the visitors come only once and might come back 20 years later with their children and again with their grandchildren. The launching this year of an annual membership might change this attitude and favour repeat visits.

In the absence of surveys, and according to site managers' observations, it may nevertheless be concluded that families to a large extent compose the cave public. Cave managers pretend that visitors visit the same cave probably maximum three times in their life. The consequence of these statements consists of a certain lack of interest in the type of visitors. This acknowledgement justifies the marketing strategy, which is attracting the widest public possible. Consequently promotion campaigns contain only very general information.

The 'Escape' from Standardisation

It is clearly a fact that caves are victims of standardisation and – even though it is not officially recognised – site managers obviously try to extend their activities. Analysing the tourism development of caves, diversification of the product has always been a goal for the people in charge. In the past, cave managers tried to diversify their product in different ways.

Firstly, they added some particular presentation features to the visit. In Han, the visit ends, for instance, since the 19th century to the present day, with a canon blast in order to hear the echo. In Lorette Cave a small balloon rising up to the top of the cave demonstrates the height of the cave and in the cave of Hotton an elevator brings the visitor back to the ground level. Furthermore, the site managers developed products for sale in relation to the cave, such as guidebooks, photos etc.

Finally, they diversified the service supply within the caves, such as opening a bar in the Han cave, or the installation of a carillon in Rochefort, or the organisation of concerts and parties within the cave. It appears though that most of these diversification attempts inside the caves constituted a real threat to the environmental integrity of the caves and many of them had to be abandoned. Some caves however still organise some specific events in order to continue diversification inside the caves: in Han, tours with torches are organised, as well as concerts; in Couvin, medieval meetings take place within the caves, the cave of l'Abime suggests special Halloween visits etc.

Either in reaction to the steadily growing visitor numbers or, on the contrary, to attract new visitors, site managers have taken the opportunity to enlarge their activities outside the caves and promote a totally different activity. For instance, archaeological or geological museums as well as deer parks are supposed to increase competitiveness of the sites. Nowadays, the majority of the caves presented above use distinctive supplementary attractions in order to compete with other caves. It should be stressed however that the possibilities of diversification depend to a large extent on the financial situation of a site. For that reason, the cave of Han, having the highest numbers of visitors, has the largest offer of diversification elements.

There are two different types of additional offers. One is integrated within the site and the visitor purchases the right to visit all elements of the site with one single ticket. The second possibility is the purchase of a combined ticket, as well as the possibility of visiting the additional element independently from the main cave site. Table 18.6 identifies these elements.

Only in the two biggest sites, in terms of visitor numbers, do the additional offers require an extra charge. This is, amongst others, due to the fact that these elements are considered as complete attractions and

Table 18.6 Present diversification elements

	Included	*Extra charged*
Han	Video presentation, tram to the entrance of the cave, playgrounds	Museum, deer park, temporary exhibitions
Hotton	Special itinerary in the countryside	–
Remouchamps	Museum	Deer park
Neptune	–	–
La Merveilleuse	–	–
Lorette	Museum, video presentation	–
Abîme	Exhibition on the problems of cave pollution	–
Pont d'Arcole	Playgrounds	–

that they appeal to a large number of visitors coming specifically to visit the deer parks. Only two caves do not have any additional offer.

Conclusion

The aim of this study was to analyse standardisation in Belgian cave sites. The sites were selected according to their visitor numbers and only the standardisation aspects of communication towards the public, such as reception including shops, presentation, interpretation and promotion have been scrutinised.

The results of the study show that from the reception area onwards standardisation is an obvious issue within the caves. Comparison between the different caves shows the similar disposition of all reception areas. The goods in the shops and especially the minerals for sale are representative of standardisation in the choice of products. Most of these mineral stones are imported, without any connection to the site.

Standardisation is equally obvious for the visits and their contents. Presentation and the interpretation provided in all examined caves (except one) by guides are similar and characterised by the use of 'specific cave presentation elements' such as nicknames, recurrent anecdotes, comparable names of spaces and the overall repeated similar presentation of speleothems.

Innovations concern mainly the technical aspects of lightning or sound and music events within the caves. Albeit being conscious about the risks of decreasing visitor numbers, there is little effort to diversify or refresh presentation and interpretation recipes that have worked for such a long time. Still, the feeling of once you have visited one cave, you have visited them all, persists.

Furthermore, it has been outlined that promotion and marketing tools are very similar and lacking individuality. The overall message is the same, referring to the 'exceptional speleothems' and highlighting specific elements, which are mainly superlatives. The use of the latter also becomes, albeit on another level, standardised.

Yet, if most aspects related to the cave visit itself stay standardised as mentioned above, cave managers tend to increase their offer in order to continue attracting old and new clients. At first, diversification attempts were situated within the caves, but with growing concern for protection and conservation issues, cave managers were compelled to extend their diversification attempts from the inside of the cave to the outside.

Even though site managers recognise standardisation in the general presentation of the caves and the reception areas, none of them acts consciously in that direction. Fashion and generally recognised tendencies of what the visitor might expect appear to be one of the origins of standardisation.

If there is an intention of encountering and preventing standardisation, one way would be to analyse the profile of the visitors and to determine their motivations and expectations.

References

Ashworth, G. and Howard, P. (eds) (1999) *European Heritage Planning and Management*. Exeter: Intellect.

Auzias, D. and Labourdette, J.P. (2001) *Petit Futé, Le guide de Belgique-Luxembourg*. Poitiers: l'Université.

Blyth, D. (2000) *Blue Guide* (9th edn). London, New York: A & C Black-WW Norton.

Cohen, E. (1979) A phenomenology of tourist experiences. *Sociology* 13 (2), 179–201.

Conty (1885) *Guide Conty*. Paris: La Belgique Circulaire.

d'Ardenne (1897) *L'Ardenne. Guide du touriste et du cycliste*. Bruxelles: Rozez.

Demoulin, D. (2003) *Les grottes touristiques en Wallonie, mémoire présenté dans le cadre de la licence en tourisme*. IGEAT: ULB.

Fielder, O. (1914) Les nouvelles grottes du pays de Liège. *Bulletin du Touring-Club de Belgique* 5, 113–114.

Hewison, R. (1987) *The Heritage Industry: Britain in a Climate of Decline*. London: Methuen.

MacCannell, D. (1989) *The Tourist*. New York: Schocken.

McDonald, G. (1999) *Frommer's, Belgium, Holland & Luxembourg* (6th edn). USA: MacMillan.

Moscardo, G. (1996) Mindful visitors – heritage and tourism. *Annals of Tourism Research* 23 (2), 376–397.

Newby, P.T. (1994) Tourism – Support or threat to heritage? In G.J. Ashworth and P.J. Larkham (eds) *Building a New Heritage – Tourism, Culture and Identity in the New Europe* (pp. 206–228). London: Routledge.

Quériat, S. (2002) Caves in the Belgian Ardennes (1830–1914): Similarities and differences between representations and perceptions. Paper presented at Tourisms and Histories: Representations and experiences, University of Central Lancashire, Preston.

Rahir, E. (1914) Abîme de Comblain-au-Pont – Chantoir de Xhoris – Abanets du pays de Couvin. *Bulletin du Touring-Club de Belgique* 7.

West, J. (1999) *Heritage Tourism in the 21st century. Tourisme et Société*. Bruxelles: Presses Universitaires de l'ULB.

Chapter 19

Liberating the Heritage City: Towards Cultural Engagement

MARION STUART-HOYLE and JANE LOVELL

Introduction

In 1995 the English Historic Towns Forum[1] (EHTF) reported its concerns regarding uncertainty of its members with respect to the future of the historic or 'heritage town' (EHTF, 1996). Despite the fact that heritage and heritage tourism remain 'an essential part of understanding and celebrating Britain' (Grant *et al.*, 1999a: 37) and that it is vital to the UK tourism industry (Swarbrooke, 2002), a glance through academic and practitioner perceptions of the status of heritage towns sees the predominance of negative and pessimistic views. At the turn of the century this view persisted, notably with regard to the commercialisation, planning and conservation debates and visitor management problems (Breakell & Human, 1999; Laws & le Pelley, 2000; Manente *et al.*, 2000) and the continuing need to balance key stakeholder needs (Grant *et al.*, 1999b; Snaith & Haley, 1999). By 2002 these key concerns had been well synthesised in the form of Swarbrooke's analysis of the key challenges facing heritage tourism in the UK (2002) and Russo's explanation of the 'vicious circle of tourism development in heritage cities' (Russo, 2002: 165), the latter pulling no punches in its honest assessment of the impossible position with which many medium-sized heritage cities are now faced.

This case study seeks to paint a more positive and balanced picture of the fate of heritage towns and their future, focusing on their ability to engage the 'sightseeing cultural tourist' (and resident) in an 'entertainment-oriented experience' (McKercher, 2002: 32). This by no means belittles the validity of the problems and challenges detailed above,

[1] The EHTF was formed in 1987 and aims to establish and encourage contact between local authorities having responsibilities for the management of historic towns and cities and between these authorities and other public, private and voluntary sector organisations.

which are further developed in the first section of the chapter. Rather it emphasises the need to be proactive in the face of those issues. The latter stages of the chapter focus on the city of Canterbury, which is adopting a proactive, positive approach to cultural tourism development and 'story-telling', while at the same time seeking to address the traditional problems of visitor management, access, product development and accommodation provision. In this way, the chapter shows how a heritage city can become 'liberated' from the age old stereotypical perceptions of a historic centre via the development, interpretation and promotion of a living, culturally engaging modern visitor destination. This work has made use of McKercher's classification of cultural tourists into five broad types, which he applies to the city of Hong Kong (McKercher, 2002), which, like Canterbury, has used the strap line 'City of Life'.

Heritage Towns: Key Challenges and Problems in the 21st Century

Although visits to some major historic buildings within heritage towns have been falling in recent years, notably Canterbury Cathedral and Windsor Castle both recording a fall in visitor numbers between 1999 and 2000 (ETC, 2002), most heritage towns are now reporting an upturn in the number of visitors staying at least one night. In the light of this encouraging situation, there follows an assessment of the four key issues that, seen in their recurrence in the literature, have been viewed as having the greatest impact upon heritage towns' ability to remain successful visitor destinations. These are accessibility and visitor management, balancing stakeholder needs, the conservation versus product develop-ment debate and conflicts surrounding appropriate accommodation provision.

For those committed to the conservation and preservation of heritage as the overriding priority, heritage tourism is a threat and is evidenced quite starkly in the fragile context of historic cities. Greater access to (if not within) historic towns has meant greater pressures of visitor numbers, and the demands of an interested, visiting public have to be reconciled with the feelings of the historic towns' local residents and businesses. Controls of some kind to manage the influx and flow of visitors are invariably needed and here the legislative responsibility lies squarely with central and local government, whilst that of effective management devolves to the site itself. Visitor and traffic management are, therefore, critical to the well-being of the two key stakeholders, i.e. the visitor and the host community.

The English Tourist Board's well publicised 'Maintaining the Balance' report of 1991 heralded the start of a range of schemes designed to ensure that a harmonious relationship between visitor, host and the environment was maintained. Ten years later, 'visitor management plans' and 'town centre managers' remain commonplace (Breakell & Human, 1999; Canterbury WHS Management Plan, 2001; Grant *et al*., 1999a) and the need for a partnership or 'joined up approach' to historic town management remains a priority (Laws & le Pelley, 2000; Swarbrooke, 2002).

As mentioned earlier, the importance of balancing the needs of the visitor, host and the environment has been critical to the development and prosperity of historic towns. Research has recently focused upon resident (host) perceptions of tourism (Gilbert & Clarke, 1997; Grant *et al*., 1999b; Snaith & Haley, 1999), focusing upon the perceived advantages and disadvantages from an economic and sociocultural viewpoint. Research has yet to materialise, however, which assesses residents' opinions of, and involvement in, the nature of the heritage 'product' on offer and of their potential expectations of a broader cultural heritage product which goes beyond the traditional attractions associated with heritage towns.

Conservation and preservation of the built heritage mindful of restrictions associated with tight planning legislation and the city landscape or medieval street layouts (see Figure 19.1) has resulted in a level of stagnation in historic towns which is not viewed as welcoming potentially lucrative homes for new businesses or commercial ventures. The fact that many historic towns are themselves Conservation Areas or homes to World Heritage Sites could be seen as a deterrent to the development of a broader cultural tourism product due to the associated planning and development restrictions at such sites. If, indeed, 'historic towns are important resources for selling Britain's future vision and potential' (Grant *et al*., 1999a), then a sea change in approaches to defining and developing the core product needs to be adopted.

This might include encouraging more 'active consumption' of 'living' heritage rather than what Swarbrooke describes as 'dead heritage' that reflects Britain's obsession with living in the past (Swarbrooke, 2002: 40). This obsession with 'oldness' and preservation 'as was' as the central Unique Selling Proposition (USP) for historic towns does not allow for modernity to be attached to heritage, for example, in the form of new buildings, the façade of which may not copy but adapt the style of surrounding heritage. There are, however, those who would be concerned about the displacement of existing traditional heritage attractions, who might go as far as hindering or blocking such developments.

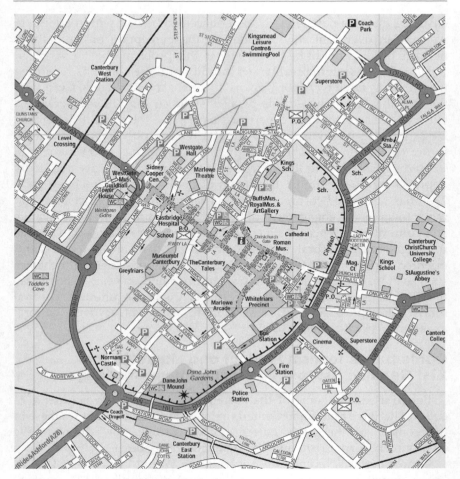

Figure 19.1 Map courtesy of Canterbury City Council

The final concern to be discussed surrounding tourism in historic towns relates to the lack of, or existence of inappropriately located, accommodation in historic towns. Grant *et al*. (2002: 147) discuss the 'particular challenges in accommodating new hotels which include limited vehicular access, lack of suitably sized sites and stringent building or design regulations in the historic core'. As increasing the number of overnight stays is a common theme within heritage towns' key objectives, it has become a question not only of providing enough accommodation, in the right location of a certain standard (for example, there are no five star hotels in the Canterbury district at all), but also of ensuring that there are enough 'experiences' to be had within a town to warrant an overnight stay. Broadening the perception of the cultural heritage product might be the answer to this problem.

Notwithstanding the reality and validity of these concerns regarding the problems faced by historic towns' planners and managers, faced with the fact that about two-thirds of all visitors to the UK are seeking a cultural heritage tourism experience as part of their trip (McKercher, 2002), perhaps it is now time to adopt a more positive approach to the future of historic towns. This chapter will now focus upon the city of Canterbury in Kent, to illustrate the ways in which the city, reputedly approaching 'the zenith of its tourism lifecycle' (Laws & le Pelley, 2000: 232), has attempted to broaden its heritage tourism product base and move towards the engagement of both visitor and resident in innovative and cultural experiences. As mentioned earlier, there is a need to engage the 'sightseeing cultural tourist' (and resident) in an 'entertainment-oriented experience' (McKercher, 2002: 32). It is possible that schemes such as those being developed in Canterbury could, in years to come, see the increasing reliance of historic towns upon the ultimate cultural tourist, the 'purposeful cultural tourist', who has a 'deep cultural experience' (McKercher, 2002: 7).

Canterbury's Tourism Product and Market in the 21st Century: Associated Management Challenges

Before assessing some of the current and planned developments of cultural heritage tourism in Canterbury, it is important to first set these in the context of the city's current visitor profile, its administrative environment for tourism and key management issues.

Canterbury was recently described in the WHS Management Plan as 'internationally renowned and in the "first division" of UK heritage destinations' (Canterbury WHS Management Plan Coordinating Committee, 2001: 64), known primarily for the historic Cathedral, its Roman walls and St. Augustine's Abbey. The current 'curriculum vitae' for tourism in Canterbury is as follows (Canterbury City Council, 2004):

- According to the Cambridge Model (one of the two main methods used by UK destinations to measure the volume and value of tourism), in 2002 there were approximately 6.3 million visitors to Canterbury district per year with a total spend of £258.9 million.
- This includes approximately 5.8 million day visitors contributing a further £153.5 million to the local economy and 585,000 staying visits to Canterbury District per year. The staying visits were

divided into 2.61 million nights, generating in the region of £105.7 million.

- Overseas visitors accounted for 24% of total staying trips and due to their typically longer length of stay, were estimated to have accounted for 43% of total visitor nights. Domestic visitors, who undertook 76% of total trips, accounted for the remaining 57% of visitor nights.

Canterbury City Council carried out a visitor survey in 2004, which found that the most frequent motivation for visiting Canterbury was sightseeing (50%) and shopping (32%). The desire to visit a specific attraction (27%) or the heritage city (24%) also indicates that the historic attractions of the city are a strong draw. The most frequent method of visitor transport was by car (44%). The majority of visitors came with their partner (26%) or other family (23%) or alone (17%), which totals 66%. This indicates that independent travellers form a larger visitor market than the group market (17%). This suggests that Canterbury attracts a high proportion of independent visitors, who like to control their visit and travel at their own pace.

Some of the facts and figures above, primarily the popularity of 'sightseeing' and the high percentage of visits by car, give rise to specific challenges for the city, as noted by Laws and le Pelley (2000), who took a nostalgic look back at Canterbury's first attempts to manage the city and balance key stakeholder needs in the form of the Canterbury City Centre Initiative (CCCI), and a 'soft system's model (Laws & le Pelley, 2000: 229). Challenges facing the city at the turn of the century were indicative of many other walled and historic cities, mirroring those outlined above.

One of the tactics for addressing these challenges is to strengthen existing partnerships and build new ones (see diagram). Canterbury's major partner is Kent Tourism, which is a subregion of the South East Tourist Board. Kent Tourism includes the Kent Tourism Alliance, a public–private marketing company formed in April 2002, which includes major contributors, such as Kent County Council and Euro-tunnel. 'The aim is to combine private and public sector interests as effectively as possible in order to grow significantly and sustainably the tourism industry's contribution to the Kent economy' (KTA, 2002). Partnership gives them the resources to fund costly campaigns such as their Spring Break campaign on the London Underground system. In the first few years, the KTA strategy has been to focus on the Transmanche and London markets, because of their proximity and the fact that they act as gateways. Canterbury exerts influence within Kent Tourism by paying a higher membership rate to the Kent Tourism Alliance in order to earn a seat on their board and is a member of the working groups, such as the Domestic Marketing group and Quality groups, defining the operational running of Kent Tourism. Canterbury is considered a 'star brand' within the subregion and therefore receives a large amount of coverage in the KTA guides and campaigns.

Like many other historic cities, Canterbury is no longer restricting its image to heritage. The connections to east Kent, Kentish countryside hinterland, including the Kent Downs Area of Outstanding Natural Beauty, and the coast, which contains landmark tourist sites such as Dover Castle, are maximised. The most tangible example of this interconnectivity is the Canterbury and Coastal Kent Holiday Guide, which links Thanet, Shepway and Canterbury Districts, classifying them under an umbrella brand and replacing the separate guides. There are plans to combine the Canterbury and Kent holiday guides and reduce duplication between the Local Authority and County even further. This widens the available markets from heritage-only to include tourists whose interests are sports and activities tourism, walking, cycling, green tourism or seaside. Canterbury is also a part of the Region Transmanche, Kent and Nord pas de Calais, which is unique in the UK, because unlike twinning, the geographical connections to France and accessibility of cross-channel travel give Canterbury closer links to France than to Northern England (Figure 19.2).

The strategic vision for Canterbury District (Canterbury, the rural area, Herne Bay and Whitstable) is:

> to enable tourism to benefit the community, visitors and environment, economically, culturally and sustainably. (CCC, 2002)

Linked to this, a key objective is to change visitor patterns, providing an 'experience' to engage visitors, which will hold them in the Canterbury District and the region of east Kent for a weekend break or holiday, as opposed to a daytrip to a 'magnet' attraction such as the cathedral. In line with the campaigns of the Kent Tourism Alliance, Canterbury district aims to increase the volume and value of visitors by 2% over 3 years. This is necessary because group travel coach figures and visitor numbers to the cathedral have fallen in recent years (see Table 19.1). It is estimated that coach visitors contribute £8,719,358/year to the local economy.

Specific to Canterbury are problems associated with its very small tourist-historic core, outside which visitors seem loath to venture. Additionally the city is not perceived to be easily accessible (despite the Channel rail link to Ashford) due to the relatively slow and unreliable

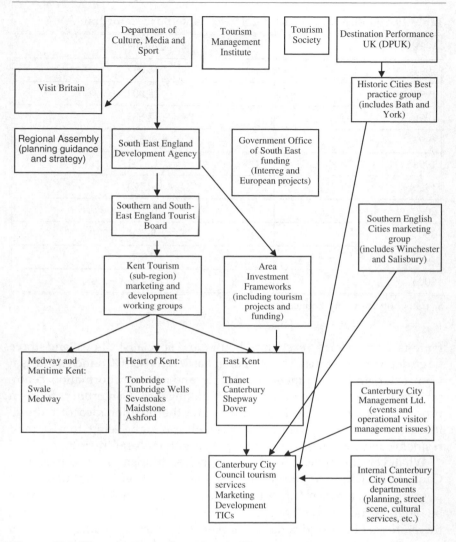

Figure 19.2 The structure of tourism in Kent

train services to and from London. Furthermore, the attraction base within the city has remained static for years and existing attractions (apart from the Cathedral) are losing out to the city's enticing range of shops, set to expand even further when the ambitious Whitefriars Shopping Development comes to fruition in 2006. Canterbury City Centre has more than 320 retail premises offering a diverse selection of

Table 19.1 Group travel coach figures to Canterbury Cathedral

Year	Coaches
1994	14,097
1995	18,002
1996	17,531
1997	16,544
1998	15,261
1999	12,174
2000	10,623
2001	8,798
2002	8,856
2003	8,456

Source: Canterbury City Council (2004)

famous name stores, exclusive boutiques, specialist shops and three large department stores. This situation has left the City Council's tourism team (tourism development, marketing and visitor information centre services) with the daunting task of taking the Canterbury tourism product and 'stretching' it to encapsulate the broader idea of cultural tourism which would appeal to the cultural sightseeing tourist (and resident) and eventually even the 'purposeful cultural tourist'.

Whatever the trends for heritage cities, tourism is a constant in Canterbury, which for the past 1000 years has been a destination for pilgrims, with a core market of heritage tourists. Cultural tourists tend to be older, spend more money and stay longer (Hughes, 2000). They are, therefore, a highly desirable market for tourism managers. New competition for tourist leisure time in terms of day trips, short breaks and long holidays has emerged from regional regenerated destinations such as Newcastle and Manchester, which use public art, lighting, new attractions and interpretation centres such as Urbis and other capital projects to stimulate urban renaissance. Canterbury Cathedral was the 10th most visited paid attraction in the UK in 2002, with 1,110,529 visitors. It acts as a magnet attraction in Canterbury ETC (2002), but Millennium projects such as the London Eye have forced Canterbury

Cathedral further down the list of nationally significant paid attractions. Cultural tourism is also fragmenting into various niche markets, such as heritage tourism and arts tourism and the heritage market (Richards, 2001). These markets have specific requirements and need investment in functions such as interpretation to ensure that their expectations are met.

Canterbury's Vision as a Cultural Centre

'Canterbury in East Kent', the city's bid to be European Capital of Culture in 2008 (CCC, 2002b) shaped the focus of development in Canterbury, adding culture to the economic and social drivers for change. The bid identified a number of 'priority projects' designed to bring cultural benefits to the area and in 2004, as a direct result of the Capital of Culture bid, Canterbury won £820,000 from the urban Cultural Programme to invest in these projects. The result will be an improved environment for tourism, which already makes a valuable contribution to regeneration in the Canterbury district. The new high-speed rail link joining London to Ashford in 2009 and the proposed expansion of Ashford as a major new housing focus for the South East will also make Canterbury accessible to a wider catchment area.

The vision for 'cultural engagement' is delivered through a programme of seven projects (from capital projects to events) in partnership with the public and private sectors. The projects will be designed to make the range of products in the Canterbury district more competitive in the destination market, increasing visitor numbers. The project categories, which all relate to the interpretation of a city in the broadest sense, are Heritage Accessibility, Cultural Facilities, Visitor Management, Shopping, Events and Festivals, Hotel Development and a wider identity, which are now detailed in turn.

Heritage Accessibility

Canterbury has a wealth of heritage, made up of no less than 1586 listed and 126 locally listed buildings. Of those listed buildings, 47 are Grade 1 and 78 are Grade II*. This is in addition to a World Heritage Site and connections to Chaucer and Marlowe, a fact that is rarely communicated to visitors except through restricted channels such as guided tours and serious textbooks. Canterbury has a range of interpretation media including destination branding in the Holiday Guide and City Centre Management inspired magazine Freedom, literary connection leaflets, re-enactment events, heritage open days, interpretation panels, trails and guided walks. The interpretation provision in Canterbury is characterised by its fragmentation. The providers include a range of individuals, for example historians like the Guild of Guides with limited resources for modernising their approach and with no strategic overview.

The challenge is to interpret and commodify the stories of the city in ways that appeal to a broad range of people. Some components of broad destination interpretation are in place in Canterbury, for example the development of the five 'Canterbury Quarters', created in 2001 by Canterbury City Management Ltd., as a marketing tool. 'Cultural events have been supplemented by Cultural Quarters and other areas in which small-scale production can be encouraged. Attractions based purely on historic cultural production, such as heritage attractions, have been "put on the back burner" in favour of creative activities and uses of urban space' (Richards, 2001). This type of destination interpretation is designed to engage visitors by giving them a sense of place, essential for historic cities working to emphasise local distinctiveness to establish their product placement and attract inward investment. The repackaging may be superficial, but it is more sustainable and carries less risk for many destinations than investing capital resources in new attractions. In 2004 a consultant was commissioned to evolve the five quarters and develop a new 'cultural quarter' for Canterbury including the Marlowe Theatre, Royal Art Gallery and Museum of Canterbury, which, with the Whitefriars shopping complex and the World Heritage Site forms three identifiable areas for tourist consumption. Recently the 50 'top' heritage points in Canterbury were identified by the City Council, Canterbury Christ Church University College students. Local historians provided the knowledge that supplied the content of the interpretation, which is a phenomenon noted by Richards (2001: 57) as 'the attempts of regions to develop their local knowledge as a form of "intellectual property" and cultural competitive advantage', to add to the visitors' experience of living history, arts and culture. The visitor survey of 2004 demonstrates that the majority of people come to Canterbury to sightsee and their trip can, therefore, be shaped by impulse decisions made on location and influenced by publications such as the heritage quarters. As time has changed the cityscape, elements of the past have blended with different layers and textures of history. The heritage points will be used on the website and in various publications such as the visitor guide. The visitor guide is being reworked in categories, as opposed to themes, which will include shopping, food, and elements of interpretation and the categories immediately address the issue of satisfying niche cultural markets.

Cultural Facilities

There are a broad range of new cultural facilities in East Kent within a short distance of the city of Canterbury. The Turner Centre is a proposed £17 million contemporary visual arts centre commemorating J.M.W. Turner's life-long association with Margate, Kent. Located on a site on the seafront, with links to the Tate, it will attract new cultural visitors to East Kent. Whitstable was already a popular destination for Londoners in search of seaside authenticity and has been linked to Southwold and Whitby in terms of its unique and popular appeal. The Horsebridge Centre was completed in March 2004 and offers a high-quality art gallery with ancillary accommodation for art workshops and display; a cafe with balcony area; a learning centre aimed at those not naturally drawn to the various established learning institutions; a performance space capable of being used for a variety of activities; and a selection of rooms available for seminars, meetings and workshops. The Museum of Canterbury has been redeveloped in a £650,000 project to offer a wider range of educational facilities such as a medieval discovery gallery and new themes for children. The feasibility of expanding the Marlowe Theatre and the Royal Museum and Art Gallery is also being researched.

The reuse of heritage buildings is being demonstrated by a study of audience development for the Norman castle, which is already used, like St Augustine's Abbey, as a venue for theatre productions. This typifies the new urban renaissance in Canterbury, mixing contemporary styles with heritage roots.

Recent Developments in Cultural Provision

The number of visitors to Canterbury shows an increase from 360,040 in 2002 to 520,000 in 2003. This is a result of both a range of new initiatives in the city to support tourists and developments in the provision of cultural attractions. These include a rebranded tourist information centre, a new Destination Management System, and an expansion of retail opportunities. Despite the development of the new Cathedral International Education Centre, provision for tourist accommodation remains an issue, especially for business tourism.

In addition, the City has stepped up its programme of cultural festivals and events, partly in response to the Capital of Culture bid. These include the Canterbury Festival (an established arts event), the first British Food Festival in 2002, a Christmas Euromarket, a sculpture festival and Son et Lumiere events.

Conclusions

Canterbury experiences all of the problems and challenges common to many of the UK's most visited and 'heritage-rich' historic cities. It would be very easy for the City Council and the tourism businesses to slide into a perpetual sense of doom and gloom faced with overcrowding and access problems. However, even if the recent resurgence of development within the city was triggered by a desire to become Capital of Culture, there is evidence that this city has adopted a more positive outlook towards broadening the appeal of the heritage city through the 'cultural engagement' of its visitor and resident markets. Canterbury does not have all the answers with regard to increasing the value of the tourist market whilst reducing some of the more unwelcome sociocultural implications of the very high resident–visitor ratio experienced in heritage cities. It has, however, started to show some of its key competitors around the country that the fate of the heritage city might depend in the future on more subtle and innovative methods of encouraging the 'sightseeing cultural tourist' and residents to engage positively in 'culture' in its broadest sense.

References

Breakell, M. and Human, B. (1999) *Practical Guidance for Tourism Management in Historic Towns: Making the Connections*. Conference Proceedings, Oxford Brookes University, Oxford, England: EHTF.

Canterbury City Council (2002a) *Canterbury District Tourism Strategy 2002*. Canterbury: Canterbury City Council.

Canterbury City Council (2002b) *Odyssey: A Journey from a Great Past to a Greater Future*. Capital of Culture bid document, Canterbury: Canterbury City Council.

Canterbury City Council (2004) Coach parking figures 2004, Festival survey figures and visitor survey figures courtesy of Canterbury City Council. Tourism Development Fact Sheet available on WWW at http://www.canterbury.gov.uk/cgi-bin/buildpage.pl?mysql = 1545. Accessed 4.4.06.

Canterbury WHS Management Plan Coordinating Committee (2001) *Canterbury World Heritage Site Management Plan*. Canterbury: Canterbury WHS Management Plan Coordinating Committee.

Carter, R., Hodgson, M. and Renault, G. (2001) Towards E-business – Best practice in tourism destination systems. Tourism Intelligence Papers. *Insights* London: ETC, July, A1–14.

English Historic Towns Forum (1996) *State of the Heritage; Survey of the Members 1996. UWE*. Oxford, England: EHTF.

English Tourism Council (2000) *English Heritage Monitor 1999*. London: ETC.

English Tourism Council (2002) Trends in visitor attractions market in 2000. UK Statistics, *Insights* London: ETC, March, F35–44.

English Tourist Board (1991) *Tourism and the Environment: Maintaining the Balance.* London: ETB/DOE.

Gilbert, D. and Clarke, M. (1997) An exploratory examination of urban tourism impact, with reference to residents attitudes, in the cities of Canterbury and Guildford. *Tourism Management* 14 (6), 343– 352.

Grant, M., Human, B. and le Pelley, B. (1999a) Heritage and making the most of it. Tourism Intelligence Papers *Insights* London: ETC, September, A37– 42.

Grant, M., Human, B. and le Pelley, B. (1999b) Making the connections – Joined up thinking in action. Tourism Intelligence Papers. *Insights* London: ETC, July, A20– 23.

Grant, M., Human, B. and le Pelley, B. (2002) Embracing tourism – Cambridge tourism strategy review case study. *Insights* London: ETC, March, C41– 50.

Hughes, H. (2000) *Arts, Entertainment and Tourism*. Oxford: Butterworth-Heinemann.

Kent Tourism Alliance (2002) *Kent Tourism Alliance Prospectus.* Canterbury, England: Kent Tourism Alliance.

Laws, E. and le Pelley, B. (2000) Managing complexity and change in tourism: The case of a historic city. *International Journal of Tourism Research* 2, 229– 246.

Manente, M., Minghetti, E. and Celotto, E. (2000) Visitor and mobility management in tourism destinations: A cross analysis of strategies, projects and practices. *The Tourist Review* 2, 5– 25.

McKercher, B. (2002) Towards a classification of cultural tourists. *International Journal of Tourism Research* 4, 29– 38.

Richards, G. (ed.) (2001) *Cultural Attractions and European Tourism.* Wallingford: CABI.

Russo, A. (2002) The 'vicious circle' of tourism development in heritage cities. *Annals of Tourism Research* 29 (1), 165– 182.

Snaith, T. and Haley, A. (1999) Residents' opinions of tourism development in the historic city of York, England. *Tourism Management* 20 (6), 595– 603.

Swarbrooke, J. (2002) Heritage tourism in the UK – a glance at things to come. Future for... *Insights* London: ETC, May, D35– 48.